WILLIAM CABELL RIVES

A COUNTRY TO SERVE

W C Rives.

William
Cabell
Rives

A COUNTRY TO SERVE

Barclay Rives

ATELERIX
New York, New York

William Cabell Rives, A Country to Serve
Copyright 2014, Barclay Rives.

ISBN: 978-0-9899263-2-4

Cover and text designed by Josef Beery.
The text is set in Adobe Jenson.

First paperback edition: 2014.

ATELERIX
288 Park Avenue South
New York, NY 10003

For information about special discounts for bulk
purchases, please contact Atelerix Press Special Sales at
contact@atelerix.com

ATELERIX and design are trademarks of Atelerix Press,
the publisher of this work.

COVER PORTRAIT

William Cabell Rives, 1839, lithograph by Charles Fenderich.
Courtesy of the American Antiquarian Society.

COVER PAINTING

George Inness, *Harvest Scene in the Delaware Valley*, ca. 1867.
Oil on canvas. (Detail on front.)
Courtesy the National Gallery of Art.

FRONTISPIECE

Etching of Senator William Cabell Rives by William W. Bannerman which
appeared in the January, 1838 *U.S. Magazine and Democratic Review*. The
editors apologized that it portrayed Rives with uncharacteristic "harshness
and even moroseness of expression," though otherwise it was a "faithful
resemblance in point of feature."
Image provided by iStock.

For Aggie:
Rives men discussed herein made advantageous
marriages, but none married better than I have.

Contents

The Rives Family

William Rives
1736-1777
+
Lucy Shands
1740-1815

William Cabell
1730-1798
+
Margaret Jordan
1742-1812

Thomas Walker
1715-1794
+
Mildred Thornton
1721-1778

Hugh Nelson
1750-1800
+
Judith Page
1755-1827

Robert Rives + Margaret J. Cabell
1764-1845   1770-1815

Francis Walker + Jane Byrd Nelson
1764-1806   1775-1808

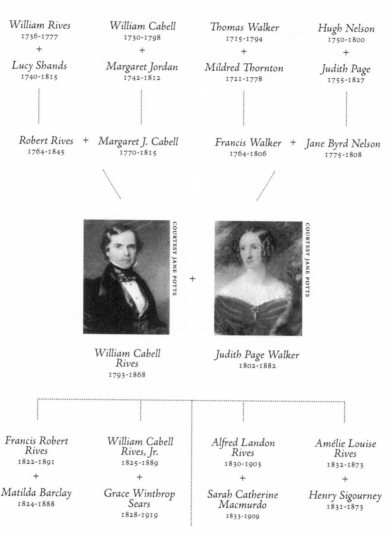

COURTESY JANE POTTS

COURTESY JANE POTTS

+

William Cabell
Rives
1793-1868

Judith Page Walker
1802-1882

Francis Robert
Rives
1822-1891
+
Matilda Barclay
1824-1888

William Cabell
Rives, Jr.
1825-1889
+
Grace Winthrop
Sears
1828-1919

Alfred Landon
Rives
1830-1903
+
Sarah Catherine
Macmurdo
1833-1909

Amélie Louise
Rives
1832-1873
+
Henry Sigourney
1831-1873

Ella Rives
1834-1892

SOME DATES VARY AMONG SOURCES, WHICH INCLUDE:
*Reliques of the Rives, Genealogical Notes, The Cabells and Their Kin,
Genealogy of the Page Family and web sites.*

CHAPTER ONE

Introduction: Giant in Intellect

MR. RIVES. MR. WILLIAM C. RIVES?

President-elect Abraham Lincoln expressed surprise that the former Senator was so short. Rives' lofty reputation had led Lincoln to believe he was at least six feet tall.

The 5'8" Rives replied to the 6'4" Lincoln, "I feel a small man in your presence."

Lincoln assured him, "You are any how a giant in intellect."

The introduction took place in Washington, February 23, 1861. Rives (rhymes with leaves) reported the exchange in a letter to his son the following day. "This piece of Western free & easy compliment passed off among his admirers for first rate Parisian cleverness and tact."[1]

Having twice served as U.S. Minister to France, Rives knew Parisian cleverness, but he believed this was no time for repartee. Rives had come to Washington as one of five Virginia delegates to the Peace Conference, an eleventh hour attempt to prevent Civil War. The 67-year-old Rives was another old man at what was derisively nicknamed the "Old Gentlemen's Convention." He had first been elected to public office in 1817. He was a protégé and friend of Jefferson and Madison. He had long sought to preserve their ideals and especially the Union, from which seven states had seceded by February 1861. Rives had witnessed revolution and bloodshed in France. He wanted to save his country from similar destruction.

When first elected to the Senate in 1832, William Cabell Rives (1793-1868) had been a staunch supporter of President Andrew

Jackson, hero of the common man. However, he was not thrilled by Lincoln's rustic charm. Rives wrote his son, "He seemed to be good-natured & well-intentioned, but utterly unimpressed with the gravity of the crisis & the magnitude of his duties. . . . He seems to think of nothing but jokes & stories. I fear, therefore, we are to expect but little from his influence with the Convention."[2]

Four days later, at nine in the evening, Lincoln met with five members of the Conference, including Rives. He told them an anecdote about how a client had once stopped his arguing a hopeless case by telling him in court, "Guv it up." Lincoln said that at this time he did not want to "guv it up," implying his permitting states to leave the Union. Former Kentucky Governor Charles S. Morehead replied it would be better to "guv it up" than to drench the land with bloodshed. Lincoln then recounted an Aesop's Fable. A lion fell in love with a young lady. He wanted to marry her, but her relatives demanded, for her protection, that the lion submit to having his claws and fangs removed. The lion was so deeply in love that he consented. Then the relatives beat the lion over the head with a club.

According to Morehead, whose account of the meeting was published in *The Liverpool Mercury* October 13, 1862 as well as the *New York Herald* November 11, 1862, William Cabell Rives rose to speak after Lincoln's fable. With "unsurpassed dignity and eloquence," Rives declared his love of the Union and stated he had done all in his power to support it. However, if Lincoln resorted to armed coercion of the seceded states, Virginia would leave the Union. "Sir, old as I am, and dearly as I have loved this Union, in that event I go, with all my heart and soul."

Lincoln jumped up from his chair. He advanced one step toward Rives who had remained standing and said, "Mr. Rives, Mr. Rives if Virginia will stay in, I will withdraw the troops from Fort Sumter."

Rives stepped back and said, "Mr. President I have no authority to speak for Virginia. I am one of the humblest of her sons, but if you do that, it will be one of the wisest things you have ever done. Do that, and give us guarantees, and I can only promise you that whatever influence I possess shall be exerted to promote the Union and to restore it to what it was."[3]

Historians have disputed Morehead's tale. Some doubt Lincoln would have made such an explicit promise regarding Sumter.[4] Rives' talk of leaving the Union with all heart and soul may also have been dramatic license. He remained vehemently opposed to secession until Virginia made her ultimate decision two months later.[5] While facing Lincoln, Rives' heart and soul were still committed to saving the Union.

Rives told Lincoln when they were first introduced, "I can do little. You can do much. Everything now depends upon you."[6] Lincoln's inauguration took place March 4. He and Rives would not meet again.

Lincoln knew William C. Rives by reputation in 1861, because Rives had been a prominent political, diplomatic and intellectual figure for three decades. Lincoln had quoted Rives during a speech in 1839, delivered when Lincoln was a little known Illinois state legislator.

Rives counseled other leaders during moments of crisis. Lafayette sought his approval before proceeding to install Louis Philippe on the French throne, after the Paris Revolution of 1830. John Tyler appreciated Rives' firm support when others doubted whether the Vice-President should become President, following the death of William Henry Harrison in 1841. Jefferson Davis summoned Rives to Richmond to discuss delicate and sensitive matters in 1864. In March 1865, General Lee conferred with Rives about how to preserve the Confederate cause while ending the conflict.

Thomas Jefferson tutored Rives during his youth. James Madison mentored Rives' political maturation. Both Jefferson and Madison predicted Rives' ascension to the nation's foremost rank of leaders. Throughout his career Rives attempted to maintain the government Jefferson and Madison had conceived. Rives helped facilitate Congressional purchase of Madison's papers. He wrote a three-volume biography of Madison and edited a four-volume edition of Madison letters.

Rives' marriage to Judith Page Walker gained him a devoted life companion, who was also a gifted diplomatic and intellectual force. Judith charmed Washington and Paris society, while gathering information important to her husband's work. The Rives were a Washington "power couple" long before there was such an expression. Judith published works of non-fiction as well as novels, including *Home and the* World, which offered a more serene portrayal of 1850s plantation life than the sensational *Uncle Tom's Cabin*.

Rives negotiated a reparations treaty with France for damages to American shipping, incurred decades before, during the Napoleonic Wars. His conference with Britain's Lord Palmerston led to the Clayton-Bulwer Treaty, regarding construction of a canal through Central America. As head of the Senate Foreign Relations Committee, Rives helped secure approval of the Webster-Ashburton Treaty, which delineated the U.S. and Canadian border.

First appointed Minister to France by Andrew Jackson, Rives stood with Jackson in his fight against Calhoun and the Nullifiers. Rives' support of Jackson's Force Bill permanently antagonized some of his fellow southerners, and gained him an actual black eye. Rives' concurrence with Jackson's dismantling of the National Bank forced him to resign from the Senate rather than obey the Virginia legislature's instructions to censure the President. Rives later infuriated Jackson by daring to express disagreement with

Jackson's controversial financial policies, which many claimed were provoking panic. Rives was unafraid to defend his principles and act for the good of the country, even when his actions were unpopular or politically damaging.

Rives' loss to Richard Mentor Johnson in the contest for the 1836 Democratic Party Vice-Presidential nomination caused bitterness that lingered from the convention past election day. While Martin Van Buren received sufficient electoral votes to be certified as President, Virginia electoral votes withheld from Johnson caused him to be the only Vice-President who required certification by the U.S. Senate, according to Amendment XII of the Constitution.

Along with Senator Nathaniel Tallmadge of New York, Rives led an 1838 revolt of Conservative Democrats against the policies of President Van Buren, who had once been Rives' close friend and political ally. Rives opposed Van Buren's Sub Treasury plan, which he considered worse than a National Bank. He especially disliked Van Buren's wielding of party discipline and power, and proclaimed in the Senate that he had a country to serve as well as a party to obey. Rives worked strenuously to ensure Van Buren was a one-term president.

Rives was a celebrated orator. A witness declared that, on at least one occasion, Rives triumphed in a debate with Henry Clay, who was the acknowledged Master of the Senate. Consistent with the style of his day, Rives' speeches sometimes lasted over three hours. Rives, Clay, Webster, and their fellow congressmen spoke to attentive full galleries. Speechmakers faced no competition from electronic media.

Rives witnessed the conception of early electronic communication, when he stood beside Samuel Morse during a trans-Atlantic voyage. Morse was discussing application of Benjamin Franklin's electrical experiments, which led to Morse's subsequent invention of the telegraph.

Rives was an inventive and dedicated agriculturalist. He earned great acclaim for his importation of a Cleveland Bay stallion in the 1850s, as well as for his prize-winning sheep and cattle.

Though he declared in the Senate that slavery was a great evil, Rives grappled unsuccessfully with the problem. He tried to arrest the country's descent into dis-union. Rives bestowed the name Constitutional Union upon the only party attempting to attract national rather than sectional support in the four-way 1860 election. Rives applied all of his political skill and energy to the February 1861 Peace Conference, which he viewed as the country's last hope.

Unable to abandon or oppose his native state, Rives joined the Confederate cause and served in its Congress. After the war, in the final act of a long life of public service, Rives served as a trustee of the Peabody Education Fund, along with General Grant, Admiral Farragut, and other distinguished northern and southern leaders. The fund aimed to restore southern educational institutions and was a symbol of reconciliation.

Love of country, of Virginia, of his home, and of his family motivated Rives' actions, along with his admiration of Jefferson and Madison. Rives also adhered to a code of behavior understood and upheld by propertied men of his time. Elements of the code included honor, duty, loyalty, dedication to family, honesty, truthfulness, forthrightness, faith and bravery. During desperate times in 1861, Rives repeatedly summarized it as "manliness."

Rives was not always allied with the winning side during his political career. However, minority opposition often helps shape legislation and events. Rives was influential, if not always decisive, during his decades of participation in national political life.

* * *

1 William Cabell Rives to William Cabell Rives, Jr. February 24, 1861, Rives MSS, LOC, box 36.

2 Ibid.

3 Unpublished biography of William Cabell Rives by William Cabell Rives, Jr., (henceforth noted as "WCR, Jr., Biography") Ibid, box 103, 140.

4 David S. Heidler, Jeanne T. Heidler, David J. Coles, editors, *Encyclopedia of the American Civil War: A Political, Social and Military History*, New York, W. W. Norton and Company, 2000, Vol. IV, 1659.

5 Rives to George W. Summers, April 15, 1861, Rives to John Janney, May 1, 1861, Rives MSS, LOC, Ibid, box 92.

6 Lucius E. Chittenden, *Recollections of President Lincoln and His Administration*, New York, Harper and Brothers, 1891, 73.

ABBREVIATIONS

Rives MSS, LOC:

William Cabell Rives Papers, Rare Book and Special Collections Division, Library of Congress (various box numbers)

Rives MSS, UVa.:

Rives Family Papers, Special Collections Department, (Albert and Shirley Small Special Collections Library), University of Virginia Library, (various accession numbers)

CHAPTER TWO

Wayward and Idle Boy

RIVES' PROSPEROUS FAMILY, and privileged upbringing influenced his outlook and enabled him to choose a life of public service.

William Cabell Rives was born at Union Hill, overlooking the James River in Nelson County, Virginia, March 24, 1793.[1] Union Hill was the home of his maternal grandfather and namesake Col. William Cabell (1730-1798). Col. Cabell fought in the French and Indian War, served in the colonial House of Burgesses, later in the Virginia Senate, and helped supply the Continental Army. He was a member of the Virginia State Convention of 1788, where he voted against ratification of the Federal Constitution, a document his grandson would regard more favorably.[2] After having given away considerable amounts of land to his children, Col. Cabell left an estate of 30,000 acres upon his death. He and his wife Margaret Jordan had seven children. Their sixth child, a daughter named Margaret Jordan Cabell, known as Peggy (1770-1815), married Robert Rives (1764-1845).

Rives is a French name which denotes river banks. Paris is divided by the Seine into *rive gauche* and *rive droite*, its left and right banks. Robert Rives' ancestors emigrated from France to England sometime before 1500, and changed the spelling to "Ryves" to help maintain the French pronunciation among the English. The Ryves reverted to the original spelling after the first American of the family William Rives, arrived in Virginia circa 1650 amid the Cavalier emigration. The Ryves/Rives were allied with the losing Royalist side in the English Civil War. A

William Cabell Rives was born at Union Hill on March 24, 1793.

family member Brune Ryves had been chaplain to the ill-fated Charles I.[3]

Robert Rives was born in Sussex County, Virginia. He joined the Continental Army in 1781 when he was 17 years old, serving as a private at the battle of Yorktown. He started his business career in the store of Col. Richard Baker in South Quay, which is near Suffolk in southeast Virginia. A few years later he moved to the store of Blow & Barksdale at Charlotte Court House. There, in February 1789, Robert Rives met Margaret Jordan Cabell, who was visiting relatives in the area. Though Miss Cabell had other suitors and was even engaged to another man for a time, Robert Rives won her hand with his "resolute energy of will and purpose which enabled him always to reach the goal he aimed at." During his courtship, he once rode 105 miles from Richmond to Union Hill to dine as a guest. His horse died from the exertion. He was a rapid rider and later in life would regularly ride 40 miles to Charlottesville on Court Day, transact business and return that evening.[4]

*Edgewood, built by Robert Rives in 1790, sold in 1807
to Joseph Carrington Cabell.*

After marrying on January 25, 1790, Robert and Peggy Rives constructed and inhabited Edgewood, near the homes of many Cabell relatives along the James River in Nelson County. Members of the Cabell family were prominent in nineteenth century state and national politics. Joseph Carrington Cabell (1778-1856) served in the Virginia Legislature for 30 years. His support was invaluable to Jefferson in the founding of the University of Virginia. Joseph C. Cabell purchased Edgewood from Robert Rives. Another Cabell cousin was John Cabell Breckinridge (1821-1875), Vice President during the Buchanan administration, Confederate General and Secretary of War. James A. Seddon (1815-1880) married Rives' Cabell cousin Sarah Bruce. Seddon served in the U.S. Congress, was a member of the Peace Convention, and served the Confederacy as Congressman and Secretary of War before Breckinridge.

As ladies often did in that era, Peggy Rives returned to her childhood home Union Hill to give birth to William C., who was the third of eleven children. Producing such a large brood in 16 years adversely affected Peggy's health. Her life was almost despaired of in October 1790, shortly after she bore her eldest. Dr. George Gilmer of Pen Park, near Charlottesville, spent six days at Union Hill to help save her. She died at age 45. Peggy's obituary stated, "Her mind was masculine and sentimental, her heart generous, benevolent and kind."[5] In 1803 the couple moved a few miles to newly built Oak Ridge, which was later the estate of Gilded Age financier Thomas Fortune Ryan. Robert Rives established stores throughout the upper James River basin, exchanging goods with farmers for their tobacco, which he shipped overseas. He profited on both transactions. One of his stores stood at the Rivanna River port of Milton, near Monticello, home of Thomas Jefferson, who was a regular customer.

According to contemporaries, Robert Rives "was a small man about 5 feet 9 inches high, well set; very neat in dress; very inquisitive and talkative; very polite; very hospitable; very much respected by all who knew him; and very much beloved by his slaves, of whom he owned a large number. . . . Although remarkably well versed in political information, and an ardent politician, he yet never would allow himself to be a candidate for a political office, and the magistracy was almost the only public office held by him. Many thought, however, that he would have been as successful in the political arena as he was as a merchant and farmer. Many . . . thought he would have been more successful in politics even than his son William."[6]

Near the end of his life, William Cabell Rives was persuaded by Virginia historian Hugh Blair Grigsby (1806-1881) to write an account of his early life. He began the letter modestly claiming that the narrative would be of no interest to anyone but the closest friend. However, the letter that resides in box 93 of the enormous Library of Congress Rives collection (50,400 items) is in his wife's handwriting with corrections added by him. The eight pages were carefully sewn together. He retained this copy for his own voluminous files and for posterity. As Madison's biographer and the President of the Virginia Historical Society, he was mindful of posterity.

In his April 6, 1866 letter, Rives described himself as "a very wayward and idle boy." His father wished to bestow the best available education on all of his children and engaged private tutors for their early years. Rives was tutored along with his older brother Landon Cabell Rives (1790-1870), who later became a physician and moved to Cincinnati. One of the tutors was Reuben Grigsby, an uncle of Hugh Blair Grigsby. Another was George Washington Varnum, a Massachusetts native who moved to Nelson County and was elected to the state legislature. These and other worthy instructors failed to excite his interest. "I was too idle and full of play." He also believed that the quality of their instruction was "far below what it had been in the time of our fathers or has been in the time of our children."[7]

Rives was sent to Hampden-Sidney College in 1805 and 1806. He and his brother Landon lived with the family of the college president Dr. Archibald Alexander. He remained uninterested in his studies.

The pair then attended James Ogilvie's school at Milton, a couple of miles east of Charlottesville. Ogilvie taught without books, delivering a long lecture followed by an examination on its contents the next day, after which came another lecture. Ogilvie was "a scotchman by birth," an eccentric and a drug addict.[8] His unusual method "enlisted all the intellect and attention of his youthful auditors, while it created a constant demand on their intellectual resources." Rives said Ogilvie quickened in him his first interest in learning. Though he was still "an idler," he felt a "waking up of the faculties" and a "desire of mental improvement, which a wild and thoughtless nature had been proof against under the old systems of routine."[9]

One of his classmates at Ogilvie's was Thomas Jefferson Randolph, a grandson of Thomas Jefferson. T. J. Randolph often invited his schoolmates up to Monticello. Jefferson's former overseer Edmund Bacon mentioned "Willie" Rives in his reminiscences as "an uncommonly fine boy" and always the peacemaker among his schoolmates. A group of boys, who had not been invited, tried to crash the party one Saturday. They broke fences and tree limbs and threw stones at the gardener. When Bacon arrived to find the attackers had fled, he asked Rives, "Willie, why didn't you settle this matter without all this fighting?"

Rives replied, "Why sir, you know that I am a little fellow and couldn't do much fighting, but I called them all the hard names I could think of, and then I started to turn Rompo loose on them, and they all ran off." Rompo was a very fierce dog. Bacon said that Rives was a modest boy, and would not join his classmates in evening forays among the slave dwellings. Thomas Jefferson Randolph later disputed these recollections of Bacon. Bacon once suggested to young Ellen Randolph that she consider Rives as a husband. "Oh, he is too much of a runt to make anybody a husband," she answered.[10] Rives saw Ellen in the summer of 1813 when he visited Monticello, and there is no evidence her opinion had changed. Ellen later married Joseph Coolidge of Boston.

In the autumn of 1808, Rives and his brother were sent to William and Mary, where his schoolmates included future President John Tyler, future Senator Benjamin Watkins Leigh, and future General Winfield Scott.[11] Rives' son's account explained that he was "carried away on several occasions by the contagious example of some of his frolicsome and disorderly associates." He once "wiped his bleeding finger, accidentally cut in a college spree, on the magnificently starched and frilled shirt bosom of a dandy fellow student."[12] He became involved "according to the fashion of the place and time in a boyish affair of honor," which only the intervention of friends prevented from escalating to a duel. He was expelled from the college. Bishop James Madison, a second cousin of the fourth President, was then President of William and Mary. Despite Rives' misbehavior, the bishop saw promise in the lad. He wrote a letter to a friend who had just retired from public life and was interested in tutoring young men of his neighborhood, Thomas Jefferson.

In a letter to Jefferson dated May 31, 1809, Bishop Madison stated Rives "has been richly gifted by Nature with fine Genius ... I ... am persuaded, that under your Auspices, we may expect that he will become one of the ornaments of his Country."[13]

* * *

1   A Virginia History sign on Route 29 south of Lovingston, Virginia, erroneously states that Rives was born at Oak Ridge, which was not constructed until 1803.

2   George Lockhart Rives, *Genealogical Notes*, (New York, 1914), (Privately Printed), 20-21. See also Alexander Brown, *The Cabells and Their Kin*, (reprinted 1994, Randolph W. Cabell, Genealogy Publishing Service, Franklin, N.C.) 81-141.

3   James Rives Childs, *Reliques of the Rives*, J. P. Bell Co., Lynchburg, Virginia, 1929.

4   Alexander Brown, Ibid, 236-246.

5   Ibid, 239.

6   Ibid, 243.

7   William Cabell Rives to Hugh Blair Grigsby, April 6, 1866, Rives MSS, LOC box 93.

8   Raymond C. Dingledine, Jr., *The Political Career of William Cabell Rives*, Charlottesville, Virginia, 1947. PhD Dissertation, page 9. This is the most thorough study of Rives' political career, and an invaluable guide to the enormous Library of Congress collection. Dingledine was later a Professor at James Madison University. He does not say what drug Ogilvie was addicted to.

9 William Cabell Rives to Hugh Blair Grigsby, Rives MSS, LOC, box 93.

10 Rev. Hamilton Wilcox Pierson, *Jefferson at Monticello, The Private Life of Thomas Jefferson*, University of Virginia Press, Charlottesville, Virginia 1967 (8th printing 1988) 87-89.

11 Philip Alexander Bruce, *The Virginia Plutarch*, Vol. II, Chapel Hill, UNC Press, 1929, 153.

12 WCR, Jr. Biography, Rives MSS LOC, box 103, page 5.

13 Dingledine, Ibid, 13.

CHAPTER THREE

My Young Élève

Monticello, 6 Aug. 1809
Dear Sir,

Under the constant hope of an early departure for Bedford, I have been hitherto detained by the prevalence of a disease in our neighborhood, and particularly among my own people. Although abated, it still has not left us, and the importance of attention to it still detains me here, and for a time which cannot be ascertained. The expectation that every case might be the last, has prevented my sooner informing you of the delay, and proposing that my intended absence should no longer postpone the commencement of the course of study which you propose to undertake with us. Should the situation of my people permit me to set out on my journey before you come, I will leave with Mr. Bankhead the books which I would first recommend for your reading. With every desire to be useful to you, I pray you to accept the assurance of my great esteem and respect.

Th. Jefferson[1]

This letter came to sixteen-year-old William Cabell Rives from his distinguished teacher. Rives moved in with a friend in the village of Milton and at least once a week visited Jefferson at his mountaintop home. Jefferson loaned him books from his library and directed him in a "general and diversified course of reading." Titles included Locke's *Essay on Human Understanding*, Joyce's *Scientifical Dialogues*, Vattel's *Law of Nations*, and Turgot's *Réflexion sur la Formation et la Distribution de Richesses*.[2] After a year, Rives moved to Charlottesville and began studying law. Jefferson recommended he begin with "Coke on Littleton," a 1628 treatise by Sir Edward Coke (1552-1634) that included Sir Thomas Littleton's 1481 treatise on property. Works by Coke were required reading for English and American lawyers well into the nineteenth century. Jefferson insisted Rives master this particular text "thoroughly, in all its black letter obscurity and abstruseness," before proceeding to "light reading of the law." Rives diligently applied himself and by the second year of his study had "successfully surmounted this *pons asinorum* of the profession."[3] This imposing material put Rives in the lifetime habit of always reading carefully and thoroughly. He was unable to read lightly for enjoyment and consequently "read less than many of my contemporaries." The dense legal material also seems to have affected his prose. While some of his letters are more readable and concise, his written speeches, diplomatic dispatches and Madison biography are challenging in their prolixity.

Rives remembered that Jefferson and his family were invariably welcoming and kind during his two years of study. Despite his friendly courtesy, the great man intimidated Rives by "the vastness of his intellectual powers, enhanced by the serene and abstract air of a philosopher which belonged to him, in combination with a very imposing person and appearance." Young Rives was shorter and less brilliant than his tutor. He could not hope to duplicate Jefferson's grasp of the assigned material, which provoked feelings of "constraint and embarrassment." His conversations with Jefferson prepared Rives for later audiences with European statesmen and monarchs, as well as U.S. leaders, whom he found less impressive than "this unpretending but most

imposing republican citizen of my native state." After struggling
to reach Jefferson's intellectual level, discourse with anyone else
seemed easy.[4]

William and Mary lifted Rives' sentence of expulsion, and he
returned to study in the fall of 1811, after autumnal frosts permitted a safe return to that "Malarious region."[5] He refrained from
further youthful mischief and remained there until the following summer. Jefferson had him carry two papers to the college for
Mr. Blackburn, a William and Mary Mathematics professor. The
papers contained Jefferson's new solutions to complex problems.
The professor was amazed that any man in Virginia had such
command of "the exact sciences." Even more amazing, that man
was Virginia's "busiest and most successful practical politician."

At William and Mary, Rives continued reading books Jefferson
recommended to him. While at Oak Ridge, before he left for
William and Mary, Rives received an instructive letter from
Jefferson.

> Monticello Sep. 18. 11
> Dear Sir,
>
> . . . Nothing can be sounder than your view of the
> importance of laying a broad foundation in other
> branches of knolege [sic] whereon to raise the super-
> structure of any particular science which one would
> desire to profess with credit and usefulness. The lam-
> entable disregard of this since the revolution has filled
> our country with Blackstone lawyers,[6] Sangrado[7] phy-
> sicians, a ranting clergy, and a lounging gentry, who
> render neither honor nor service to mankind; and
> when their country has occasion for scientific services,
> it looks for them in vain over its wide extended sur-
> face. The particular sciences too, which you propose to

yourself, are certainly well allied to that of the lawyer, who has many occasions at the bar for mathematical knolege, and cannot, without disreputation, be ignorant of the physical condition of the subjects which surround him. History the closest adjunct of the law, can be acquired in our cabinet, but mathematics and natural philosophy require academical aids and I know no place where this can be had to greater profit than at William and Mary. It possesses the double advantage of as able professors and a better apparatus than any other institution I know.

Inasmuch therefore as you are not pressed in time to begin the practice of your profession, I entirely approve your idea of going there to perfect yourself in these sciences. I would not however, while there, lose time in attending to branches which can be as well acquired by reading in retirement as by listening to lecturers, such are history before mentioned, ethics, politics, political economy, belles letters etc. Considering the progress you have already made in the law, and that it's [sic] greater difficulties are now surmounted, the habit of reflection in that line should not be lost by an entire disuse. I would devote an hour or two of the four and twenty to maintain the ground gained and even to advance it. This would be done by reading the reporters which may really be considered as but the light reading of that science. But you should common place them as you go, and doing that, take great pains to acquire the habit of condensing your matter and of considering ideas in the fewest and most correct words possible. They will thus occupy less space in the mind and leave more room in it for other aphorisms.

Among the modern languages to be attended to the

Spanish is important. Within your day, our country will have more communication with that than with any other language but it's own. All our antient [sic] history too is written in that language. Spanish, English and French cover the whole face of our continents and islands and the last as the language of science and of general conversation is an universal passport. They are therefore the languages exclusively which every American of education ought to possess. I think it useless to lose time on Italian, German etc. which . . . are rather beyond the limits of utility for us. I have thus hazarded my thoughts to you frankly because you desired it, believing at the same time that your own judgement and appetite for science would be sure guides for you.

Be assured in all situations of my friendship and respect,

Th Jefferson[8]

Jefferson's words about the increasing importance of the Spanish language seem prophetic in twenty-first century America. French was the language of diplomacy throughout the nineteenth century. As previously mentioned, Rives did not always compress ideas into the fewest words possible as an author, nor did Jefferson himself abide by twenty-first century standards of brevity. "When in the course of human events . . ." are stirring and memorable words that might have been deleted by a modern editor.

When war with England was declared on June 18, 1812, 19-year-old Rives wanted to enlist in the army as his father had done at age 17. However, his father counseled the young man to postpone military service and continue learning the law. He entered the law office of George Hay, though he spent more time observing court cases involving "most distinguished practitioners" than he did in the office. While in Richmond Rives met Supreme Court Chief Justice John Marshall as well as legendary orator John Randolph of Roanoke. He enjoyed the company of fellow aspiring lawyers Abel Parker Upshur, later Secretary of State and Francis Walker Gilmer, son of the Doctor George Gilmer who had tended to Rives' mother. Francis Walker Gilmer became a Professor of Law at the University of Virginia.[9]

On May 2, 1814, Rives obtained his law license. His first legal action was addressing a grand jury in his native Nelson County. Two days later he turned 21, "the age of legal maturity." Before settling down as a country lawyer, he wanted to travel. He carried letters of introduction from Thomas Jefferson to prominent figures along the east coast, which Jefferson wrote May 17 and 18, 1814. Rives was likely a guest at Monticello those two days. Because Rives only got as far as New York, some of the letters remained in his possession and became treasured family keepsakes. Intended recipients included The Honorable John Langdon of New Hampshire, Governor Daniel Tompkins of New York, General Henry Dearborne of Boston (Secretary of War under Jefferson), and John Adams.

> Monticello May 18. 14.
> My dear Sir,
>
> This will be handed you by Mr. Rives a young gentleman of this state and my neighborhood. he is an *élève* of mine in law, of uncommon abilities, learning and worth. When you and I shall be at rest with our friends of 1776, he will be in the zenith of his fame and usefulness. Before entering on his public career he wishes to visit our sister states and would not conceive he had

seen any thing of Massachusetts were he not to see the venerable patriot of Braintree. I therefore request your indulgence of his wishes to be presented to you, a favor to which his high esteem for your character will give double value. But his wishes would be but partly gratified were he not presented to Mrs. Adams also. may I then ask this additional favor of you, which I shall value the more as it will give him the opportunity which I hope of bringing back to me a favorable report of both your healths. Accept as heretofore the assurances of my affectionate esteem & respect

Th Jefferson[10]

Jefferson mailed a similar letter to Adams on the same day. He wrote Adams a longer letter July 5, saying Rives was on his way. In that letter he commented on Adams' reported illness saying their "machines" have been running over 70 years and parts will inevitably fail, a wheel, a pinion or a spring until "all will at length surcease motion." Adams replied on July 16, "Whenever Mr. Rives, of whom I have heard nothing, shall arrive, he shall receive all the cordial civilities in my power."[11]

Rives recorded in his journal that Washington D.C. in early summer of 1814 seemed like a dependency of the older city of Georgetown. The British would burn the city on August 24. He admired New Jersey farmland and churches. The College of New Jersey at Princeton seemed inferior to William and Mary in his opinion. He found the city of New York impressive from a distance, but dirty and architecturally deficient upon closer examination. News of British invading forces made him decide to return to Virginia.

The burning of Washington stiffened American resolve to fight, and thousands of Americans, including William Cabell Rives, volunteered for service. Rives became aide de camp to General John Hartwell Cocke, who commanded a force of Virginia militia. They drilled and trained for an invasion that never happened. After the burning of Washington and the bombardment of Fort McHenry, the British sailed to Jamaica and then to the January 8, 1815 battle of New Orleans that, unbeknownst to its combatants, took place after the Treaty of Ghent had been signed on December 24.

Rives favorably impressed General Cocke, with whom he maintained a long friendship. Cocke was another vital supporter of Jefferson's establishing the University of Virginia. The general later shared Rives' interest in colonization of freed slaves, in agriculture, and he provided crucial advice when Rives and his wife sought to build a stone church in their neighborhood. General Cocke wrote a letter to Rives' cousin Joseph Carrington Cabell on September 21, 1814 saying, "My staff promises to do credit to themselves and afford me the greatest satisfaction, My choice of an aid I shall enumerate among the lucky moments of my life. I think Rives is one of the very finest young men I have ever known."[12]

After the militia was disbanded in February 1815, Rives returned to Oak Ridge and began practicing law in Nelson, Amherst and Buckingham counties. He filed a lawsuit on behalf of his father and business partner James Brown over the 1813 loss of a large shipment of flour to Cadiz, Spain. Rives and another lawyer recovered a settlement of over $100,000, an enormous sum at the time. He also supervised cultivation of a 991-acre tract of land near Oak Ridge given to him by his father. He named it Ranston after a Rives ancestral estate in Dorset, England.

Margaret Jordan Cabell Rives died August 19, 1815. After the death of his wife, for the remaining thirty years of his life, Robert Rives gradually retired from his larger commercial affairs to devote more time to his farms. He did not remarry. His oldest daughter Margaret Jordan Rives (1792-1862), known to her numerous nieces and nephews as Aunt Peggy, did not marry and "became the stay of her father's declining years."[13]

Rives' political debut took place on July 4, 1816 when he delivered a speech to the people of Nelson County. Residents of Nelson County and all western portions of Virginia wanted more equal representation and more attention to their needs from the state government. One of the problems was the three fifths rule used in the U.S. and State Constitutions specifying that slaves could not vote, but counted as three fifths of a person for political districting purposes. This gave white residents of Tidewater disproportionate political power because of its large slave population. The problem would continue through Virginia's 1829 Constitutional Convention and after.[14] Rives and his brother Landon were elected delegates to an August convention in the Shenandoah Valley town of Staunton. The convention, attended by "the most experienced and distinguished public men of the State" addressed methods of amending the state constitution.[15]

In January 1817, Rives traveled to Washington and Baltimore. He carefully and critically observed sessions of Congress. He would become very familiar with the place and the participants over the next thirty years. He was not entirely impressed. During sessions, legislators lived and dined in boarding houses. Rives was a guest of Senator James Barbour, a former Virginia governor whom Rives had met when he lived in Richmond. Barbour's "messmates" included Nathaniel Macon of North Carolina, Senator Charles Tait of Georgia, John C. Calhoun of South Carolina, and Thomas Telfair of Georgia. Rives found their conversation dull. After dinner Telfair, Tait and Calhoun fell asleep, snoring in "horrible discord, without seeming to arouse any notice among the rest of the group."[16]

Manners, class, refinement and character were crucial to Rives. He was often snobbish and condescending in his appraisal of those he found deficient in gentlemanly attributes. Rives found Macon "coarse and savage" in manner, unjustifiably confident of his wisdom and the infallibility of his opinions. Later encounters would revise his first impression of Calhoun, who seemed "silent and apparently unsociable." Though Rives speculated that some temporary weariness may have caused this behavior, he wrote that Calhoun's "character would be improved by infusing a little more ardour & vivacity into it."[17] Calhoun summoned more ardour and vivacity than Rives desired when the two would later strenuously oppose each other on the Senate floor on a number of issues.

John Randolph of Roanoke failed to live up to Rives' expectation. Rives thought his speeches were not well organized. He wrote that the famed orator held his audience with an intense concentrated style and a brilliant sentence or two, but afterwards the audience could not remember the argument. Most of Randolph's contemporaries regarded his oratory more favorably.[18] Famous for his stinging eloquence, Randolph once characterized Jackson's Secretary of State Edward Livingston as "a man of splendid abilities, but utterly corrupt. He shines and stinks like rotten mackerel by moonlight."[19] That sentence trumped any amount of organization.

Speaker of the House Henry Clay, whom Rives would often oppose but would also come to respect, also disappointed. Rives found him animated and eloquent, but lacking "reasoning or force of argument in his speech." Rives compared him to a hunting hound, who "overruns his game in the heat of the chase, & is compelled to retrace his steps & begin the pursuit anew." As Clay repeated and redeveloped his themes, Rives noted that his voice and energy would sink, which deflated the effect.[20]

Clay's reputation survives as a gifted orator and political genius. Rives was self-critical, and seldom satisfied with his own speechmaking. Of the three famous antebellum politicians Clay,

Calhoun, and Webster, Rives would have the most cordial relations with Webster. He praised fellow Virginian Philip Pendleton Barbour for his "clarity & cogency" of argument, "propriety & elegance" of diction in the "most "erudite & philosophical" speech he heard at the time. He also noticed Col. Richard Mentor Johnson of Kentucky, who would best Rives in the 1836 Vice-Presidential contest. He considered Johnson a bad speaker, "confused, awkward & inelegant," but a man of "good plain sense," respected for his firmness and honesty, though lacking first-rate talent.[21]

The most significant introduction during Rives' trip took place at a New Year's Day reception in Baltimore for President James Madison. This was the beginning of a nearly 20-year friendship between Rives and Madison. Rives' relationship with the fourth president would influence his politics and occupy much of his post-political life.[22]

In April 1817 Rives offered himself as a candidate for election to the Virginia House of Delegates. He promised to support principles of Jefferson and Madison. He was elected in November to a four-year term in what Virginians proudly call the "oldest continuously meeting legislative body in the Western Hemisphere." The election also brought James Monroe to the presidency. Monroe asked Rives to serve as his private secretary, but Rives declined because of his election to the legislature.[23]

Despite his youth and freshman status, Rives was appointed chairman of a committee to investigate the James River Company for non-fulfillment of its charter to improve navigation of the river. Nelson County and the Cabell family lands lay along the James, making the issue important for his constituents and family. The committee's report faulted the company, but recommended a legal trial to reveal all the facts before the legislature should take action. Several veteran legislators opposed this deliberate method. They wanted to throw out the old company immediately and incorporate a new one. One of this faction, Mr.

Archibald Thweatt of Chesterfield, repeatedly referred to Rives as "the young gentleman." The majority voted to follow Rives' recommendation. The legal proceeding took place, followed by the incorporation of the James River and Kanawha Company, which constructed a canal that remained an important commercial artery for the next 50 years.[24] Rives' cousin and Virginia State Senator Joseph Carrington Cabell was called "Father of the James River and Kanawha Canal" for his efforts.[25]

In his second Virginia General Assembly session, Rives argued for locating the University of Virginia in Charlottesville. This was repayment of kindness to his former instructor Jefferson. The originally named Central College had been approved by the General Assembly in 1814. Jefferson designed its buildings and the cornerstone of the first structure, Pavilion VII also known as the Colonnade Club, was laid in 1817 with Jefferson, Madison and Monroe present. Jefferson through his supporters in the General Assembly, including Cabell and Rives, pushed for establishment of a state university. The College of William and Mary opposed the idea. Some advocated locating the school in Lexington or Staunton. The General Assembly voted in Charlottesville's favor and the University of Virginia was officially chartered January 25, 1819.[26] The young *élève* had already proven his usefulness.

* * *

1 Quoted by W. C. Rives to Hugh Blair Grigsby April 6, 1866, Rives MSS, LOC, box 93.

2 William C. Rives Memorandum, August 24, 1809, Rives MSS, LOC, cited in Raymond Dingledine, Jr., "The Political Career of William Cabell Rives," 14.

3 Ibid. "Coke on Littleton" is explained on the website www.http:legal-dictionary.thefreedictionary.com. Coke's name is pronounced "cook." *Pons asinorum* (asses bridge) refers to the fifth proposition of the first book

of Euclid, and the expression means a difficult but essential problem for beginners.

4 Ibid.

5 WCR, Jr., Biography, Rives MSS, LOC, box 103, 13.

6 English Judge Sir William Blackstone (1723-1780) wrote a four Volume *Commentaries on the Laws of England* that invoked Judeo Christian foundation to the law. Some contemporaries felt that Blackstone was presumptuous in trying to compress centuries of English common law into four volumes. (Special thanks to Georgetown Law Professor James Oldham.)

7 Dr. Sangrado was a quack physician in the 18th century novel *Gil Blas*.

8 Rives to Grigsby, April 6, 1866, Ibid. The letter is also available at the Library of Congress web site under The Thomas Jefferson Papers Series www.http://hdl.loc.gov/loc.mss/mtj.mtjbib020706.

9 *Genealogy of the Page Family in Virginia*, Richard Channing Moore Page, Second Edition 1893, Reprinted C. J. Carrier Co., Harrisonburg, Va. 1972, 222.

10 University of Virginia Special Collections microfilm 3375 M-510 of original in Library of Congress.

11 *The Adams-Jefferson Letters*, Edited by Lester J. Capon, Vol. II, 1812-1826, University of North Carolina Press, 1959. 430-434.

12 General John H. Cocke to Joseph C. Cabell 9-21-14. Joseph C. Cabell papers, Special Collections Department, University of Virginia Library.

13 James Rives Childs, *Reliques of the Rives*, 569-570.

14 *The Last of the Fathers, James Madison and the Republican Legacy*, Drew R. McCoy, Cambridge University Press, 1989 see Chapter 6: 217-252.

15 W. R. Rives to Hugh Blair Grigsby, 4-6-66, Ibid.

16 W. C. Rives Journal, 1817, Rives MSS, LOC, quoted in Dingledine, Ibid, 32.

17 Ibid. 33.

18 Ibid.

19 William Cabell Bruce, *John Randolph of Roanoke 1773-1833*, Vol. II, 197.

New York, G. P. Putnam's Sons, 1922. Randolph coined the term "Kitchen Cabinet" to describe Jackson's inner circle. Randolph was accusing Livingston of being the author of Jackson's Nullification Proclamation during a speech at Charlotte Court House. (Special thanks to Jean Martin, Senior Editor of *Harvard Magazine*).

20 Ibid.

21 Ibid.

22 WCR, Jr., Biography, Ibid., 30.

23 Ibid. 31.

24 W. C. Rives to Hugh Blair Grigsby, April 4, 1866, Ibid.

25 Alexander Brown, *The Cabells and Their Kin*, 28.

26 Virginius Dabney, *Mr. Jefferson's University, A History*, Charlottesville, University Press of Virginia, 1981, 3-4.

CHAPTER FOUR

Full Blown Rose

William Cabell Rives achieved his life's greatest and happiest success March 24, 1819. On that day he married Miss Judith Page Walker of Castle Hill, Albemarle County. Rives' wife would be his thoughtful and constant supporter. Whenever they were apart they corresponded incessantly. Letters between the two of them, which survive in the Library of Congress, the Library of Virginia, the University of Virginia Library and other collections number in the thousands. Their letters brim with affectionate expressions, indicating a love interrupted only by death.

According to one of their sons, "Mrs. Rives' part in her husband's successful career was no insignificant one. He was of a delicate, nervous, excitable diathesis [susceptibility to disease]; she of a calm equable temper with deep and strong feelings but under admirable control and of a religious faith of an intensity which rose superior to all the ills and sorrows of life and was her unfailing support in all circumstances of trial."[1]

By birth and by marriage, Rives was connected to families of many Virginia political leaders, past and present. He and his bride believed in an aristocracy, perched atop a well-defined social order. They felt members of the upper class were qualified and obligated to govern. In her unfinished autobiography, Judith commented on her husband's ascendant early political career, "In those days, education, talent, a noble nature, and even advantages of birth and fortune, instead of being disqualifications for the public service and favor, were considered the best requisites."[2] Only wealthier citizens could afford to travel to the state or

Castle Hill, West Front, 1764.

national capital and reside there during legislative sessions of the early 1800s. The right and power of the aristocracy to rule diminished during Rives' lifetime. His conservative nature hindered his ability to adjust to the change.

Judith Page Walker was born March 24, 1802 at Castle Hill, which had been built in 1764 by her grandfather Dr. Thomas Walker (1715-1794). Dr. Walker explored and named the Cumberland Gap in 1750. He served with Rives' grandfather Col. William Cabell in the colonial legislature and French and Indian War. Walker became 14-year-old Thomas Jefferson's legal guardian after Peter Jefferson died in 1757. Walker moved to the eight thousand acre Castle Hill property in 1741, when he married Mildred Thornton (1721-1778), who was the widow of Nicholas Meriwether. Relations of explorer Meriwether Lewis, the Meriwether family had obtained a grant of over 17,000 acres in the area by King George II in the 1720s. Dr. Thomas Walker founded the town of Charlottesville in 1762, and was active and influential in politics, business and agriculture.

Thomas and Mildred Walker had twelve children. Their eleventh child and youngest son Francis inherited Castle Hill. Francis Walker (1764-1806) represented the counties of Albemarle and Orange in the U.S. House of Representatives 1793-1795. Francis married Jane Byrd Nelson (1775-1808), whose pedigree included Byrd, Carter, and Page ancestors.[3] Francis and Jane Walker had two daughters and a son, but their happiness was short lived. Francis' death was followed a year later by the death of his seven-year-old son Thomas Hugh Walker. The next year Jane died, leaving two young orphan daughters.

Jane Frances Walker (1799-1873) and her younger sister Judith clung to each other following their loss, and remained cherished companions and confidants. The two girls spent most of their childhood in Richmond with their maternal grandmother Judith Page Nelson. After both girls were married, Castle Hill was divided into two tracts of approximately 4,000 acres, which were "assigned by lot." Judith gained the portion with Thomas Walker's house while Jane and her husband Dr. Mann Page settled the adjoining parcel, which they called Keswick.[4]

Judith and Jane were educated by a series of tutors engaged by their grandmother. Subjects included English, French, Italian and music. Judith devoured the novels of Sir Walter Scott, and apparently read with greater speed and pleasure than her future husband. Her prose, though sometimes over-ornamented, is generally more accessible than her husband's.

Judith was only ten when she first met 19-year-old William Cabell Rives, who visited her grandmother's house while he was in Richmond. She liked to steal his law books and put her children's storybooks in their place. Judith wrote that Rives was a favorite of "the more advanced young ladies" of the household and that he was a handsome youth.

"A slight but active figure, about, or perhaps five feet eight may be called a little below the middle stature, eyes of clear

William Cabell Rives   *Judith Page Walker Rives*

hazel, whose sparkling glance allumined the dark brows above a forehead so symmetrical and fair that it looked as if just from a sculptor's hand, shaded by a profusion of dark waving hair. In repose, the features might have seemed almost stern, even at that youthful day; but their thoughtful expression was often contradicted by a smile of peculiar sweetness, revealing beautiful teeth, and even calling dimples into play, which he denied, as being ornaments too effeminate for a man, as he already thought himself. . . ."[5]

Two years later Rives appeared in his militia uniform. His bearing had become "more manly, the eagle glance more penetrating," and his cheek had been "embrowned by camp life."[6]

Despite these favorable impressions, Judith rejected Rives' first serious proposal in 1818. She was impressed that he was a barrister and legislator, but she protested that she was only sixteen and too young to commit herself. His face was pale when they bade each other "adieu," with mixed emotions.[7] Judith had other suitors, and turned down seven marriage proposals.[8]

Months later Judith was a guest at Farmington, home of George Divers, husband of Judith's Aunt Martha Walker Divers.

A few miles west of Charlottesville, the Farmington home is now the clubhouse of Farmington Country Club. It has an octagonal wing designed by Thomas Jefferson, who was a friend of Divers. William Cabell Rives accepted an invitation to Farmington at the time of Judith's visit, and he renewed his courtship over the course of several days. He and Judith read aloud the story of Gaudentio di Lucca that described how Italian suitors hundreds of years before would propose to their ladies fair. A lover would offer a rosebud. The lady's acceptance signified encouragement. If she accepted a half opened rose, his hope increased. If she took his proffered full-blown rose and wore it, they were betrothed. Rives enacted the sequence with trembling hands. Judith accepted the flowers in their turn, placing the two full-blown roses offered last in the belt of her corsage on the left side.[9]

Judith insisted however that they could not be married until she reached the "respectable" age of seventeen. Her ardent fiancé insisted that the ceremony take place March 24, her seventeenth birthday. She protested that the weather and condition of the roads that time of year would be unfavorable, but eventually she agreed to the plan. When the day arrived, rivers were swollen and roads nearly impassable. The bridegroom faced a 50-mile journey from Oak Ridge. According to the expectant bride, "people in earnest are rather stimulated than deterred by obstacles."[10] When the coach and four, intended to convey bride and groom back to Oak Ridge, had to turn back at a swollen river ford, Rives plunged in on horseback and was nearly swept away in the current. Apparently Rives' younger brother Robert Rives, Jr. followed suit and the pair safely reached Castle Hill. Robert took his brother aside and confided that he did not find Judith as attractive as he had imagined. "It's too late now," exclaimed the happy groom.[11]

Portraits and photos show Judith was not a great beauty. Her nose was conspicuously large. She described her younger self as "a delicate child, with a complexion like bleached wax, hands that could not compass much more than half an octave on the piano, and feet that seemed to be made more for ornament than use."[12] In portraits of later years, she appears to have maintained a trim figure even after bearing six children. Her intellect and charm enabled her to shine in Washington and Paris society. Rives knew he was a lucky man. 47 years later he called his marriage "the connection to which I owe the happiness of my life."[13]

The Reverend Samuel Wydown, an English clergyman visiting the neighborhood, performed the wedding ceremony at Castle Hill. In her will, Judith noted that she was married in the same first floor room of the old house in which she later gave birth to William C. Rives, Jr., and his youngest sister Ella.[14]

A spell of sunny weather enabled the arrival of the wedding coach. Judith received a warm welcome from the Rives household at Oak Ridge. The couple then toured Virginia by coach. They visited Natural Bridge to the south and the various mineral springs in the western part of the state including White Sulphur, Salt Sulphur, Warm Springs and Stribling's (Augusta) Springs. Judith noted that the company at the springs was aristocratic because it was limited to owners of carriages, horses and servants. The lodgings were not luxurious, but the spring baths were "as clear as a diamond and as large as the sea, varied and wonderful in every degree of temperature, and bubbling up from the crystal depth as if a troop of genii were about to appear dancing and singing among the waves."[15]

The newlyweds returned to Oak Ridge and then to Castle Hill. Thomas Jefferson called upon them on his way to visit Madison at Montpelier, some 15 miles to the north. Jefferson offered pleasant recollections of previous visits to Castle Hill and Judith's grandfather Thomas Walker. "Mr. Jefferson was far advanced in life at this period, but his manners were pleasing, his voice and general conversation very attractive, his eye bright, and his tall figure had lost none of its uprightness. With his back turned, and especially on horseback, no one would have suspected that nearly eighty years had passed over such a form."[16] They accepted Jefferson's invitation to visit him at Monticello, which Judith found pictur-esque and impressive.

After much deliberation whether to build a home at Ranston in Nelson County or live at Castle Hill in Albemarle County, the couple decided on Castle Hill. A principal factor in the decision was that Albemarle seemed to offer better political prospects.

Judith accompanied her husband to Richmond their first winter together for the Virginia legislative session. The General Assembly debated issues, which would inflame the entire nation: the National Bank and the Missouri question.

Virginia had taken a stand in 1799 opposing the plan of Congress to incorporate a National Bank. Rives remained staunchly Anti-National Bank for his entire political career. He supported a resolution condemning the 1819 McCullough v. Maryland Supreme Court decision, which affirmed the constitu-tionality of the second Bank of the United States. Southerners and westerners were generally opposed to the national bank for a number of reasons, including that they believed it enriched its northern investors and unfairly suppressed competition from state banks, which more freely loaned to farmers and small businessmen.

Even more portentous was the Missouri issue. Missouri applied for admission to the Union as a slave state. This would have upset the balance of eleven free and eleven slave states, giv-ing slave states control of the Senate. The Missouri Compromise, engineered by Henry Clay, brought in Maine as a free state along with Missouri as a free state. It also prohibited slavery north of the parallel extending west from Missouri's southern border in the remaining Louisiana Purchase territory. Rives supported a resolution condemning the Missouri "Restriction."[17]

Debate about the Missouri question also involved the question of whether the General Assembly could instruct or merely request how its U.S. Senators should vote on any issue. Senators were selected by state legislatures until the law for direct election by voters was passed in 1913. Rives felt the legislature was entitled to request, but not instruct its Senators. He felt instruction discounted the Senator's own intelligence and discretion. Rives' political opponents would later use his opposition to the doctrine of instruction against him. He would one day resign his U. S. Senate seat rather than obey the legislature's instruction.[18]

Having moved to Albemarle County, Rives could no longer represent Nelson County and did not serve in the 1821-22 General Assembly. He was elected as a Delegate from Albemarle in 1822. Rives wrote his old friend Jefferson a letter on February 6, telling him that the General Assembly had authorized a loan of $60,000 to the University of Virginia. This was much needed money and Rives said the amount was sufficient to fund construction of buildings on the scale Jefferson designed. The letter stated that it would be too soon to declare the $60,000 as an outright gift and for the state to assume any of the University's debt. However, he proposed to do that at a more favorable time. Many legislators, along with Jefferson and Rives, favored state supported primary schools. Trying to fund both presented a challenge.[19]

The most important issue of the ensuing session was discussion of the Virginia Kentucky Compact of 1789. The issue was whether settlers of Kentucky land, if evicted by non-resident title-holders, could claim compensation for improvements and cultivation of the land. The Virginia Senate and House could not agree on legal particulars, so a joint session was convened. Judge Henry St. George Tucker was chosen to argue the Senate's position. He spoke first. Rives was chosen to speak for the House of Delegates. At the conclusion of his speech, Tucker congratulated Rives on the way he rebutted his arguments.[20] Forty-four years later, Rives wrote, "there is no event of my public life which, for various reasons, brings back to me, in the recollection, more gratifying reflections."[21]

His career in the Virginia legislature thus ended pleasantly, and he was now ready for Washington.

* * *

1   WCR, Jr., Biography, Rives MSS, LOC, box 103,71.

2   Judith Page Rives, *Grandmama's Autobiography for Her Grandchildren*, The original handwritten copy is in Rives MSS, LOC, Box 103. A typewritten copy is in Rives MSS, UVa., Accession #2532, Box 1. Many of these typewritten copies exist, including one in the author's possession, which will be subsequently noted as Judith Page Rives *Autobiography*.

3   R. C. M. Page, *Genealogy of the Page Family in Virginia*, 230-231. Historian and genealogist Franklin H. Moore has traced Jane Byrd Nelson's pedigree back to King Edward III of England.

4   *Autobiography*, 58.

5   Ibid. 18.

6   Ibid. 27.

7   Ibid. 39.

8   Dingledine, "The Political Career of William C. Rives," 45.

9   *Autobiography*, 48.

10 Ibid. 51.

11 WCR, Jr. Biography, Ibid., 71.

12 *Autobiography*, 8.

13 W. C. Rives to Hugh Blair Grigsby, April 4, 1866. Rives MSS, LOC, Box 93.

14 Last Will and Testament of Judith Page Rives, Rives MSS UVa., Accession # 2313, Box 4.

15 *Autobiography*, Ibid. 54.

16 Ibid. 57.

17 WCR, Jr., Biography, Ibid, 32.

18 Dingledine, Ibid, 49.

19 William Cabell Rives to Thomas Jefferson, February 6, 1822, Letters
    to and from Jefferson, 1821-1822, Electronic Text Center, University
    of Virginia Library, http://etext.lib.virginia.edu/toc/modeng/public/
    Jef7Gri.html.

20 WCR, Jr. Biography, Ibid, 3.

21 W. C. Rives to Hugh Blair Grigsby, April 4, 1866, Ibid.

CHAPTER FIVE

Dolley's Diamonds

RIVES WAS ELECTED TO CONGRESS in 1823 to take the place of his neighbor Judge Hugh Nelson of Belvoir, two miles distant from Castle Hill. Having held the seat since 1811, Nelson had been appointed Minister to Spain by President Monroe. Rives addressed his prospective constituents in Albemarle and Amherst counties and said that he would uphold Jeffersonian ideals if elected. He would protect farmers from manufacturing interests of the north. He opposed tariffs and internal improvement laws that he said were not only partial and unequal, but unconstitutional as well, violating Jefferson's concept of a government with limited powers.[1] Rives was unopposed in the election, though according to his son, elder kinsman Joseph C. Cabell had coveted the seat.[2]

The Rives family was brightened and enlarged by the birth of Francis Robert Rives February 16, 1822. The first of three sons who lived to adulthood, Francis would become a New York lawyer. Along with duties of new motherhood, Judith had to prepare for a winter in Washington as congressional wife. "In those days the duties of a Virginia Housewife required as much executive talent as those of a minister of state." She wrote that there were duties in the 1820s that had become obsolete 40 years later. The mistress of a plantation house carried keys to the larder, smokehouse, and all places food was stored. Referring to slaves who worked as house servants, she wrote she had to "think of those who thought not for themselves." Quoting from the verses about the Good Wife, Proverbs 31:15, Judith recounted that her days began as in Old Testament times: "She riseth while it is yet night, and giveth meat to her household, and a portion to her maidens."[3]

Like his wife, Rives was an early riser in Washington. On occasion he was up and about before then Secretary of State John Quincy Adams.[4] Adams liked to take early morning nude swims in the Potomac, and stories abound with varying particulars about his clothes being waylaid onshore.

The journey from Castle Hill required at least two or three days. Rives traveled by horse and carriage over bad roads to Fredericksburg. There he sent the carriage back and proceeded by boat down the Rappahannock and up the Potomac to the capital.

The House of Representatives of the 18th U.S. Congress included distinguished figures Rives had previously seen in action: Speaker of the House Henry Clay, Daniel Webster, John Randolph, and future President James Buchanan. The Presidency of James Monroe 1817-1825 was marked by a national harmony in its first six years that became known as "The Era of Good Feeling." That era was drawing to a close when Rives arrived to take his congressional seat. President Monroe had proposed a system of internal improvements of canals and roads, including the Cumberland Road, in his December 2, 1823 message to Congress.[5]

Rives first speech was against the "Bill for Federal System of Internal Improvements." Like many of his subsequent performances in the House and later the Senate, the speech was lawyerly and lengthy. He abided by his promise to advocate Jeffersonian limited government. He argued that the Constitution gave the Federal Government power over "objects only in which all the States have a common interest," including regulation of commerce, negotiations with foreign powers, declaring war, regulating a national currency and establishing uniform weights and measures. He declared the Constitution did not give the Federal government power to build roads and canals. Rives invoked

statements by Patrick Henry and Alexander Hamilton supporting his position. He rebutted previous speeches on the matter by
Henry Clay "the honorable Speaker," and Congressmen McLane
of Delaware and Storrs of New York. He criticized Storrs for
using the term "National Government." Rives said their government was Federal, with defined and limited powers, as opposed
to National, which in his opinion would imply unlimited power
over the states. In his conclusion Rives said, "If the inhabitants of
the States, instead of looking to their governments at home, are
to look to the General Government (as they certainly will, if this
system should be adopted,) for the ordinary facilities of travelling
and transportation, then the State governments become useless
machines, and are not worth the expense of maintaining. . . ."[6]
The speech failed to persuade a majority and the bill passed 115
to 86.[7]

Rives voted against a bill for improvement of the navigation of
the Mississippi and Ohio Rivers. Congress also considered bills
for improvement of rifles and muskets manufactured at armories,
appropriations for the Navy, Indian affairs, and relief of distill-
ers. The house tabled a bill regarding claims from the widow of
Pierre Beaumarchais. Beaumarchais was a French watchmaker
and author of *Le Barbier de Seville* and *Le Mariage de Figaro* who
had invested his own money in securing arms and support for
the American Revolutionary cause. The claims were not settled
until 1835 by payments to his heirs.[8]

After a few weeks, Rives returned to Castle Hill for Judith and
their son. Judith brought along jewelry loaned to her by Dolley
Madison. The Rives had called upon the Madisons at Montpelier
in the fall. The Madisons had visited Castle Hill, and Rives and
Madison would later serve together on the University of Virginia
Board of Visitors. During some of those meetings Dolley would
remain at Castle Hill with Judith. When the Rives visited
Montpelier in the autumn of 1823, Dolley insisted that Judith

accept a loan of a necklace and a Maltese cross of diamonds. Dolley ordered her to wear them when attending social functions because her old friends would recognize them and "they will be as much a passport to their hearts as the letters of introduction I have given you."[9]

More important than Dolley's diamonds was the political counsel James Madison would provide. Rives would need several years to absorb Madison's teachings. As he matured politically, he would change from a Jeffersonian advocate of states rights and limited government to a Madisonian proponent of Constitution and Union. Though Jefferson and Madison maintained a legendary friendship, they had their political differences. Jefferson did not initially endorse the Constitution, and later advocated periodic conventions to revise the Constitution. Madison thought this would be unstable. Having observed the French monarchy, Jefferson feared tyranny from concentrated power. Having lived under the Articles of Confederation while Jefferson was in France, Madison feared disorder.[10] Throughout his political life, Rives shared both Jefferson and Madison's belief in the power and efficacy of reason.

Judith described Montpelier as being in a scenic location with "a beautiful horizon in front of the dwelling," and a "superb forest in its rear that bounded the grassy lawn." She was less complimentary about the house. "The building was then a massive and irregular pile with some claim to architectural taste, though evidently the combined work of several generations." James Madison's mother, then in her nineties, occupied one wing. The morning was chilly and a fire was blazing in her hearth when Judith visited her, yet her window was open. Mrs. Madison explained to Judith, "It would be impossible for me to live without air."[11]

Of the Father of the Constitution, Judith wrote, "In conversation Mr. Madison was perfectly charming, whether on subjects grave or gay, lively or severe, the vein of playful wit or grave debate seemed inexhaustible." Madison had a brightly colored parrot, a gift from a South American diplomat, which terrorized Judith and bit Madison's finger when he tried to protect her. He serenely accepted the wound.[12]

The winter of 1823-24 was severe, and the frozen Potomac prevented Rives and family from traveling to Washington by boat. The journey to Alexandria by carriage required a full week. Rives kept a pocket account book, in which he noted his travelling expenses from Washington to Castle Hill were $15.85. Expenses on the return trip were $37.08, presumably reflecting a need for more comfortable lodgings and better food with his wife and young son along. He also noted $10.00 for Tom's return expenses along with $1.00 "given Tom." Tom was evidently a trusted servant and coachman. Rives also spent $10.00 on a coat for Tom. Later expenses included $1.25 for shoeing horses, $50.00 for a "surtout [overcoat] and pantaloons" from Burns the tailor, $66.25 for portraits of himself and Judith by an artist named King along with a box to pack them in, $5.00 for washing, $5 for a green silk bonnet for Judith, and 25 cents given to a beggar. Though he noted receiving $480.00 for his crop of wheat, expenditures outweighed income from January to September.[13]

Rives largest payment was $750 to "Captain Perry on account of building."[14] The Rives authorized construction of a brick addition to Castle Hill, much larger than the wooden structure Thomas Walker had built. Their builder, Captain John Perry, was a master brick mason who had assisted Jefferson in the construction of the University of Virginia. The Federal or Roman Revival style brick portion connected to the old house by a spacious hallway or summer living room resulting in an H-shaped configuration.[15] The columned portico of the brick front faces east, overlooking a spacious lady's slipper-shaped lawn rimmed with a variety of trees and boxwood. The older wooden front faces the mountains to the west. In her autobiography Judith observed that some elder neighbors disapproved of plans to enlarge the home that her father and grandfather had considered sufficiently spacious. Disregarding the critics and pessimists, the Rives resolved to make themselves comfortable in a home that has become an architectural landmark. They turned the garden into a lawn and cut down "steeple shaped poplars already showing signs of decay."[16] Perry, a carpenter named Williams, and crew completed their work by Christmas, 1824.[17]

In Alexandria the previous January, the Rives called on Anne Hill Carter Lee, widow of General Henry (Light Horse Harry) Lee. Judith and Mrs. Lee were related through the Carter and Page families. Judith used her tiny son to brighten the invalid matron's day. Judith wrote that Mrs. Lee was "most lovely and charming," though confined by poor health to her curtained bed. Judith carried blue-eyed baby Francis into Mrs. Lee's bedchamber and held him between the parted curtains where the old lady could see him. "I shall never forget the tender sympathetic expression that lighted up her glance as she looked upon him. She seemed to regard the little visitor as one from a brighter sphere, and welcomed him as if he had been an angel."[18]

About a month later Mrs. Lee's son Robert would present himself to Secretary of War John C. Calhoun hoping to be recommended for admission to West Point. Unforeseen by either, Calhoun's later doctrine of nullification would be a significant step on the road to secession and war.[19]

Crossing the Potomac brought the Rives to Washington, which was a disappointment to Judith. Every place in the city seemed at least a mile from everywhere else. In her autobiography Judith admitted to nostalgia prevalent among older people (she was 58 when she was writing). She nevertheless argued that the House and Senate chambers of the 1820s were tasteful and respectable, unlike the "preposterous pile" of later additions, "the meretricious ornaments, the vulgar attempts at sculpture and painting" which were "unknown and unattempted in the simplicity of those happier and better days."[20]

Ladies were welcomed into the Senate chamber in the 1820s, allowed to sit in empty seats set aside for diplomats. Senators would even offer their own seats "when their gallantry disposed them to do homage to their gentle visitors." Although the privilege was "modestly used," Judith lamented that the ladies were later excluded.[21] Rives requested that his wife (playfully she said) stay at home whenever he spoke for fear that he might fail. She cited a letter of praise to her husband from John Randolph as evidence that his fears were unfounded.

> Dear Sir,
>
> On getting home last night, I found your very acceptable note and speech, [Randolph had listened to the speech with pleasure and had requested a written copy.] which last I shall read this day, *Deo volente*, [Randolph hoped that Rives had not made improvements or corrections on the written version] . . . give me a rough and vigorous sketch, a manly negligence which camps may give, but courts never can.
>
> My modesty (don't start) knows not how to reply to the very handsome, too handsome things you say to me and of me. Spare my blushes, but if your health shall permit, I will take it as a favor if you will be here by ten o'clock or as much earlier as your convenience admit you to come.
>
> I am your afflicted but obdt. servant,
>
> J. R. of Roanoke[22]

Though they had disagreements, Randolph never fired one of his lethal verbal shots at Rives. The sting would have endured and prevented Judith from including the letter in her autobiography. Although he opposed her husband on several issues, Daniel Webster, according to Judith, had "a vein of pleasantry in his nature which the portraits and busts that have survived him certainly do not present." Judith invited her intended readers, her grandchildren, to compare her husband's first Congress with "the productions of more Democratic days."[23] In her view, quality had severely declined.

Judith was pleased to see President Monroe and his wife Elizabeth. Monroe had been a friend of Judith's father Francis Walker. Their congressional careers briefly overlapped. Walker served in the House 1793-95 while Monroe served in the Senate 1790-1794. Monroe had served as Minister to France 1794-96, a post Rives was destined to occupy. Judith had not met Mrs. Monroe until presented at a White House reception. Some Americans resented the Monroes for their fluent French and the European flavor they brought to White House functions. Fully enjoying the ambiance, Judith accompanied the French Minister Comte Jules de Menou who whispered to her after she was presented to the first lady, "*Une vraie Ninon de l'Enclos! N'est-ce pas?*" (A veritable Ninon de l'Enclos, isn't she?). Ninon was a celebrated courtesan of the 17th century, renowned for her wisdom and allure. The remark appears to have been a measured compliment.[24]

Four candidates waged a bitter campaign in 1824 to succeed Monroe: John Quincy Adams, William H. Crawford, Andrew Jackson, and Henry Clay. Rives and a majority of Virginians supported Crawford of Georgia, who suffered a stroke during the campaign but still finished third.[25] Jackson won a plurality of electoral and popular votes, but not a majority. The House of Representatives was called upon to decide between Jackson,

Adams and Crawford, the three top finishers. Henry Clay threw his considerable support as Speaker of the House to Adams, drawing charges of a "Corrupt Bargain" when Adams named Clay as his Secretary of State after being chosen as president. The Era of Good Feeling gave way to an era of hard feeling.

The country was able to unite in welcoming the venerable revolutionary hero General Lafayette. He arrived in New York on August 16 and made his way from city to city towards Monticello to see his old friend Jefferson. Lafayette was escorted by an honor guard from Fluvanna and met at the Albemarle County line at eleven a.m., November 4 by the "Albemarle LaFayette Guards," and an enthusiastic crowd. Indicating his political stature, William Cabell Rives had been chosen to deliver a welcoming speech:

General LaFayette,

We are come hither, in the name of the people of Albemarle, to meet you, at the threshold of our country, with a cordial and affectionate welcome . . . we cherish the most grateful recollection of the generous and devoted zeal, which, in the darkest aspect of our revolutionary fortunes, enlisted you in the support of our cause, and which, at the sacrifice of every present enjoyment and at the hazard of all your future prospects, retained you in it, 'till, by your aid, it was crowned with the most glorious success.' . . . In peace as well as war, in prosperity and adversity, through every change of our political destinies, you have been the constant friend, the faithful guardian of America. The diplomatic records of the nation show that, after the close of our revolutionary struggle, your influence with the government of your native country was zealously and efficiently exerted, in aid of the illustrious citizen, who now waits to receive you, under his hospitable roof, with the enthusiasm of antient friendship, in securing for us important advantages in the future commercial intercourse of the two countries. . . .

In addition to these obligations, . . . we owe you, as citizens of Virginia, a particular and extraordinary debt of gratitude. To your care was entrusted by the confidence of Washington, (and the fact itself is your best eulogy,) the defense of Virginia against the legions of an invading foe; and so happily did you prove your-self worthy of his choice, that, although your force scarcely amounted to one-sixth of the enemy's, yet by the sagacity and promptitude of your maneuvers you kept him perpetually in check, and extended the shield of protection over every part of our territory. . . . In the neighborhood of this spot, you terminated a painful and laborious march through a then trackless forest, and by the terror of your approach, rescued our habitations and our fields from impending deso-lation. History has recorded the movement as one of consummate enterprise and judgment, and the faithful tradition of our ancestors has identified the scene of it by the adjunct of your name, which has continued to distinguish it, to the present day, and by its interest-ing associations, has tended to preserve in our hearts a lively remembrance of the service of our benefactor. [A nearby road called The Marquis Road]

We are proud, General, exultingly proud, of this opportunity of testifying to you, in person, the sen-timents of gratitude, veneration and affection, with which these, your various and exalted merits, have inspired us: and if we could venture, for a moment, to

intrude upon the privacy of your domestic feelings, it
would be, to breath a wish that we might be permitted in some small degree, to requite the generous care
you took of our infancy, by tending your age, with filial
assiduity, in the bosom of a country, which would feel
itself honored by your residence, as it has been blessed
by your exertions."

Lafayette grasped Rives' hand and replied:

When after an absence of three and forty years, I find
myself in this county of Albemarle, inhabited by a dear,
and honored friend, the recollections, and feelings
that crowd upon my mind, cannot but be enhanced
by your kind welcome, and your flattering expression.
The honor I had to be early admitted among the soldiers of our sacred cause, the choice made of me by
our venerated commander-in-chief, to defend this, his
native State, the smallness, in the beginning of the
campaign, of our forces, a disproportion so honorable
to the troops I had the honor to command, are circumstances you have been pleased to mention in the most
gratifying manner. . . . I am happy to . . . present to you
and the citizens of Albemarle, the acknowledgments
of a grateful heart, whose old devotion to this country,
delights in their actual tranquility and happiness.[26]

After three spontaneous loud cheers from the troops and the
crowd, the General and dignitaries enjoyed a sumptuous meal
at Mrs. Boyd's Tavern. Rives, Lafayette, and Thomas Jefferson
Randolph boarded a Landau [four wheeled convertible carriage]
belonging to Jefferson, pulled by four gray horses for the ascent
to Monticello. Two carriages followed carrying Lafayette's family

and "suite" along with a wagon carrying his baggage.[27] Jefferson and Lafayette staged an emotional reunion before an adoring crowd after two o'clock.

Rives apparently saved all correspondence and records. This simple handwritten note must have been among his favorite keepsakes:

"Th Jefferson asks the favor of Mr. Rives to dine at Monticello to-day with Gen. LaFayette

Nov. 6. 24"[28]

Lafayette insisted on speaking English during his tour of America except at Monticello where Jefferson requested he speak French. Hopefully Rives had learned enough of "the language of conversation" Jefferson had recommended, so that he could fully enjoy the occasion.[29]

During his visit, Lafayette, Jefferson and Madison toured the unfinished University of Virginia. Lafayette left Monticello November 15 and continued his national tour, made even more triumphant by an award by Congress of $250,000 and 25,000 acres of Federal lands. Lafayette addressed Congress December 10, the first foreigner ever invited to do so.[30]

Jefferson would never again see Lafayette, but Rives would. Lafayette would entertain him at his chateau and consent to become godfather to Rives' youngest son.

★ ★ ★

1 W. C. Rives, Address to Citizens of Albemarle County, April 1823, Rives MSS, LOC, box 119.

2 WCR, Jr. Biography, Rives MSS LOC, box 103, 32. This may be unfounded family lore. J. C. Cabell limited his career to the Virginia State Legislature.

3 J. P. Rives, *Autobiography*, 70.

4 Raymond Dingledine, "The Political Career of W. C. Rives," UVa. dissertation, 1947, 67.

5 Proceedings of the 18th Congress, memory.loc.gov.

6 Annals of Congress, House of Representatives, 18th Congress, 1st Session, 1343-1361.

7 Dingledine, Ibid, 72.

8 www.encyclopedia.com/topicPierreAugustinCarondeBeaumarchais.

9 J. P. Rives *Autobiography*, 69.

10 Drew R. McCoy, *The Last of the Fathers*, Cambridge, Cambridge University Press, 1989, 45-55, 143-45.

11 Ibid. 67.

12 Ibid. 68.

13 William C. Rives pocket account book. Rives MSS, UVa., Accession # 11375, box 1.

14 Ibid.

15 K. Edward Lay & Martha Tuzson Stockton, "Castle Hill: The Walker Family Estate," *The Magazine of Albemarle County History*, Vol. 52, Charlottesville, Albemarle County Historical Society, 1994, 39.

16 J. P. Rives, Ibid, 61.

17 WCR, Jr., Biography, Ibid, 34.

18 Ibid. 71.

19 Douglas Southall Freeman, *R. E. Lee A Biography* Vol. I, Charles Scribner's Sons, New York, 1934, 40.

20 J. P. Rives, Ibid, 72.

21 Ibid.

22 Ibid. 75.

23 Ibid. 77.

24 J. P. Rives, Ibid. 78.

25 Henry H. Simms, *The Rise of the Whigs in Virginia 1824-1840*, Richmond, William Byrd Press, 1929. 15.

26 Charles Downing, "Reception of General Lafayette in Albemarle," *The Magazine of Albemarle County History*, Charlottesville, Albemarle County Historical Society, Volume 24, 1965-1966, 53-66, This account was reprinted from the *Richmond Enquirer*, November 16, 1824.

27 Ibid, 56.

28 Jefferson to Rives, November 6, 1824, original in Rives MSS, LOC. Microfilm copy in "Papers of William Cabell Rives in the Library of Congress," University of Virginia Alderman Library, old accession # Mss 3375 M-510, new call # Microfilm 7523.

29 Olivier Bernier, *Lafayette, Hero of Two Worlds*, New York, E. P. Dutton, Inc., 1983, 292-296. Also John Hammond Moore, *Albemarle, Jefferson's County, 1727-1976*, University of Virginia Press 1976, 158.

30 Bernier, Ibid. 295.

CHAPTER SIX

Blister and Mercury

PERSONAL JOY, TURNED TO SORROW, distracted Rives during the national electoral struggle and Lafayette's visit. Judith gave birth to a son October 6, 1824 who was christened William Cabell Rives, Jr. The infant died in January 1825 of unspecified causes. Both parents were devastated. Rives traveled about western Virginia the following summer with a heavy heart and in feeble health. The untimely death of his son prompted his increasing interest in religion. He decided to be confirmed into the Episcopal Church. Judith heavily relied on her religious faith to overcome the loss. She gave birth to another son, also christened William Cabell Rives, Jr. December 19, 1825. This boy would live a long life honoring his father's name.[1]

The election of 1824 revived the two party system. The Federalist Party had virtually disappeared during the Monroe administration and all four candidates in 1824 were nominal Democratic-Republicans. After the election, Clay and Adams led the National Republicans, later called Whigs. They stood for a strong federal government, a national bank, protective tariffs, and were generally supported by business and propertied interests. Andrew Jackson led the Democratic-Republican Party, which stood for limited federal government, and was generally supported by small farmers, emerging businesses and city workers.

Rives was a firm Jackson supporter throughout the 1820s. He opposed Adams and his administration whenever possible even though Judith established cordial relations with Mrs. Adams.[2] Henry Clay was now Secretary of State, but as a congressman he had proposed the American System of bank, tariffs and internal improvements to unify the nation and make it self sufficient. Rives voted against tariffs and appropriations for roads and canals. When Adams and Clay proposed to send delegates to an 1826 Panama Conference of Latin American nations, Rives spearheaded Congressional opposition. His speeches described the project as dangerous and part of the dreaded American System.[3] Democrats wanted to embarrass the Adams administration, but southerners also feared the conference might include discussion of slavery as some of the South American wars of liberation also included emancipation. Northeasterners favored the conference as an economic opportunity and saw a need to protect against British economic competition. After four months of debate, Congress authorized two delegates to attend the conference. One died en route and the other was detoured to Mexico.[4]

Rives based his politics of obstruction on his understanding of the Virginia and Kentucky Resolutions of 1798-1799. During the administration of John Adams (1797-1801), Virginia and Kentucky had, at the urging of Jefferson and Madison, passed resolutions condemning the Alien and Sedition Acts. The Alien and Sedition acts empowered the government to deport aliens and prosecute critics. The Virginia and Kentucky Resolutions proclaimed the federal government was created by the states to serve them and that state legislatures could declare laws of Congress unconstitutional. John C. Calhoun would later refer to these resolutions to support his doctrine of nullification. James Madison would endeavor to convince Rives and Calhoun that they had misunderstood.[5]

Rives heeded Madison. Calhoun did not. During the latter half of the 1820s, Madison helped Rives and others understand that the Virginia and Kentucky Resolutions were expressions of opinion, meant to rally support from other states, rather than proclamations of fact.[6] Furthermore, Congress had been levying

Castle Hill, East Front.

protective tariffs since its original 1787 session, and Madison stated that their fairness or appropriateness could be questioned, but not their constitutionality.[7] Finally, Madison drew a sharp distinction between tariffs, which might be economically painful, and the Alien and Sedition Acts, which violated fundamental freedoms of speech and security. A congressman had been imprisoned in 1799 for delivering speeches opposing the Federalist administration, and Madison himself had been fearful he would be prosecuted.[8]

Rives rushed to Madison's defense when the editor of the *Richmond Enquirer* Thomas Ritchie criticized Madison's support of the right of Congress to levy tariffs. Ritchie proclaimed, "The day of prophets and oracles has passed." Another writer urged Virginians to ignore a confused old man. Rives answered with a column declaring that Madison was the unquestioned authority on constitutional matters. In a letter to a state legislator he said Virginia was nothing "without her great men," and that Madison had shielded him from storms of heresy and misunderstanding.[9]

On a less controversial matter, Rives continued to support the establishment of the University of Virginia. He wrote Jefferson that he had spoken to the Postmaster-General about establishing a post office at the university. Rives also ushered a bill through Congress to refund duties paid on 31 cases of marble destined for university buildings amounting to $394.32. Rives concluded the letter with "most cordial wishes for your health."[10] Jefferson died the morning of July 4, 1826 (Adams died a few hours after), on the 50th anniversary of the signing of the Declaration of Independence.

Rives had his own health problems at the time. In a July 11, 1826 letter to Henry Harris of Nelson County, he described his symptoms and medical treatment for the benefit of Harris' brother who, Rives had learned, was afflicted with similar symptoms. Dr. George Holcombe of New Jersey, Rives' fellow congressman, prescribed the treatments. Rives claimed Holcombe was famous for his successful treatment of diseases of the stomach and the liver. Mercury, an ingredient in his medicine chest, was also the main ingredient in cure-all pills carried on the Lewis and Clark expedition. Mercury is a lethal poison.

Rives described his "morbid symptoms" to Harris. After even light meals he felt "a sense of weight and oppression in the stomach . . . a consequent heaviness and confusion in the head, a most distressing fullness and distension of the whole cavity of the body arising from wind and a general prostration of strength." Although Rives felt sick to his stomach, his physicians blamed his problems on "derangement in the function of the liver." When he admitted that he also felt occasional slight pain in his right side and shoulder, the doctors stated that was additional proof of "a disordered state of the liver."

Dr. Holcombe (sounds like hokum) prescribed a course of mercury to stimulate salivation. Rives endured the poisonous remedy for "three or four weeks till my strength was utterly prostrated."

The desired effect of increased salivation never occurred. Giving up on the mercury, the doctor decided to blister the right side of the patient to stimulate liver function. Rives believed this treatment was effective, although he still complained of "distressing flatulence . . . and general debility of the whole system."

Rives tried an additional remedy: a diet exclusively of milk and stale bread. He was not able to adhere to the diet very long, because milk upset his stomach. Present day physicians would pronounce him lactose intolerant. The doctor did not explain why stale bread was better for the liver than fresh bread.

Dr. Holcombe's most useful prescription was "gentle exercise, especially on horseback, and never prosecuted to fatigue." Horseback riding remained a pleasure for Rives throughout his life. Holcombe also advocated "tranquility and agreeable occupation of mind." Rives followed his dietary preferences, which excluded all vegetables except rice, sweet potatoes, and raw tomatoes prepared with vinegar and pepper. He enjoyed the benefit of occasional "mild tonics, such as bitters made with gentian." Rives urged Harris to tell his brother "that time and patience are not the least important ingredients in the cure of chronic complaints."[11]

In spite of his blister and mercury treatment, Rives survived past threescore and ten years. Exercise, tranquility of mind, time and patience were the most beneficial medicines involved. Medical advances and discoveries occurred during the Civil War, but even then surgeons did not wash their hands between patients. A prescription for Rives' 16-year-old grandson and namesake from 1866 seems primitive to later generations:

Prescription For Master Willie Rives June 4th, 1866

Diet: Nourishment to be taken every 2 hours consisting of strong broth, thickened with rice, boiled milk, arrowroot or tapioca, rice milk.

A teaspoonful of spirit at the same time. Suspend it if the fever should rise & the pulse become strong.

Keep the feet & hands warm.

Large mustard poultices constantly over the whole abdomen. Omit the mustard if too much irritation should be produced & continue the simpler poultices.

Drink: A little mucilage of any kind.

He must not be disturbed when asleep.

Operations oftener than twice in 24 hours if very copious, or annoying in their frequency must be checked by an enema of Starch & Laudanum (15 drops) Sugar of Lead (3 Grains)

Give a teaspoonful of the mixture well shaken every four hours without regard to the time of eating."[12]

"Master Willie" survived this treatment and became a doctor, hopefully employing more enlightened techniques.[13] Rives visited the western Virginia springs as often as he could, believing in their therapeutic effects. Thomas Jefferson advocated a mostly vegetarian diet with meat consumed sparingly. Limited to rice, sweet potatoes, and tomatoes as his only vegetables, Rives was more carnivorous.

In the years following the death of Jefferson, Madison persuaded Rives to abandon extreme states rights positions he had earlier professed. Under the guidance of the Father of the Constitution, Rives came to believe that Virginia should align herself with northern states more than those of the Deep South. He would repeat this point while arguing with Virginia secessionists in 1860. He advocated development of manufacturing industry in Virginia to increase her prosperity and to avoid exclusive reliance on agriculture. In letters to his relative William Mason Rives in the Virginia legislature, Rives stated that, "the great desideratum in Virginia politics" was "prudence, moderation, forecast and practical counsels."[14] When South Carolinians and Georgians became increasingly vocal in their opposition to tariffs, Rives urged Virginia to disregard their disloyal calls. Rives wrote, "Her [Virginia's] interest must ever be to remain in that union, of which she may be considered, emphatically, the founder."[15] Rives also declared that the tariff was a gross abuse of power, but not unconstitutional. Though many Virginians disagreed with Rives' opinion, Madison wrote Rives, agreeing that Congress did possess a constitutional power to regulate trade by use of tariffs.[16]

Rives and his wife befriended New York Congressman Martin Van Buren, who was energetically developing a network of support for Andrew Jackson's candidacy in the 1828 presidential contest along with a sympathetic post-election Congress. Van Buren wrote Rives October 17, 1827.

Mr. McLane & myself will take our lodgings together. We invite you & Mrs. Rives to join our mess. Barbour will not do for speaker. I greatly prefer Stevenson. If I had the making of the speaker & was to be governed by my own conviction of the superior fitness & worth etc. of the candidate I should unhesitatingly say thou art the man. Every day adds to the conviction of us northerners that the country has more to expect from you than from any southern man of your age and circumstances.[17]

Despite his flattering words to Rives, Van Buren did have the power of "making of the speaker," and he employed all of his power to secure the election of Andrew Stevenson (1784-1857) to be Speaker of the House.[18] Van Buren earned his nickname

"the Little Magician" by crafty political maneuvering. Stevenson
lived in central Virginia, in southern Albemarle County not too
far from Rives. When Stevenson served as the US Minister to
Great Britain 1836-1841, his wife Sarah Coles Stevenson gave
Queen Victoria a basket of Albemarle Pippin apples that became
the queen's favorite variety.[19]

Rives expressed his hopes for a Jackson presidency in a letter to his friend Thomas Walker Gilmer (1802-1844). Gilmer's
father was a first cousin of Judith Page Rives. In a July 22, 1827 letter to Gilmer, Rives said that Jackson was "a most orthodox and
thoroughfaced republican of the Jefferson school." Rives believed
Jackson favored use of a tariff to enable competition between
domestic and foreign industry, while Adams used prohibitory
tariffs to completely exclude foreign competition. High tariffs
were consistent with Clay's "American System," which Rives continued to oppose. Rives said Jackson was for states rights and
strict construction of the Constitution. Jackson offered hope of
restoring the country to "the golden age of the republic" that was
the Jefferson administration.[20] Rives was a boy during Jefferson's
presidency, which had its share of political upheaval and was
probably less of a golden age than he imagined. Rives reflexively
compared every president to Jefferson and Madison. He would
not witness their second coming.

Jackson defeated Adams in 1828. Calhoun was re-elected
Vice President, having held the office under Adams. Van Buren
assumed a dominant role in Jackson's so-called "Kitchen Cabinet"
as Secretary of State. On May 5, 1829 Van Buren offered Rives
the post of Minister to France.[21] Distinguished predecessors in
the position included Thomas Jefferson, Benjamin Franklin and
James Monroe. Van Buren selected Rives to placate Virginians,
who wanted more of their own in high ranks of the administration. He was also confident that Rives could help resolve a
lingering dispute between the U.S. and France.[22]

WILLIAM CABELL RIVES

* * *

1 J. P. Rives, *Autobiography*, 80. See also Dingledine, "Political Career of William Cabell Rives," 76.

2 Dingledine, Ibid, 83.

3 McCoy, *The Last of the Fathers*, 333.

4 Americanforeignrelations.com Panama Conference.

5 McCoy, Ibid, 334.

6 Ibid. 141. McCoy cites 1830 letters from Madison to Edward Everett, Nicholas Trist, and others.

7 Ibid. 123.

8 Ibid. 142-43.

9 Rives to William M. Rives, January 8, 1829, Rives MSS, LOC, box 45, cited in McCoy, Ibid. 119-123. William Mason Rives was a member of the Virginia House of Delegates from Campbell County 1821-23, 1826-32.

10 Rives to Thomas Jefferson, May 13, 1826. Letters to and from Jefferson, 1826 Electronic Text Center University of Virginia Library, http://etext.virginia.edu.

11 Rives to Henry Harris, July 11, 1826, Special Collections Department, University of Virginia Library, Papers of James McDowell, Accession # 1755, box 2.

12 Prescription, June 4, 1866, Rives MSS, LOC, box 93.

13 William Cabell Rives III (1850-1938), known as Dr. William C. Rives was also an eminent ornithologist.

14 McCoy, Ibid, 334, and Dingledine, Ibid, 106.

15 McCoy, Ibid, 335. Rives to W. M. Rives, Jan. 1 and Jan. 8, 1829, Rives Mss, LOC Ibid, box 45.

16 James Madison to William C. Rives, December 20, 1828, *Letters and Other Writings of James Madison*, [Rives and Fendall editors] Philadelphia, J. B. Lippincott and Company, 1865, Vol. III, 663-664, and Madison to Rives, January 10, 1829, Ibid, Vol. IV, 3-5.

17 WCR, Jr. Biography, Rives MSS, LOC box 103, 40.

18 John Niven, *Martin Van Buren The Romantic Age of American Politics*, New York, Oxford, Oxford University Press, 1983, 193-196.

19 The Albemarle Pippin was first grown in Virginia by Dr. Thomas Walker at Castle Hill. Walker carried cuttings of the variety in his saddlebags on his way home from the 1755 French and Indian War expedition with General Braddock and George Washington.

20 William C. Rives to Thomas Walker Gilmer, July 22, 1827, reprinted in *Tyler's Quarterly*, Vol. V, 237.

21 WCR, Jr. Biography, Ibid, 4.

22 Niven, Ibid, 237 refers to a May 5, 1829 letter from Van Buren to Rives in Van Buren papers, Library of Congress.

CHAPTER SEVEN

Revolution and Reparations

THE RIVES SAILED FOR FRANCE IN AUGUST aboard the
warship USS *Constellation*, which was a sister ship to the USS
Constitution. The *Constellation* was rebuilt in 1854, using some
material salvaged from the old 1797 vessel and is now docked in
Baltimore harbor.[1]

Before his departure, Rives visited Ranston, his Nelson
County farm and spoke with his overseer there, Mr. Mitchell.
He instructed Mitchell and his Castle Hill overseer Mr. Parsons
to keep the fields in a corn/wheat/clover rotation and to send
the tobacco crop to the Richmond firm of Rives and Ferguson.
According to his son, Rives instructed his overseers to properly
clothe his slaves and treat them "with humanity." The overseers
were also advised to rely on advice from Robert Rives (Sr.) and
Martin Dawson if necessary.[2]

Also before the voyage, Daniel Webster congratulated Rives
on his appointment and introduced Rives and his wife to Mr. and
Mrs. David Sears of Boston. This was the beginning of a long
and productive friendship. The Rives traveled to Niagara Falls
where they met Mr. George Peabody, a London Financier, whose
friendship would also be important.[3]

Secretary of State Van Buren advised Rives that one of his
most important duties was to gather and transmit information
about the French government, including its domestic and foreign
policies. He should be a "steady and impartial" observer, in order
to "discriminate between that which is authentic and that which

is spurious." He should also cultivate "friendly social relations" with diplomats from other countries he encountered.[4]

Joining the Rives aboard the *Constellation* were Mr. and Mrs. Louis McLane. The former Delaware Congressman was the new Minister to Great Britain. Van Buren advised McLane and Rives to maintain close relations and communications with each other once they reached London and Paris. McLane's primary mission was to settle disputes regarding British and American trade in the West Indies. Rives faced a more formidable task of securing reparations payments from the French for damages to American shipping that occurred during the Napoleonic wars decades before.[5]

American merchants claimed over $15 million in damages by Napoleonic forces, who had seized or destroyed American ships in French ports or on the high seas. When Napoleon was finally defeated at Waterloo in 1815 and exiled, the French treasury was empty and strapped by other demands for reparations from Great Britain and its allies. The kings Louis XVIII and Charles X, who followed Napoleon, along with their ministers, admitted the American claims but contrived to delay serious discussion and settlement. The French also made a counterclaim that the U.S. had violated the Louisiana Purchase Treaty. Its Article Eight entitled France to most favored nation status; however, the French charged that the U.S. was illegally trading with other nations under the same terms. Trade between the two countries amounted to many millions of dollars by 1829, including U.S. imports of French wines and silks. Rives' task was to convince the French that it was in their interest to settle the dispute.[6]

The warship *Constellation* had not been constructed for passenger comfort. Stormy weather and rough seas rendered the transatlantic voyage rough and uncomfortable. Judith had terrible seasickness, exacerbated by her being in the first trimester of her fourth pregnancy. Rives wrote Van Buren when they reached England September 12, 1829: "We arrived here yesterday morning after a passage of about thirty days from New York, the latter part of which was rendered very disagreeable by the state of the weather. . . . Mrs. Rives' sufferings from seasickness have been extreme and unintermitted during the whole voyage. . . ."[7]

Along with instructions for his negotiations, Van Buren designated new formal diplomatic attire: "A black coat with a gold star on each side of the collar near its termination, the underclothes to be black, blue or white, at the option of the wearer; a three-cornered *chapeau a bras*, a black cockade and eagle and a steel-mounted sword, with white scabbard." Rives accessorized the outfit with "black satin breeches, with silver buckles on his shoes, relieving any severity at the neck with a voluminous cravat of lace-edged white cambric, and being a handsome man with a high complexion the dress well became him."[8]

Rives had preliminary audiences with the new Minister of Foreign Affairs Prince Polignac as well as with King Charles X. Rives wrote Van Buren of his negotiations with Polignac, who tried to deny any connection between the present monarchy and the Napoleonic regime that had inflicted the damage. Rives was ready for this expected tactic. He pointed out that Napoleon's government had enjoyed the support of the French people and had been recognized by all foreign powers as the legitimate government of France. Rives said it was a well-established principle of international law that acts of the existing government of a country "devolve" upon every succeeding government and that France seemed to have admitted this by recent reparations payments to the British and their allies.

Polignac replied that those claims were different than the American ones.

Rives countered that the claims were not identical in their particulars, but they rested on the same principle. Furthermore, the United States had been more considerate of France, patiently waiting "until she had recovered from her embarassments." Rives also mentioned favorable treatment of French silks and wines under the current U.S. tariff.[9]

Polignac raised the Louisiana Purchase Treaty trade issue along with the matter of unpaid debts to the heirs of Beaumarchais for his assistance to the Americans during the American Revolution. Van Buren authorized Rives to deduct one million francs from the American claims for those concerns. Van Buren and Jackson also approved of Rives' offer to Polignac to reduce duties on French goods if the French would renounce the Louisiana Treaty claims. The negotiations proceeded slowly over the course of several months, but Rives was confident they were moving toward a satisfactory conclusion.[10]

Though Rives had not achieved his goal, Jackson and Van Buren were pleased with his work. Rives had followed instructions about keeping in touch with McLane in London. Rives also informed Van Buren that Judith had been of invaluable assistance in finding out court gossip and in helping him with his dispatches.[11]

Judith developed a much closer bond of friendship with the Princesse de Polignac than Rives had with the Prince. The Princesse was an English lady who remained a friend and correspondent.[12] In a letter to her sister Jane Frances Page back in Virginia, Judith described how the Princesse presented her to King Charles X. The 72-year-old Charles was the brother of Louis XVIII and also the brother of the beheaded Louis XVI. Judith had hoped to wear her blue and silver dress designed by "the celebrated Victorine, whose taste and prices are the talk of all Paris." However, because the Court was in mourning, she had to wear a black outfit, "looking more like a wintry cloud than was altogether desirable." She rode alone in a coach to the Palace of the Tuileries, because the king did not receive gentlemen and ladies at the same time. Judith met the Princesse in the palace, along with many other ladies who were waiting to be presented. When her turn arrived, Judith entered an oblong room and made "a most profound courtesy," to the king seated on his throne at the far end. Her gesture was "returned by a bow from His Majesty equally profound." She advanced to the center of the salon and repeated her "most profound courtesy," which was "answered by as polite a reverence." The business was repeated a third time when Judith had nearly reached the king.

Judith had been warned that she might be "dazzled even to blindness by the majesty and splendor of it all." Instead she reported that the ceremony seemed so ridiculous that she could barely refrain from laughing. The old king, perceiving her bemusement, "accosted me very merrily, laughing heartily at his own jokes, and spoke entirely in English, which the Princess told me was a peculiar compliment." After a brief conversation, "we made one more bow, and retired through a door opposite the one by which we had entered."[13]

Judith gave birth to Alfred Landon Rives in Paris March 25, 1830. Alfred would later earn an engineering degree from the French *École des Ponts et Chaussées*.

Rives continued to meet regularly with Polignac who was doing everything possible to stall the negotiations. In May, Rives approached him at a reception of the diplomatic corps for the visiting King and Queen of Naples. Rives told Polignac that it was time to quit stalling: "I endeavored to impress on him the expediency of turning his attention at once to maturing the details of some practical arrangement, instead of renewing a profitless, and possibly a mischievous discussion. . . . He promised to consider my suggestion."[14]

The Rives attended a grand ball held in honor of the King and Queen of Naples by Louis Philippe the Duke of Orleans. The great number of guests invited caused a traffic jam of carriages half a mile from the Duke's palace. Judith did not like the look of the mob of people on foot who were glaring at the carriages. Judith wrote her sister that she "could not help recognizing in the dark ferocious countenances of the men and the hardened faces of the women the same spirit which had wrought such horrors in the Revolution." Judith was relieved to reach the palace and leave the rabble outside.

Judith noticed that the Duke of Orleans and his family were upstaging Charles X and the King of Naples. "I could not help thinking they assumed rather too much the airs of royalty, so that if the Duke should one day or other take possession of the crown of France, I shall claim the credit of being a prophetess, for I had this idea in my mind all the evening."[15] Judith's keen observation and intuition were accurate. The mobs in the street and Louis Philippe would soon make history.

In July the Rives family visited Lafayette at his home La Grange, 40 miles from Paris. Judith described the chateau as "very old, and the outside being flanked with round towers in the antique style." The interior contained a large map of Virginia as well as portraits of Washington, Jefferson and other prominent Americans, along with "a few of the General's countrymen." Lafayette had a large family with several grandchildren, who invited eight-year old Francis Rives and five-year-old Will Rives to join in their activities, including expeditions on donkeys. Judith said her two older boys were delighted to be in the country, "like birds out of a cage."

On the evening of July 26, guests were seated inside La Grange. The ladies were knitting and the gentlemen were reading newspapers. A letter came for Lafayette from his granddaughter in Paris informing him that the Chamber of Deputies was dissolved, the Law of Elections changed, and liberty of the press was suspended. Judith wrote, "These few words, read in a calm and steady voice by the General, had the same effect which the

*Lafayette in drawing by Eugène Devéria for a
painting of the accession of Louis Philipe.*

report of a pistol in the midst of the salon would have produced."
Everyone started talking at once, expressing opinions about what
was to be done. General Lafayette sat silently for a few minutes
before leaving the room. The next morning he told his guests he
had to hasten to Paris.

Revolution had begun in Paris. The mobs, whose discontented
stares had bothered Judith, armed themselves with weapons
seized from royal arsenals and threw up barricades of stones, trees
and overturned carriages in the streets. Rives noted in a dispatch
to Van Buren, "the contest on Wednesday [July 28] assumed a
more serious and sanguinary character."[16]

That same day the Rives family headed for Paris, although
Judith felt "lurking anxiety" about the trip, traveling in an open
landau with three small boys. As they neared the city, drivers of

other carriages warned them to turn back. Some gave the coachman specific instructions about which routes to avoid. In the city, Judith noticed the *réverbères* [street lamps] were broken and so their coachman had to navigate by light of the moon. As they crossed the Seine on a bridge near the *Jardin des Plantes* [Botanical Gardens], their footman had to lead their horses past a fallen horse, who lay dying of freshly received wounds. Sounds of canon fire and musketry sounded in the distance throughout the night. The Rives reached their home at 82 *Rue de l'Université* after eleven p.m.

Thursday morning, July 29, Rives ventured out to witness the conflict despite his wife's fears that he might encounter a stray musket ball, like the bullet that had shattered one of their windows. The Paris citizens stormed the Louvre and Tuileries palaces where the king's forces made their last stand. After hours of fighting, members of the royal forces either retreated or joined the citizens.[17]

Rives wrote Van Buren that negotiations would have to begin again under a new government, because "of one of the most wonderful revolutions which has ever occurred in the history of the world." After three days of "commotion and bloodshed," the tricolored flag waved over the palaces and Paris was as tranquil "as I have ever seen it under the royal authority."[18]

General Lafayette was called to command the re-established National Guard, and also to join several others at the head of the Provisional Government. Lafayette was the hero of the hour and powerbroker when the shooting stopped. Some urged him to declare himself king, others wanted a Second Republic of France. Lafayette had fought to bring democracy to America, but he had his doubts about whether the French were ready for such a government. On July 31, Lafayette proclaimed Louis Philippe, Duke of Orleans, Lieutenant-General of the Kingdom. Then Lafayette conferred with the American Minister.

Louis Philippe (1773-1850) bearing the tricolore flag on the barricades during the Revolution of 1830.

Lafayette asked Rives what Americans would think of the establishment of a constitutional monarchy in France. The general declared that he was a republican, but a majority of the French were monarchists. Lafayette believed the people would support Louis Philippe as their new king. Would Americans approve, or would they condemn Lafayette for failure to establish democracy? Rives answered that "a popular throne surrounded by republican institutions" seemed to be the most practical and stable form of government under the circumstances. Rives also assured Lafayette that most Americans would accept their decision. Historian Beckles Willson claimed that Rives told Lafayette what he wanted to hear, but he did not answer as his predecessors Jefferson or Monroe would have. Willson speculated that an impassioned tirade by Rives against monarchical rule at that moment might have changed Lafayette's mind and actions. Lafayette and Rives weathered criticism in France and America for abandoning their ideals when news of their conference was publicized.[19]

Louis Philippe was crowned King of the French on August 7 with little advance notice. Rives received an invitation from Louis Philippe to attend a meeting of the Chamber of Deputies that morning. Rives and Judith, along with their friend, author and diplomat Washington Irving,[20] suspected that something important was going to happen. Even though Irving and Judith did not have tickets to the event, Irving said they could gain admittance because the French would not turn away a lady and he would pretend to be an attaché. When their carriage arrived, a crowd of citizens was gathered in front of the building. According to Judith, they were "looking at every one as they descended from their carriages with a degree of familiarity that was far from being agreeable."

One old ruffian pointed to his own red, white and blue ribbon and demanded of Rives *"Où est votre tricolore?"* [Where is your tri-color?]

Rives smiled, placed his hand on his heart and replied, *"C'est dans mon coeur."* [It's in my heart.]

"Bravo," replied the man, and the crowd parted to allow the three Americans to pass. They were admitted to an upper gallery reserved for members of the diplomatic corps. Seats were available because some diplomats had not had time to receive orders from their governments, authorizing them to attend the ceremony. The two most notable French dignitaries seated below were Lafayette and Prince Talleyrand. Talleyrand was a remarkable political survivor, having managed to retain power and influence for decades while French governments were toppled by revolution and war. Napoleon once called him *"merde en bas de soie."* [sh** in a silk stocking]

An English officer pointed to the two of them and told Judith, "There are two men whom I would recommend to the new King to bind hand and foot and put into the Seine without further delay, as there is certainly no security for any government so long as they are extant, for the one [Talleyrand] has sworn fidelity to eight different governments, and the other [Lafayette] is a revolution in himself."

Louis Philippe took his place on the stage. The Charter of the new government was read, which authorized the King and legislature to govern the country together. Louis Philippe swore allegiance to it. He and his family then rode in their carriage through cheering crowds in the streets of Paris.[21]

Rives wrote Van Buren asking for a new letter of credence authorizing him as U.S. Minister to the new monarch and government. Rives worried that the Liberal French who had come into power were even more opposed to the U.S. claims than the Royalists had been.[22] Rives dined with the King, who assured him that he was a friend of the United States and would make every effort to settle. In an official dispatch to Van Buren a month later, Rives described how his French counterpart Louis Serrurier said that an agreement "would depend on a material reduction of the extent of our demands, and that, in the amplitude we had given them, their admission would be impossible." Rives replied to Serrurier "that I regretted exceedingly to hear what he had just communicated to me." Despite the King's gratitude for Rives' backing his accession to the throne, the French were determined to haggle and stall. Rives summarized: "While, therefore, they are compelled to admit the principle of responsibility, a reluctance, or a fear to touch the purse of the nation, disposes them to dispute the consequences of its application, by every sort of pretext."[23]

In a personal letter to Van Buren written the same day, Rives stated the matter more plainly: "Nothing can exceed the reluctance of a Frenchman or of the French government to pay money."[24] Rives continued to negotiate with no end in sight. Nevertheless, in his December message to Congress, President Jackson praised Rives' work. "The negotiation with France has been conducted by our Minister with zeal and ability, and in all respects to my entire satisfaction."[25]

Jackson was tired of the French stalling tactics, and so was Rives. In April, Rives sent a note to the new French Foreign Minister Count Sebastiani. Rives suggested no two governments have "more motives" for cordial relations than France and the U.S., but the "unhappy influence of this long and protracted question" makes those relations "equivocal and precarious." It was past time for French action to suppress "this germ of discord."[26]

Sebastiani finally made an offer. He told Rives he realized that the process had dragged on far too long, and rather than argue over each specific item, France *"avec une bonne foi extrême"* [with extreme good faith] was willing to pay 15 million francs to settle the entire matter. Rives rejected it with indignation. The $15 million American claims amounted to approximately 50 million francs. Rives wrote Van Buren:

> I replied that I was altogether astonished at such a proposal, that my Government, instead of seeing in it an evidence of good faith, could regard it in no other light than as a mockery and equivalent to an absolute refusal of justice; that if it was to be considered as a definitive proposition on the part of France, I had only to say

that the negotiation was at an end, and that it would
be for each Government to recur to its rights, and its
sense of its own dignity and honor"

Rives was implying that a trade war or a real war loomed
ahead. Sebastiani protested that Rives should reflect upon the
offer. Rives wrote Van Buren, "I replied that such a proposal did
not require a moment's reflection."[27]

At their next meeting, Sebastiani raised the figure to 24 million francs to be paid over six years, and stated that was *"le dernier
mot"* [the last word, (his final offer)]. Rives was not satisfied.
A few days later Rives spoke with Sebastiani at a royal celebra-
tion at Palais Royale. After speaking with the King, who again
professed his "very cordial sentiments," Rives told Sebastiani the
U.S. would accept 40 million francs. Sebastiani said that was out
of the question. Rives proposed that the matter be submitted to
an international commission for arbitration, a situation he knew
would bother the French more than the Americans.[28]

As the bargaining continued, Rives suggested they split the
difference between their respective demands. Sebastiani refused
and brought up the matter of the unsettled Beaumarchais claims.
He also submitted his own list of claims of damage inflicted
on French shipping by Americans. Rives proposed French payment of 25 million francs to be paid in six annual installments.
Sebastiani accepted.

Rives wrote the new Secretary of State Edward Livingston,
"I have the honor to transmit herewith, the treaty which has
been concluded with the government of France. . . . The result
which has been gained in the interest of the claimants has not
been achieved without the greatest difficulty." Rives noted that
Article 7 of the Treaty, which promised current low duties on
French wines would be maintained or else reduced under a new

general tariff, was an essential part of the agreement that had been insisted on by the French.[29]

Livingston replied to Rives:

> [President Jackson] instructs me to say that the manner in which you have carried on the negotiation meets his entire approbation, and that he is convinced the result has been quite as favorable as we could have expected, and my own opinion coinciding perfectly with his I congratulate you on the success of your persevering and talented exertions, and on the great advantages they have procured to your country.[30]

The treaty was signed in Paris July 4, 1831. Jackson praised Rives' success in his December 1831 message to Congress.[31] The treaty was unanimously ratified by the U.S. Senate February 2, 1832.[32] However, the treaty required approval by the French Chamber of Deputies before payments could begin.

Having accomplished his main assignment, Rives traveled with Judith to points of interest in Italy, Germany, Switzerland and France. Judith wrote a book *Tales and Souvenirs of a Residence in Europe*, based on their travels. The prose is highly ornamented and lacks the directness and interest of her letters. Apparently she felt it would have been un-ladylike for her name to appear on the cover and so the author is listed as "a lady of Virginia."[33] Rives visited England and was thrilled to witness debates in Parliament. He met with Foreign Secretary and future Prime Minister Lord Palmerston (1784-1865).[34]

Judith gave birth to a daughter in Paris July 8, 1832. The girl was christened Amélie Louise, in honor of her godmother Queen Amélie, wife of Louis Philippe. The godfather of Amélie's youngest brother Alfred was Lafayette. Alfred would have a daughter,

THE BRIDGEMAN ART LIBRARY

Queen Amélie

also named Amélie, who claimed Robert E. Lee as her godfather. The younger Amélie, a popular novelist of the late 19th and early 20th centuries, observed that the Rives were "happy in godparents."[35]

Among many prized objects at Castle Hill was a needle and thread used by Queen Amélie. Judith had paid a visit to the Queen who asked what keepsake she could give her American friend. As the Queen was sewing, Judith asked for the needle and thread that had been held by royal fingers.[36] Queen Amélie was the mother of eight children including Louise, who married Leopold of Belgium. Their daughter Charlotte (Carlotta) married Austrian Archduke Maximilian, ill-fated Emperor of Mexico.[37] When Judith bade farewell to Queen Amélie before returning to America, the queen broke the rules of royal ceremony and flung her arms around Judith in a "warm and tearful embrace."[38]

Rives' work on the treaty had greatly enhanced his political prospects. Returning home would allow him to press his advantage. There was talk of Rives as a possible Vice Presidential

*The Rives children in the Tuileries Garden, 1831. Painting
by George Cooke. The Tuileries Palace signifies their father's
diplomatic position.*

candidate under Andrew Jackson who was seeking a second
term. However, Van Buren secured the Vice Presidential nomination after the Senate refused to confirm Jackson's appointment
of Van Buren as Minister to Great Britain.[39]

The Rives were unharmed by the cholera epidemic sweeping
through Europe that killed thousands in Paris in 1832. Bacteria
spread through water and poor sanitation caused the disease,
which therefore was more prevalent among the poor and disad-
vantaged. Lafayette wrote Rives in September that the "fury of
the cholera" was abating in Paris and in the neighborhood of La
Grange. He said that though he had heard reports of cholera in
the U.S., he believed that its enlightened citizens would better
withstand the disease than superstitious Europeans. Lafayette

sent a petition with Rives for payment to French soldiers who had fought in the American Revolution under General Rochambeau. Lafayette also requested Rives to "Remember me most affectionately" to Mr. and Mrs. Madison.[40]

.The Rives and their four children sailed from Le Havre aboard the Sully on October 1, 1832 and did not reach New York until November 16. The westward crossing of the Atlantic was rougher and more miserable than the eastward voyage on the *Constellation* had been. One of the Rives' fellow passengers was their friend Lewis Rogers, who ran a successful tobacco export business in Paris. Other passengers were artist Samuel F. B. Morse and Dr. C. T. Jackson, who both later claimed to be inventor of the telegraph. During their patent dispute, Morse appealed to Rives for support, because during the voyage Rives had heard him suggest how Benjamin Franklin's experiments demonstrated electricity could be used to transmit information instantaneously. Morse ultimately won his claim for the invention that he described to Rives on the storm tossed decks of the *Sully*.[41]

* * *

1 www.historicships.org/constellation.html.

2 WCR, Jr., Biography, Rives MSS, LOC, box 103, pages 157, 42 .

This is likely the same Martin Dawson who died in 1835 and bequeathed his farm to the University of Virginia. This was a substantial gift because the University sold the property for $19,000 and erected student dormitories known as "Dawson's Row." Virginius Dabney, *Mr. Jefferson's University*, Charlottesville, University Press of Virginia, 1981, 24. A gristmill built by Martin Dawson on his land on the Hardware River was dismantled and moved in the 1960s, and became the nucleus of the Boar's Head Inn west of Charlottesville.

3 WCR, Jr., Ibid, 43.

4 Martin Van Buren to William C. Rives, July 20, 1829, quoted in: Beckles Willson, *America's Ambassadors to France (1777-1927)*, London, John Murray, 1928, 167-168.

5 John Niven, *Martin Van Buren The Romantic Age of American Politics*, New York, Oxford, Oxford University Press, 1983, 276-281.

6 Ibid, 276.

7 William C. Rives to Martin Van Buren, September 12, 1829, Letterbook, Rives MSS, LOC, box 15.

8 Willson, Ibid , 167.

9 William Cabell Rives to Martin Van Buren, November 7, 1829, Gales and Seaton's Register of Debates, 22nd Congress, 2nd Session, Appendix, 232 (related documents occupy pages 210-297).

10 Niven, Ibid, 282-283.

11 Ibid, Niven cites letter from William C. Rives to Van Buren, September 8, 1830, Van Buren Papers Library of Congress.

12 WCR, Jr., Biography, Ibid., 44 (In an early 1861 letter, the Princesse asked Judith how she liked the new president. Judith did not like Lincoln. Rives MSS, LOC, box 93, misfiled with 1867 letters).

13 Judith Page Rives to Jane Frances Page, December 1829, "A Woman in the Paris Revolution of 1830," *Harper's Monthly Magazine*, Volume CIV, December 1901 to May 1902, 33-34.

14 William C. Rives to Martin Van Buren, May 18, 1830, Register of Debates, 22nd Congress, 2nd Session, Appendix, 246-7.

15 Judith Page Rives to Jane Frances Page, May 1830, *Harper's Monthly Magazine*, Ibid, 35.

16 Rives to Van Buren, July 30, 1830, Register of Debates, Ibid, 265.

17 Judith Page Rives to Jane Frances Page, July 30, 1830, *Harpers*, Ibid, 40.

18 Rives to Van Buren, July 30, 1830, Register of Debates, Ibid, 264-265.

19 Willson, Ibid, 173-175.

20 Irving had published his *Sketchbook* that included "Rip Van Winkle" and "The Legend of Sleepy Hollow" in 1819. He was Secretary of the U.S. Legation in London 1829-1832 and U.S. Ambassador to Spain 1842-46.

21 Judith Page Rives to Jane Frances Page, September 20, 1830, *Harpers*, Ibid, 43-44.

22 Rives to Van Buren, August 8, 1830, Register of Debates, Ibid, 266.

23 Rives to Van Buren, September 8, 1830, Register of Debates, Ibid, 267.

24 Rives to Van Buren, September 8, 1830, Van Buren Papers, Library of Congress, quoted in Jon Meacham, *American Lion, Andrew Jackson in the White House*, New York, Random House, 2008, 288.

25 President Jackson's Message to Congress, December 7, 1830, Register of Debates, 21st Congress, 2nd Session, Appendix, iv.

26 Rives to Count Sebastiani, April 21, 1831, Register of Debates, 22nd Congress, 2nd Session, Appendix, 279-280.

27 Rives to Van Buren, April 28, 1831, Register of Debates, Ibid, 279.

28 Rives to Van Buren, May, 7, 1831, Register of Debates, Ibid, 280-281.

29 Rives to Edward Livingston, July 8, 1831, Register of Debates, Ibid, 296-297.

30 Livingston to Rives, September 26, 1831, Register of Debates, Ibid, 224.

31 Gales and Seaton's Register of Debates, 22nd Congress, 1st Session, Appendix, 1.

32 Raymond, L. Dingledine, Jr., "The Political Career of William C. Rives," University of Virginia, Phd dissertation, 1947, 162.

33 *Tales and Souvenirs of a Residence in Europe, by a Lady of Virginia*, Philadelphia, Lea and Blanchard, 1842.

34 Dingledine, Ibid, 174.

35 Louis Auchincloss, *A Writer's Capital*, Boston, Houghton Mifflin, 1979, 135.

36 WCR, Jr. Biography, Ibid, 51, Amélie Rives Troubetzkoy recounts the story in an autobiographical sketch. Rives MSS, UVa., Accession #2532, Box 1.

37 William L. Langer, *An Encyclopedia of World History*, Boston, Houghton Mifflin Company, 1968, 675, 680.

38 "Obituary of Judith Page Walker Rives," Rives MSS, UVa., Accession # 38-348.

39 Dingledine, Ibid, 164-165.

40 Lafayette to Rives, September 17, 1832 and September 29, 1832, Letterbook, Rives MSS, LOC, box 20, 88, 90.

41 Samuel F. B. Morse to William C. Rives, November 14, 1837, Letterbook, Ibid, 210, also, WCR, Jr., Biography, Ibid, 51, also Dingledine, Ibid, 176.

CHAPTER EIGHT

Lieutenant Randolph Outrage

LESS THAN A MONTH after his return home, Rives was elected U.S. Senator by the Virginia legislature December 10, 1832. Accepting this Senate seat placed him in a political war zone. Dispute had arisen over the tariffs of 1828 and 1832 and the fight escalated until the nature and even the survival of the U.S. government were at stake.

In 1828 when John Quincy Adams was still President, Congress passed a bill containing high duties on woolen cloth, as well as raw materials including flax, hemp, iron, lead, molasses, and raw wool. Southern congressmen were generally opposed to tariffs, which raised the price of manufactured goods in their agrarian region, but they had voted against reducing the high rates. Since the 1828 bill also raised costs of raw materials for New England manufacturers, the southerners thought that Adams would veto the bill and that New England congressmen would join them in opposing it. When their tactic backfired and the bill passed, the southerners cursed it as "the Tariff of Abominations."[1]

South Carolina led the fight against the tariff. John C. Calhoun wrote the 1828 *South Carolina Exposition and Protest*, which argued that states had the right to declare federal laws null and void. This first statement of the theory of "nullification" was published anonymously, because Calhoun was serving as Vice-President. Calhoun claimed he was following the example of Jefferson and Madison who had helped draft the Virginia and Kentucky Resolutions of 1798-1799, which opposed the Alien and Sedition Acts of John Adams' presidency.[2] Senator Robert Y. Hayne of South Carolina sent Madison copies of his speeches in support of states rights and nullification, and was shocked when Madison voiced his disagreement with the nullifiers and their interpretation of his words and actions.[3]

Daniel Webster delivered one of the most famous speeches in Senate History in reply to Hayne in 1830. Hayne had claimed dissolution of the Union was not as much to be feared as "submission to a government of unlimited powers."[4] Webster rose and spoke for three hours in reply. He declared that if the nullifiers had their way, then the Union was a "rope of sand," and the government was thrown back into the disorder experienced under the Articles of the Confederation. Webster stated that New England had opposed the embargo declared during the Jefferson administration by taking the case to the Supreme Court. If they had nullified that law, there would be no U.S. in 1830, he said. Webster famously concluded, "Liberty and Union, now and forever one and inseparable."[5]

The nullification debate raged on in 1832 when Congress passed another tariff bill that did not reduce rates to the satisfaction of South Carolina. Calhoun resigned the vice-presidency and openly supported nullification. He took Hayne's Senate seat while Hayne became governor.[6] South Carolina held a Convention November 19, 1832, which declared the tariffs of 1828 and 1832 null and void. Andrew Jackson unofficially expressed his desire to have Calhoun hanged.[7] Officially he issued a December 11, 1832 Proclamation declaring that nullification was treason, that it would lead to dis-Union, and that the law would be enforced.[8]

The Virginia Legislature engaged in heated debate over whether to support the President or the nullifiers. Rives' name had been placed in nomination for the Senate by Thomas Walker Gilmer and Charles Yancey. Some legislators opposed Rives, questioning his views on the tariff, which they strongly opposed. Gilmer assured them Rives could be trusted. Gilmer wrote Rives:

> The battle has been fought and won. You are a Senator of Virginia....
>
> We had some difficulty as to your opinions on the tariff. The impression generally prevails that you are a luke warm state right man....
>
> You will see that I was interrogated much as to your course.... I took a prudent course for you and myself in giving no cause of offence to any, yet endeavoring to be frank and explicit as I could. Much depends on your course on your own account as well as mine. I feel no doubt however on this score....
>
> I am assured you will look to the great ends of public justice and your country's good, and by so doing be all that your friends desire....[9]

Gilmer and Rives had corresponded during the 1820s and while Rives had been in France. When Gilmer had contemplated moving to Missouri in 1828, the older Rives had encouraged him to stay in Virginia and take a seat in the Legislature. A few months later, Rives described to Gilmer his forceful reply to Congressman Ichabod Bartlett (1786-1853) of New Hampshire who had "assailed my personal character." Rives wrote, "I trust this affair will not gain for me the character of a brawling politician, for if there be any character which would be more my aversion than all others it is this."[10]

Rives had missed the buildup of the nullification crisis while in France. His father had written him that he considered Calhoun and his nullification "equally exceptionable as Aaron Burr."[11] Rives had to decide his position on the issue quickly, because Andrew Jackson had his supporters in Congress introduce a "Force Bill," authorizing the President to use the army and navy to insure revenue collection. Rives initially told Silas Wright of New York "that the southern men could not vote for any provisions of force."[12] Thomas Jefferson Randolph wrote Rives that the Force Bill would turn Virginians away from Jackson and make them support the nullifiers. "The condition of Virginia is very critical. The reprobation of South Carolina would have been decided; but the proclamation has thrown the nullifiers in principle but not in name from utter prostration into a majority."[13]

On February 14, 1833, Senator Moore of Alabama delivered a speech strongly opposing the Force Bill, also known as the Revenue Collection Bill. Moore criticized Jackson as dictatorial, enforcing at the point of a bayonet "the collection of odious, unjust, unequal and unconstitutional taxes. . . . You cannot enforce this bill. . . . We know our rights, and knowing them, dare maintain and defend them."[14]

Rives rose at the conclusion of Moore's remarks. He apologized that he had been out of the country while much of the discussion occurred. He said he disagreed on the issue with his fellow Senator (John Tyler) and many others from his quarter of the Union. He stated he was opposed to the tariff, and believed that appeals from Virginia and other states would cause the law to be changed. However, he did not support the right to nullify the law that South Carolina claimed. He stated that if the Federal Government permitted South Carolina to refuse to abide by the law, "The example would inflict a mortal wound on the Constitution." The country would return to the disorder of the Articles of Confederation, if it survived at all.

Rives continued that the Constitution contained no state veto or nullifying provision. He quoted Madison: "The Constitution of the United States being a compact among the states in their highest sovereign capacity, and constituting the people thereof one people for certain purposes cannot be altered or annulled at the will of the states individually, as the constitution of a state may be at its individual will."

Rives also quoted Federalist Paper 15 that "sovereignty of the Union and complete independence in the members are things repugnant and irreconcilable." Rives explained that sovereignty resided where the power of amending the Constitution resided: in a three fourths majority of the states. Rives also pointed out that, unlike the Articles of Confederation, the Constitution acted directly upon each citizen, not through the states.

Rives was interrupted twice by Calhoun who said the Senator from Virginia had "misapprehended" his remarks. Calhoun claimed he had not said that, "the people of a state might resume the powers which had been granted by the General Government, but that they had had a right to judge of the extent of those powers and whether they had been exceeded."

Rives replied that in repeating Calhoun's remarks, he was not only aided by his recollection, but also by a printed report "which seems to have been very carefully prepared and I presume under his own eye."

Turning to his fellow Virginian, Rives said Tyler had called the Constitution a "league" of states. Rives explained that Articles of Confederation was a league of states, but the Union under the Constitution possessed greater authority. Rives said Tyler had asked, "Who has ever seen a citizen of the United States?"

Tyler interrupted and said, "I said, 'Who has seen a citizen of the government of the United States?'"

Rives replied, "My honorable friend will perceive that this is but an evasion, not a solution. 'Who, Sir, has seen a citizen of the Government of Virginia?' There is no more a citizen of the government of Virginia than there is a citizen of the government of the United States." Rives explained that the Federal Government protected its citizens from abuse of law by states and ensured impartial administration of justice. Rives stated he was proud to be a Virginian, but even prouder to be a U.S. citizen.

Rives implored his fellow citizens to join him in changing the tariff "in harmony not in discord and hostility." He stated that the Union was "our only security for Liberty." He pointed to the current condition of South Carolina as proof that dis-union into separate states would bring anarchy and economic ruin. He said the state had been converted into an armed camp and had given its governor dictatorial powers.

> Sir, this is but a prefiguration of the evils and calamities to which every portion of this country would be destined, if the Union should be dissolved. Let us then rally around that sacred Union, fixing it anew, and establishing it forever on the immutable basis of equal justice, of mutual amity and kindness, and an administration at once firm and paternal.[15]

Rives' predictions of the "evils and calamities" of dis-union would seem understated 28 years later, when the Civil War raged. He would repeat the warning during the intervening years.

James Madison expressed enthusiastic approval of Rives' speech, which expressed his own concept of the U.S. government under the Constitution. Madison disagreed with the nullifiers, but he also disagreed with Daniel Webster's view of the Union that insufficiently recognized powers retained by the states. Madison envisioned a government that occupied a middle ground between extremes of states rights and nationalists.[16] In his March 12, 1833 letter to Rives he stated:

> I have found as I expected, that it [Rives' speech] takes a very able and enlightening view of its subject. I wish

it may have the effect of reclaiming to the doctrine and language held by all from the birth of the Constitution, and till very lately by themselves, those who now contend that the States have never parted with an Atom of their sovereignty, and consequently that the Constitutional band which holds them together, is a mere league or partnership, without any of the characteristics of sovereignty or nationality.

It seems strange that it should be necessary to disprove this novel and nullifying doctrine, and stranger still that those who deny it should be denounced as Innovators, heretics and Apostates. Our political system is admitted to be a new Creation—a real nondescript. Its character therefore must be sought within itself, not in precedents. . . .

The words of the Constitution are explicit that the Constitution and laws of the U.S. shall be supreme over the Constitution and laws of the several States, supreme in their exposition and execution as well as in their authority. Without a supremacy in those respects it would be like a scabbard in the hand of a soldier without a sword in it. . . .

The conduct of S. Carolina has called forth not only the question of nullification, but the more formidable one of secession. It is asked whether a State by resuming the sovereign form in which it entered the Union, may not of right withdraw from it at will. . . . One thing at least seems to be too clear to be questioned, that whilst a State remains within the Union it cannot withdraw its citizens from the operation of the Constitution and laws of the Union. In the event of an actual secession without the consent of the co states, the course to be pursued by these involves questions painful in the discussion of them. God grant that the menacing appearances which obtruded it may not be followed by positive occurrences requiring the more painful task of deciding them?

In explaining the proceedings of Virga in 98-99, the state of things at that time was the more properly appealed to, as it has been too much overlooked. The doctrines combated are always a key to the arguments employed. It is but too common to read the expressions of a remote period thro' the modern meaning of them, and to omit guards agst misconstruction not anticipated. A few words with a prophetic gift, might have prevented much error in the glosses on those proceedings. The remark is equally applicable to the Constitution itself.....[17]

Many Virginians disagreed with Rives and Madison. Some political enemies never forgave Rives for his support of the Force Bill. Rives wrote Van Buren, "the nullifiers, noisy, turbulent, and untiring in their efforts, have made me the butt of their most venomous attacks."[18] Opponents of Jackson's tactics, including John Tyler, deserted the Democratic Party in early 1833. Madison's concurrence with his speech and opposition to the nullifiers was sufficient validation for Rives. Rives owed his diplomatic appointment and success to Jackson and Van Buren, and his sense of loyalty would have prevented his turning against them in the crisis. Rives also could not have easily ignored his father's opposition to Calhoun's "exceptionable" doctrines. However, his assertion that he was prouder to be a citizen of the U.S. than of being a Virginian would cease to be true in 1861.

The national crisis was diffused in March mostly through the efforts of Henry Clay, who consulted with Calhoun and negotiated a compromise tariff that lowered rates over the next ten

NAVAL HISTORICAL CENTER

Thomas Walker Gilmer

years. South Carolina withdrew its Nullification Ordinance. Jackson signed the new Tariff Bill on the same day he signed the Force Bill, which had been rendered unnecessary. The struggle over state versus Federal power under the Constitution was not over. Rives wrote Jackson's private secretary Nicholas Trist in April, "we still want light very much in Virginia, where, I am sorry to tell you, both nullification and secession are much more current, than you seem to imagine at Washington."[19]

Thomas Walker Gilmer supported the nullifiers and was furious at Rives for what he considered a betrayal on the tariff issue. Rives took offence when Gilmer dismissed Madison's recent writings disavowing the nullifiers as "trash."[20] Gilmer published newspaper essays under the name "Buckskin," that denounced Rives. Gilmer had recently opposed Rives' youngest brother Alexander in an election. Rives and Gilmer exchanged letters that lacked the cordial sentiments of their previous correspondence. They encountered each other in a tavern on Charlottesville's Court Square on July 1, 1833. After an exchange of words,

Gilmer pulled Rives' nose, an affront known as "The Lieutenant Randolph Outrage."

The gesture was named for Lieutenant Robert Beverly Randolph, whom Andrew Jackson had removed from the U.S. Navy in 1828. Years later, Randolph had approached Jackson, removed his glove as if to shake hands, then reached out to tweak Jackson's nose. Jackson tried to beat the retreating Randolph with his cane, but was restrained by people around him. Then Jackson swore that Randolph had not actually touched him. The masculine code of the era dictated that a nose pull or any offensive touch of a man's body was an attack on his honor. A gentleman was supposed to defend himself against such insults even if that required a duel to the death.[21]

Rives answered Gilmer's provocation by striking him with his horsewhip. When Gilmer tried to grab Rives by his coat collar, Rives bit his finger. Gilmer punched Rives in the face, grabbed the whip and used it on Rives before the two could be separated. Rives bore a black eye from the encounter. Different versions of the fight appeared in issues of the *Charlottesville Advocate* and the *Richmond Enquirer*. An apparently crucial point of honor, in dispute, was whether Rives had been seated and not suspecting attack when Gilmer inflicted the outrage and threw the first punch.

Gilmer claimed in the July 9 edition of the *Enquirer* that he called Rives a hypocrite; Rives answered with "language equally offensive." Gilmer said they were both rising from their seats when he committed the "Lieutenant Randolph Outrage."

> This done, Mr. Rives commenced striking him with the butt end of his horsewhip, and inflicted with it one or two slight blows. That whilst this was passing, he attempted to seize Mr. Rives by the coat with his

left hand, but in doing so, was so unfortunate as to get his finger into Mr. Rives' mouth, a circumstance which resulted in the only injury that Mr. Gilmer received in the affray. And it was at this juncture — Mr. Gilmer alleges, whilst his finger was undergoing a most painful operation, that he struck Mr. Rives two blows in the face; and that he did this with a view of extricating the luckless member. Having succeeded in this, he wrested the horsewhip from Mr. Rives' hands, and struck him, or rather cut him several times, with the small end of it. They were then separated.[22]

The August 9 issue of the *Enquirer* stated that a witness corroborated Rives' assertion that Gilmer had sprung a surprise attack, and that he had done so while he was standing and Rives was seated. Gilmer had insisted that his opponent was rising, because Rives was not so "deficient in the spirit of manhood" that he would remain seated under threat of violence.

The instant before Mr. G. used the offensive epithet, and attempted to inflict the Lieutenant Randolph Outrage, which were, of course, simultaneous, Mr. Gilmer was upon his feet, and Mr. R. in his chair, totally unsuspicious of an attack, and furthermore, that Mr. G. took care to press his advantage so instantaneously as to strike him while he was still sitting, and before he had time to rise. Every fact which we have heard is in corroboration of this statement of Mr. Rives. We had supposed at first, that no white person was present at this affray; yet we understand, that it has since been ascertained, that a respectable person from an adjoining county was a witness of it, who fully confirms this statement, particularly as to the important fact of the violent blow given Mr. Rives, before he had yet risen from his chair. Under these circumstances, we are content to leave to the public to decide, which one of these parties proved himself "deficient in the spirit of manhood.[23]

Gilmer and Rives were both required by an Albemarle Court to give one thousand dollars bond to live peaceably with each other. The high amount indicated the seriousness of the matter.[24] Rives had become a "brawling politician" despite his inclination. An even bloodier street fight had taken place on Charlottesville's Court Square in 1819 between Thomas Jefferson Randolph and his brother-in-law Charles Bankhead. Randolph was seriously wounded, having only a whip to defend himself, while Bankhead was armed with knives.[25] Rives' behavior fell short of the example of Madison who was opposed by James Monroe in a 1789 congressional election. Madison's ear was frostbitten during a wintry outdoor debate in Culpeper. Madison playfully referred to the injury as a battle scar, but was proud to note that his friendship with Monroe was not diminished by the campaign.[26]

Perhaps the most famous duel of the era took place between John Randolph and Henry Clay in 1826. Henry Clay fired a shot that barely missed Randolph and pierced his coat. Randolph purposely missed Clay, and the two participants then embraced. Randolph said, "You owe me a coat Mr. Clay." Clay responded, "I am glad the debt is not greater." Eyewitness Thomas Hart Benton declared the duel "among the highest toned that I have ever witnessed."[27] Rives' and Gilmer's brawl was not high-toned. Serving in the Senate would bring Rives more conflict. His attempts to occupy a moderate position between extreme factions often gained him enemies from both sides.

* * *

1   Richard N. Current, T. Harry Williams, Frank Friedel, W. Elliot Brownlee, *The Essentials of American History*, 3rd Edition, New York, Alfred A. Knopf, 1980, 134-135.

2   Ibid, 136-137.

3   Drew R. McCoy, *The Last of the Fathers*, Cambridge, Cambridge University Press, 1989, 140-141.

4   Robert Y. Hayne speech in U.S. Senate, January 26, 1830, Gales and Seaton's Register of Debates, 21st Congress, 1st Session, 57.

5   Daniel Webster speech in U.S. Senate, January 26, 1830, Gales & Seaton's Register, Ibid, 58-80.

6   Current, Williams, Friedel, Brownlee, Ibid, 140.

7   Ibid.

8   Henry H. Simms, *The Rise of the Whigs in Virginia*, Richmond, The William Byrd Press, Inc. 1929, 65.

9   Thomas Walker Gilmer to Rives, December 10, 1832, Rives MSS, LOC, Letterbook, box 20.

10 Rives to Glimer, April 22, 1828, June 12, 1828, *Tyler's Quarterly Historical and Genealogical Magazine*, Vol. VI, #1, (1924-1925), 9-12. Volumes V and VII contain additional letters from Rives to Gilmer.

11 Robert Rives to Rives, May 3, 1831, Rives MSS, LOC, box 22.

12 Silas Wright to John Dix, February 4, 1833, Dix Papers, Columbia University, quoted in John Niven, *Martin Van Buren The Romantic Age of American Politics*, New York, Oxford, Oxford University Press, 1983, 327.

13 T. J. Randolph to Rives, February 21, 1833, Rives Mss, LOC, quoted in Niven, Ibid.

14 Senator Moore of Alabama, Senate speech, February 14, 1833, Gales and Seaton's Register of Debates, 22nd Congress, 2nd Session, 491.

15 William C. Rives, Senate speech, February 14, 1833, Ibid, 491-516.

16 McCoy, Ibid, 148-9, quotes Madison to Andrew Stevenson, November 27, 1830 and Madison to Daniel Webster, March 15, 1833, from *Letters*

and Other Writings of James Madison, [edited by Rives and Fendall], Philadelphia, J. B. Lippincott & Co., 1865, Vol. IV, 121-139, 293-294.

17 Madison to Rives, March 12, 1833, [Rives and Fendall], Ibid, 289-292 Madison's last remark indicates he considered the Constitution less perfect than some 21st century "originalists," or even than Rives, who often invoked it as sacred.

18 Rives to Van Buren, undated, Van Buren Papers, Library of Congress, quoted in Simms, Ibid, 74.

19 Rives to Trist, April 15, 1833, Trist Papers, Library of Congress, quoted by McCoy, Ibid, 155.

20 McCoy, Ibid, 154, cites December 22, 1832 and January 29, 1833 *Richmond Enquirer* .

21 www.shmoop.com/antebellum/gender.html (with thanks to Daniel Morrow).

22 *Richmond Enquirer*, July 9, 1833.

23 *Richmond Enquirer*, August 9, 1833.

24 Rev. Edgar Woods, *Albemarle County*, Charlottesville, The Michie Company, 1901, 110.

25 John Hammond Moore, *Albemarle, Jefferson's County*, Charlottesville, University of Virginia Press, 1976, 104.

26 William Cabell Rives, *Life and Times of James Madison*, Boston, Little, Brown and Company, 1866, Vol. II, 657.

27 *Thomas Hart Benton, Thirty Years View*, New York, D. Appleton and Company, 1854, Vol. I, 77.

CHAPTER NINE

Bank War

HAVING SUPPRESSED THE NULLIFIERS, Jackson directed his attention to the National Bank. The Second Bank of the United States, headquartered in Philadelphia, had been chartered in 1816. Four-fifths of its stock belonged to private investors and one-fifth to the federal government. The bank served as the official depository for government funds and sold government bonds. It also held private deposits and made loans. Its bank notes were trusted as sound currency. Northeasterners, especially its investors who profited, generally supported the bank and used its services. Residents of the south and west were less supportive. Some preferred state banks, which provided easier credit and inflated the value of farm crops. Others of the so-called "hard money" philosophy opposed all paper money, including National Bank notes, and believed silver and gold coins (specie) were the only safe currency. Rives was initially in the hard money camp, though his views would evolve.

Andrew Jackson despised the bank and was determined to destroy it. Clay, Webster and other bank supporters advised president of the Bank Nicholas Biddle to apply to Congress for a recharter of the Bank in 1832, four years before the 1816 charter was due to expire. Seeking to bolster support for the Bank, Biddle extended loans on easy terms to politicians, newspaper owners and editors.[1] Congress passed the bill, but Jackson vetoed it, denouncing the Bank as unconstitutional, un-democratic and un-American. Congress was unable to override the veto. The Bank was the main issue of the 1832 Presidential contest between

Jackson and Henry Clay. Jackson interpreted his election as an anti-Bank mandate.

Although the Bank's charter would last until 1836, Jackson sought to cripple it by ordering in September 1833 that federal funds would no longer be deposited in the Bank of the United States but in state banks. The Bank had been functioning effectively. Removal of the federal funds caused financial crisis throughout the country, and prompted resentment of Jackson as dictatorial. In the winter of 1833-34, Henry Clay led the consolidation of Jackson's opponents into the Whig party[2], named after the party in England, which had traditionally stood for limiting the power of the King and his court (Tory) party. Some sources erroneously claim that the term Whig sprung from an acronym for We Hope in God. English historians trace its origin to Scots Gaelic "whiggam," a term for horse thieves, which was applied to late 17th century supporters of Parliament.[3] The names "Whig" and "Tory" were suggested at an Anti-Administration meeting in New York's Masonic Hall, April 1, 1834. Because "Tory" was a name associated with Revolutionary War loyalists, no American party ever adopted the Tory name.[4] During the Jackson and Van Buren administrations the terms Democratic and Republican were both used to describe the administration party. The modern Republican Party arose in 1854, which has resulted in the two party system of Democrats versus Republicans.

Jackson opponents criticized his removal of the "deposites," as they are called in the Congressional Register. They called for the federal money to be returned to the Bank and its 29 branches, instead of being distributed among Jackson's "pet banks," as his critics called the state banks. They viewed his funneling of money to favorite banks as an outrageous expansion of Jackson's political spoils system and the mark of a corrupt and imperial presidency. Calhoun, stung over nullification, had joined with Clay to oppose the president on the Bank issue. Though many historians consider Jackson's economic policies misguided and damaging, Rives steadfastly supported the president during weeks of debate in the Senate in late 1833 and early 1834.

On January 17, 1834, Rives delivered a speech in support of Jackson of a length that seemed calculated to bludgeon if not persuade his opponents. It filled 32 pages of the Congressional Register. He began by declaring his reluctance to speak in a chamber where he was more disposed to listen. He admitted there was financial distress in the country, but he claimed the cause was not Jackson's order of the removal of the "deposites." The problem was the size and concentrated power of the Bank, a "powerful, remorseless overshadowing monopoly." He quoted Jefferson and Madison's cautions about the First Bank of the United States. Citing Madison was problematic, because the Second Bank was chartered in 1816 during Madison's administration.

Rives spoke in favor of "simple, solid, hard-money Government." He preferred gold and silver coins for small transactions and advocated suppression of bank notes of less than twenty dollars. Restoring the deposites to the Bank would, according to Rives, aggravate the situation and the country would be at the mercy of the Bank in 1836 when its charter came up for renewal.

He condemned the Bank's "extension of its accommodation to individuals" in 1831 and 1832 when outstanding loan amounts rose from over 42 million dollars to over 70 million. Intended by Biddle to increase support for the Bank, the arrangement caused inflation and over-trading. Rives also criticized the Bank for printing and distributing self-promotional pamphlets during the re-charter debate.

Rives quoted Calhoun's remarks delivered in the House in 1816 that the federal government should retain control over its deposites to assure some degree of control over the Bank. He quoted Clay's recent criticism of Jackson's conduct as a usurpation. When he mentioned Calhoun's name, Calhoun rose and

objected that he did not consider the president's action a usurpation, but a gross abuse of power.

Rives answered, "Sir the only question presented by the resolutions under consideration is a question of the existence, not the
abuse of power." He continued that Clay had said "with his char-
acteristic eloquence" that Jackson, by wielding his power over the
Treasury, had united "power of the purse and power of the sword."
Those words were taken from a Patrick Henry speech and,
according to Rives, were "calculated to excite jealousies of a free
people." Rives argued that the power of the purse, the ability to
levy and collect taxes and duties, resided in Congress. Executive
officers merely received, kept and disbursed that public money.
Likewise the power of the sword rested with Congress who alone
could declare war, raise and supply armies and navies of which
the president was Commander-in-Chief.

Rives argued that the president had control over cabinet officers under the Constitution, a power Clay had disputed. Rives
cited a Jefferson letter to the French M. de Tracy to support his
argument.

Clay interrupted and asked if the letter was written before or
after Jefferson's presidency.

Always careful with his Jefferson citations, Rives replied the
letter was written in 1811 after his retirement. He quoted from
the letter Jefferson's reflection on having experienced both superior and subordinate roles.

Rives began his two pages of conclusion by quoting Senator
Clay's assertion that "We are in a revolution." Rives said, "I
agree, a happy and auspicious revolution." The country had seen
internal improvements under federal authority returned to the
states. The Bank had been foiled in its attempt to perpetuate
its existence. Directly confronting Clay, Rives said, "We have
seen the American system which we in the south feel is a system not of protection but of oppression partially overthrown

and abandoned." Singing his praise of Jackson, Rives said, "We are indebted to the firmness, vigor, patriotism of the individual who now presides over the administration of the Government sustained by the virtuous confidence of a free people."

He concluded, the people "call upon us for the rescue of their liberties from the grasp of a selfish and unrelenting moneyed despotism . . . and worthily I trust will the call be answered by the firmness, the constancy, and the patriotism of their representatives."[5]

Having read a pamphlet copy of the speech, James Madison wrote Rives a letter expressing both praise for his eloquence and gentle disagreement with his position:

> Montpelier
> Feb. 15, 1834
> Dear Sir,
>
> I have received the copy of your speech on the 'Removal of the Deposits,' kindly forwarded in pamphlet form. It has certainly treated the questions embraced by it with the distinguished ability which was looked for. Whilst I feel a pleasure in doing it this justice I must not forget, as I presume you are aware, that some of them are not viewed by me in the lights in which your reasoning presents them.[6]

Despite Madison's differing view, Rives remained opposed to a National Bank throughout his political career. Rives' speech also revealed his continuing loyalty to Jackson.

As was the case during the nullification crisis, residents of western portions of Virginia were more supportive of Jackson than those in the east. In January, Rives' brawling antagonist Thomas

Walker Gilmer, now firmly in the Whig faction, proposed resolutions that were passed by the Virginia House of Delegates declaring the President's action to be "an unauthorized assumption and dangerous exercise of executive power" although it also condemned the Bank as unconstitutional.[7] Virginia Senators Tyler and Rives were instructed by the Virginia legislature to vote for the restoration of federal deposits to the Bank of the United States.

On Saturday, February 22, 1834, Tyler in the Senate presented resolutions adopted by the two houses of the Virginia Legislature expressing their views of the conduct of the President regarding the Bank and the removal of deposits. Rives opposed the resolutions and rose to explain why he had only one honorable course.

His remarks were brief compared to his January speech. Rives noted Tyler's resolutions were a "legitimate expression of the opinion of my State." It was his "misfortune to have entertained and expressed very different opinions." He could not vote against the instruction of the legislature. He could not follow the instruction of the legislature and vote against his conscience and beliefs. Therefore he proceeded to "surrender his trust into the hands from whom he derived it." However he suggested that the "sentiments of the people in the present instance are not in unison with the proceedings of the legislative authority."

[Rives concluded,] I abandon what I have ever regarded the highest honor of my public life, an honor than which none higher in my opinion can be presented to the ambition of an American citizen. I sacrifice social and kindly relations with many members of this body, I would fain hope with all, which has been the source of the highest satisfaction to me here, and the remembrance of which I shall cherish with sincere pleasure in the retirement whither I go. I know and feel the weight of these sacrifices; but great as they are, I make them without a sigh, as the most emphatic homage I can render to a principle I believe vital to the republican system, and indispensable to the safe and salutary action of our political institutions.[8]

The Virginia Legislature chose Benjamin Watkins Leigh over Philip Pendleton Barbour to succeed Rives.[9] Rives would return. President Jackson wrote Rives expressing his regret over the loss of such a strong supporter:

I have just been informed that you felt it necessary to resign your seat in the Senate. It is a matter of supreme regret to me, as I do not doubt it will be to others, that a difference of opinion between your Legislature and yourself on a single point, should have assumed a shape by which the country is at this very interesting moment deprived of the services of a gentleman who has evinced so much willingness and ability to aid her . . .[10]

Andrew Jackson, his niece Emily Donelson, and her three children visited Castle Hill in the summer of 1834. Jackson had been in poor health and reportedly suffered "bilious colic" en route from the White House. Heavy rains, unusually hot weather and bad roads complicated the trip. When the carriage stopped at a tavern in Gordonsville (seven miles north of Castle Hill) Jackson saw Senator George Poindexter of Mississippi who was afraid of Jackson and hid from the President, which caused him to miss his stagecoach.[11] Jackson also visited Castle Hill in 1836. One of Rives' sons later recalled the sight of Old Hickory seated in the Castle Hill parlor smoking a corncob pipe.[12]

Being out of office allowed Rives to visit his brother Landon, a physician living in Cincinnati. Rives was impressed with the western city. Landon had two sons who would later serve as surgeons in the Confederate Army. One of Landon Rives' great grandsons was Congressman Nicholas Longworth, who married Alice Roosevelt.[13]

Judith gave birth to a daughter Ella Rives September 15, 1834. She would be the youngest of five children. When parents and children were apart, they maintained a voluminous and affection-ate correspondence.

The following letter from Judith to Rives bears the date May 26, without a year. The mention of Ella's tooth seems to indicate Ella was nursing, which would indicate 1835, although Rives did not return to the Senate until 1836. Whatever the year, the letter shows Judith's affection for her husband as well as her strength and cheer while traveling with young children.

Robinson's Tavern
Thursday

We are here, safe and sound, my dearest Husband, and I hasten to obey your injunction of writing you an account of our journey before its termination. The day has been rather moist, but cool and so favorable for traveling, that I thought it best to come this far, as the horses do not appear at all fatigued. If we are as much favored tomorrow as we have been today, I hope we shall reach home without any difficulty tomorrow evening. We have had a quiet and pleasant trip so far, and there is something sweetly refreshing in the view of the woods in their gay spring garb....

... my dear Husband how much I miss you, and how like the broken half of a pair of scissors I feel without you. . . . I trust to hear from you that you take every measure to preserve your precious health, that you continue your rides before breakfast. . . .

Our dear little ones are well and merry, they appear to enjoy the fresh air very much and look better and happier already. Little Ella bit me so hard this morning, that I thought there must be something more than common in her little mouth, and I soon found a nice pearl, in the form of a sharp little white tooth. I wish you could enjoy the satisfaction of being bitten.

Offer my kindest and most affectionate souvenirs to Mrs. Cambreling[14], and her dearer half, and tell her that I have many things to say to her, but I shall say them to her myself before long. Tell her I hope she misses me, and thinks of me and loves me. Need I say the same to you? No my dearest, I know you do, and I am only afraid that you miss me too much, and that you are not happy without me. Let us trust, however, that we shall very soon be restored to each other, and in the mean time, I pray that every blessing, earthly and spiritual may be yours. Forgive this unworthy scrawl, as it comes from,

Your own

JP Rives[15]

Rives had advised Judith in 1833 to travel to Washington mostly by land because of "the uncertainty and recent accidents of the Steam Boat." Judith and the children had to ride in the Castle Hill carriage to Orange Court House and spend the night at Blakey's Tavern there in order to catch an early morning Piedmont Stage Line coach. They would reach Washington in two days after spending a night in Warrenton. The chartered stagecoach would haul all baggage as well as passengers while Tom the coachman followed in the Castle Hill carriage.[16]

As the Bank war raged, Jackson threatened another war. After years of delay, on April 1, 1834 the French Chamber of Deputies voted 176 to 168 not to pay the indemnity Rives had negotiated. Perhaps America's friend Lafayette could have changed the vote. However he was too ill to attend the Chamber session and would die May 20.[17] Jackson was furious and, along with his Secretary of State Louis McLane (Minister to England when Rives served in France), devised an aggressive response. Vice-President Van Buren contacted Rives for advice. Rives suggested that imposing tariffs on French silks or wines would be appropriate, but he opposed drastic action or provocation. The measure had failed by six votes and a new Chamber of Deputies due to convene in December might deliver a more favorable result.[18] Van Buren calmed Jackson down and convinced him that Rives' proposals were sounder than McLane's. A needless war with France would reinforce Whig claims that Jackson was unstable and tyrannical. McLane resigned, and never again spoke to Van Buren.[19]

Jackson was only temporarily soothed. The President met with Rives in Richmond in late September and grew irritated when Rives continued to advocate patience and diplomacy. Rives wrote Van Buren a letter describing his meeting with Jackson and reiterated his position. Van Buren, calculating that he needed Jackson's backing for his own presidential campaign more than he needed Rives, sent Jackson a copy of Rives' letter to him with disparaging comments:

> By the enclosed you will perceive, as well, that our friend Rives is getting to be quite confident of his own success and that he has fallen into the prevailing error of the Virginia politicians, who appear to be always on the lookout for some rash act on your part, a fault

which it seems that no success of your measures can
entirely cure them.[20]

After sending this letter to Jackson, Van Buren wrote the
unsuspecting Rives to assure him that he would fully present his
views to the president:

> You may take it for granted that a strong (but I trust
> prudent) statement of the injuries we have rec'd from
> France will be made. . . . you in Virginia or I might per-
> haps rather say they are prone to apprehend rash acts
> from the Gen'l., but they must admit that after all he
> has been oftener in the right than others. . . . I have
> been a strenuous advocate for forbearance heretofore
> (more than you are aware of) and will continue to be.[21]

The Little Magician's reputation as a wily politician was well
justified. In this instance Van Buren was a Little Manipulator.
Thomas Walker Gilmer had delivered a black eye. Van Buren had
stabbed Rives in the back. War with France would have proved
much more costly than five million dollars. The amount was a
fraction of the trade between the two countries.[22] Honor of both
countries was deemed to be at stake, which made the situation
more irrational, dangerous and intractable.

Jackson sent a message to Congress in December 1834 warning
the French government he would recommend reprisals if the new
Chamber did not vote to pay the indemnity. The Whig-controlled
Senate refused to support Jackson. However the French King,
government and citizens were still outraged by the President.
King Louis Philippe ordered home his minister. The Chamber
of Deputies approved payment of the five million dollars April
18, 1835, but made it contingent on Jackson's making an apology
for impugning the honor of France. Andrew Jackson was not a

man who apologized. However, after mediation by the British and wrangling by Van Buren (who persisted in asking Rives for advice) and others, Jackson inserted conciliatory language in his December 1835 message to Congress. The French appeared satisfied, but an old note from ex-Minister Serrurier presented an affront to Old Hickory's honor. The note read:

"*Les plaints que porte M. le president contre le prétendu non-accomplissments des engagements....*"

The American translator had rendered the passage:

The complaints which the President brings against the pretended non-fulfillment of the engagements....

The problem was the word "*prétendu.*" Translated as "pretended," it slighted presidential motive and behavior, implying Jackson was not truthful or honorable. Would the President go to war over one word? The British and French foreign offices both exclaimed that the translation was faulty. "*Prétendu*" was more accurately translated as "alleged," which removed the negative connotation. The explanation satisfied the Americans and a memorandum for future translators was filed in State Department archives.[23] Payments were made into the bank of Baron de Rothschild who acted as agent for the Americans. A crisis involving four U.S. administrations and decades of diplomacy was finally resolved.[24]

★ ★ ★

1 Richard N. Current, T. Harry Williams, Frank Friedel, W. Elliot Brownlee, *The Essentials of American History, 3rd Edition*, New York, Alfred A. Knopf, 1980. 141.

2   See Michael F. Holt, *The Rise and Fall of the American Whig Party: Jacksonian Politics and the Onset of the Civil War*, New York, Oxford, Oxford University Press, 1999, 24-27.

3   Whig. www.globalsecurity.org/military/world/ukparties-whig.htm.

4   Henry H. Simms, *The Rise of the Whigs in Virginia 1824-1840*, Richmond, The William Byrd Press, Inc. 1929, 86.

5   Gales and Seaton's Register of Debates in Congress, 23rd Congress, 1st session Dec. 2, 1833 to June 30, 1834, 259-291.

6   James Madison to William C. Rives, February 15, 1834, *Letters and Other Writings of James Madison*, [edited by Rives and Fendall] Philadelphia, J. B. Lippincott and Company, 1865, Vol. IV, 339-340.

7   Simms, Ibid, 79.

8   Register of Debates in Congress, Ibid, 637-638.

9   Simms, Ibid, 80.

10 Andrew Jackson to Rives, February 22, 1834, letterbook, Rives Papers, Library of Congress, Box 104.

11 Jon Meacham, *American Lion, Andrew Jackson in the White House*, New York, Random House, 2008, 179-180.

12 WCR, Jr., Biography, Rives MSS, LOC, Box 103, 63, 67.

13 George Lockhart Rives, *Genealogical Notes*, New York, 1914, 5-6.

14 Wife of New York Congressman Churchill C. Cambreling.

15 Judith Page Rives to Rives, May 26 (no year), Rives MSS, UVa., Accession #2313, box 7.

16 Rives to Judith Page Rives, December 7, 1833, Rives MSS, LOC, box 22.

17 Beckles Willson, *America's Ambassadors to France (1777-1927)*, London, John Murray, Albemarle Street, 1928, 187.

18 John Niven, *Martin Van Buren The Romantic Age of American Politics*, New York, Oxford, Oxford University Press, 1983, 368-369.

19 Ibid, 370-372.

20 Ibid. 377 quotes Van Buren to Jackson, October 23, 1834, Van Buren Papers Library of Congress.

21 Ibid. quotes Van Buren to Rives, October 23, 1824, Rives MSS, LOC.

22 Ibid, 378.

23 Marquis James, *The Life of Andrew Jackson*, Indianapolis, New York, The Bobbs-Merrill Company, 1938, 697-698. Cites Lord Palmerston letter to H. S. Fox, British Minister to the U.S., April 22, 1836, British Foreign Office Papers (copies) Volume 307, Library of Congress.

24 See Niven 378-385 and Willson 190-197.

CHAPTER TEN

A Heartbeat Away from the Vice Presidency

WHILE THE FRENCH TREATY CRISIS proceeded towards resolution, the Bank fight between Jackson and Congress continued to rage. On Friday March 28, 1834, the Senate passed a resolution proposed by Henry Clay:

> Resolved. That the President, in the late Executive proceedings in relation to the public revenue, has assumed upon himself authority and power not conferred by the Constitution and laws, but in derogation of both.[1]

This resolution came a few days before the initial French refusal to honor the reparations treaty. Jackson was not inclined to submit to the Senate any more than he was to the French. Jackson's supporters in the Senate objected to the resolution and began a fight to have the passage removed or "expunged" from the original Senate journal. That would require a majority.

Regaining majority support in the Senate would require majority support of state legislatures. In the 1834 spring election campaign, Virginia Democrats portrayed Jackson as a man of the people who had slain the triple headed monster of tariffs, internal improvements and the Bank. Whigs declared the issue was a struggle between liberty and ruthless presidential power. In May 1834, Virginia Whigs elected 79 delegates to 55 Democratic delegates.[2]

Virginia Democrats struggled to overcome temporary defeat. They wanted to return Rives to his Senate seat in the election which would take place in 1835. Jacksonians sought to discredit Rives' replacement Benjamin Watkins Leigh as a Bank supporter and unsympathetic to western Virginians. At a September dinner for Orange-Madison district Congressman John M. Patton, a toast was drunk to William C. Rives as "one of the bright constellation of the Democratic party," while Leigh was denounced as "a Blue-light Hartford Convention Federalist of the Boston Stamp."[3] Whig orators accused Rives of being an abolitionist, a curious charge because he owned 5,000 acres farmed by scores of slaves.[4] On another occasion Whigs denounced Rives as one who would rather serve "a prince than a Republic."[5]

January 27, 1835, Charles Yancy, a Rives supporter in the Virginia legislature, moved that the Senate election be postponed until after spring elections. Rives backers wanted more time to increase their numbers. The measure was defeated. His old friend T. J. Randolph nominated Rives, but after two days of debate, Leigh won by a vote of 85 to 81.[6]

Three days later an Englishman named Richard Lawrence attempted to assassinate President Jackson. He was standing six feet away when Jackson walked into the rotunda of the Capitol. Lawrence pulled the triggers of two loaded pistols, which misfired; only the caps exploded. Old Hickory tried to club his assailant with his cane, but an army officer reached the man first. Lawrence said he was rightful heir to the British throne and that killing Jackson would strengthen his claim. He was sent to a lunatic asylum.[7]

Had the assassin's bullets found their mark, the nation would have lost a leader of matchless force and the subject of much argument in Congress. Although he would not run for a third term, Jackson proposed that the Democratic Party hold its convention early to create party unity. Jackson and Van Buren's nominations as President and Vice President had been uncontested at the first convention held in Baltimore in 1832. The second convention was also held in Baltimore in May 1835, and despite Jackson's intentions, controversy erupted.

Van Buren was Jackson's chosen successor for the presidential nomination. Southern Democrats favored Rives as their nominee for vice president. They felt Rives would strengthen the party's appeal in the South and soothe southern doubts about the New Yorker Van Buren's position on slavery. Rives' supporters were confident of his qualifications and his chances. Rives trusted that his friendship with Van Buren and his support of Jackson's policies would secure his nomination. He wrote Van Buren April 10, 1835 about how he as a Virginian would help the ticket. He said the idea of a southern confederacy was gaining adherents and that "the only means of defeating it, is to keep Virginia as the fulcrum of the South in harmonious relations with the administration of the General Government."[8]

Whether Jackson was still irritated at Rives for advocating restraint in dealing with the French, or because he wanted a rugged fellow westerner, the President's choice for Van Buren's running mate was Richard Mentor Johnson of Kentucky. Johnson had served in the House and Senate, and had campaigned for the presidency. Johnson had also fought under General William Henry Harrison and claimed to have personally killed the Indian Chief Tecumseh at the Battle of the Thames. A friend of Jackson's questioned whether the killing of Tecumseh qualified a man to be Vice President.[9]

Johnson had two daughters with Julia Chinn, a mostly Caucasian woman with a small fraction of African ancestry that prevented Johnson from legally marrying her. After her death in 1833, Johnson took another light-skinned slave as his mistress. When she ran off with an Indian, he had her captured and sold at auction, and compelled her sister to take her place. These actions were hardly uncommon or shocking to slaveholding southerners.

What they found offensive was that Johnson's conduct was so blatant.[10] One Virginia newspaper accused him of believing in amalgamation of the species for living "in shameless prostitution with a black" whom he tried to force "on genteel society."[11]

In the vice presidential contest, Van Buren and the New York delegation went along with Jackson's choice of Johnson. Andrew Stevenson, Rives' fellow Virginian and Albemarle County neighbor, was Chairman and President of the convention. W. P. Slaughter, a Virginia delegate who supported Rives, claimed that Stevenson conspired with others against Rives out of jealousy. He claimed there were "New Yorkers in our own camp."[12] Tennessee did not send delegates; however a man named Edward Rucker from Tennessee happened to be present and was allowed to cast Tennessee's allotted 15 votes. The final tally was 178 votes for Johnson and 87 for Rives. When Johnson's victory was announced, the Virginia delegation hissed in disapproval.[13]

Virginia held its grudge against Johnson through the 1836 general election. There was no national election day until 1845. Each state was allowed to choose its own convenient voting day in the fall of 1836. The electoral votes were not counted until February 8, 1837. Van Buren received a popular vote majority and a decisive electoral victory over the opposition vote split between Daniel Webster, William Henry Harrison, and Hugh Lawson White of Tennessee. The Whigs had hoped to deny Van Buren an electoral majority and have the contest decided by the House, as in 1824. In the vice presidential election, Virginia's electors voted for Judge William Smith of Alabama, which denied Johnson his needed electoral majority. Under terms of the Constitution's Twelfth Amendment, the election had to be settled by a vote in the Senate, which chose Johnson. Johnson is the only vice president to have been selected this way. Van Buren was not pleased with Johnson's performance in office and dropped him from the ticket in 1840, opting to campaign with no running mate.[14]

The bitter contest prompted Van Buren to write Rives that the Virginia delegation's actions created an impression of belligerence. Van Buren would have preferred more of a spirit of concession.[15] He hoped he could still count on Rives' support. Rives replied that after having been the target of anti-Administration attacks for two years, the honor of the vice presidential nomination would have been gratifying. He also said an acceptable southern man on the ticket would have garnered southern support.[16] Rives sought to reassure Van Buren, "Certainly on my part, nothing shall be wanting to allay every feeling of dissatisfaction which may have arisen on my account and to promote by whatever means may be in my power that hearty Republican concert which is so necessary to the ascendancy of the principles for which we have contended."[17]

These words of support did not entirely conceal Rives' disappointment. Relations between Rives and Van Buren had been damaged and would further deteriorate. Rives had to accept the defeat and serve in some other office. Democrats regained control of the Virginia Legislature in 1835, creating the possibility that Rives might regain his Senate seat. The strategy was to have the legislature instruct Senators Leigh and Tyler to vote for a measure they personally opposed. Van Buren visited Castle Hill in November 1835, and Rives met with sympathetic legislators in Richmond to discuss the plan. The Senators would be instructed to vote for Senator Benton's resolution to expunge Clay's 1834 resolution, which condemned Jackson, from the official Senate record.[18]

Thomas Hart Benton of Missouri had fought Andrew Jackson in a gunfight in Nashville in 1813. Jackson was severely wounded by two bullets fired by Thomas Benton's brother Jesse.[19] The next time Jackson and Benton met was in 1823 when they were both Senators. Defying expectations, Jackson was civil and courteous.[20] Jackson's former antagonist became his strongest ally. Benton wanted to expunge Clay's resolution, because he claimed the resolution charged the President with an impeachable offense.[21] Benton's proposal was to have a black line drawn around the resolution as it appeared in the original hand-written journal with the words "Expunged by order of the Senate." Although the words would remain in hundreds of printed copies of the proceedings, senators on both sides of the issue did not see the measure as merely symbolic. Speeches about the expunging were long and passionate.

Democrats had regained control of the Virginia legislature in 1835, and on February 11, 1836, they passed a measure to instruct Senators Tyler and Leigh to vote for the expunging. Tyler sent a brief letter of resignation, but Leigh initially refused to resign because, he claimed, he could not be instructed to do something unconstitutional.[22] Rives was elected to replace Tyler, and returned to the Senate at the end of March.

Rives' part in the expunging struggle earned him the derisive nickname "The Little Expunger" from enemies who had also opposed his support of the Force Bill.[23] Whigs dubbed Benton "The Great Expunger." Rives delivered a speech in support of the expunging March 28. Among his arguments, Rives cited a 1765 expunging that took place in the Virginia House of Burgesses. Patrick Henry had proposed five resolutions that were approved. The next day the fifth was expunged because it was deemed too inflammatory and likely to incite British force for which Virginia was not prepared. Voters for the expunging included future signers of the Declaration of Independence Edmund Pendleton, George Wythe and Richard Henry Lee. Rives cited another expunging that took place in the House of Representatives in 1822. John Randolph had been informed that Senator William Pinkney of Maryland had died, and he announced the news to his colleagues. Randolph was later informed that Pinkney was not dead when he made the announcement, though Pinkney did die several hours later. The next day Randolph explained the circumstances. The House granted his request that his premature eulogy be expunged. Rives argued that the Senate had the power to correct its mistakes and to purge its journal of improper material. He noted that eleven state legislatures had voted for the expunging, and he thought several more would join them. He vowed to "cheerfully obey their voice."[24]

His fellow Virginia Senator Benjamin Watkins Leigh expressed disagreement with his "honorable colleague" in an April 4 speech. Leigh said Rives might have been mistaken about the particulars of the 1765 Patrick Henry expunging. Leigh also disputed Rives' citation of English Parliamentary precedents. He concluded that the expunging was part of a movement in which the people would lose all rights and fall under monarchy.[25] Leigh was eventually forced to resign.

Rives and Leigh both sent copies of their speeches to James Madison. Madison wrote Rives that his speech "contains strong points, strongly sustained;" however, he stressed the importance of preserving original journals of the legislature. Madison seemed to agree more with Leigh. Madison said he had dictated his letter to Rives because of "the clumsy state of my fingers."[26]

Madison died at Montpelier June 28, 1836. Jackson sent a message to the Senate two days later that the country's fourth president had died "full of years and full of honors." Recognized as Madison's most devoted friend and disciple in the Senate, Rives rose and spoke after Jackson's message was read:

> The eulogy of Mr. Madison is written in every page of the history of his country, to whose service his whole life was devoted. . . . He was, in an especial manner, the founder and author of that glorious Constitution which is the bond of our Union and the charter of our

liberties. . . . He was the last surviving signer of that sacred instrument. . . .

In speaking of these things, Mr. President, I am but too forcibly reminded of my own personal loss in the general and national calamity which we all bewail. I was the neighbor of Mr. Madison, sir, and enjoyed his kindness and friendship. . . .

It is my melancholy satisfaction to have received, in all probability, the last letter ever signed by his hand.[27] It bears date only six days before his death. . . . In that letter which is now before me, he spoke of his enfeebled health, and his trembling and unsteady signature, so much in contrast with the usual firmness and regularity of his writing, bore a graphic and melancholy intimation of his approaching end.[28]

Rives proposed that a committee be appointed to consider proper memorial procedures. The committee included Rives, Clay, Calhoun, Grundy, Buchanan, Leigh and Tallmadge. Rives reported their recommendations: that chairs of the Speaker of the House and President of the Senate be shrouded in black for the remainder of the session, that members of both houses of Congress wear a badge of mourning for 30 days and that the people of the U.S. be recommended to wear black armbands on the left arm for 30 days. The President was asked to transmit a copy of the resolutions to Mrs. Madison and offer condolence and respect.[29]

In his will, James Madison bequeathed his manuscript notes from the 1787 Constitutional Convention to his wife Dolley for her to sell. Though they lived a privileged lifestyle on their plantation Montpelier, the Madisons were often short of cash. Bad harvests, and debts incurred by Dolley's son and Madison's stepson John Payne Todd, caused them major financial problems.

Madison hoped that the sale of his papers would provide financial security for his wife.[30]

Estimating that the papers could be sold for $100,000, which would be more than enough for Dolley, Madison bequeathed $9,000 to be divided between his nieces and nephews and $12,000 to institutions including the University of Virginia, his alma mater in Princeton, New Jersey, and the American Colonization Society.[31] Madison had been President of the last named organization, whose aim was to "colonize" or transport freed slaves to Africa. Madison's bequest to the Colonization Society was controversial. Northern abolitionists were disappointed Madison had not freed his slaves in his will as George Washington had done. Deep South slaveholders viewed the ACS as a threat to the institution of slavery.[32]

Dolley tried unsuccessfully to sell her husband's papers to private publishers in the summer and fall of 1836. Madison friend and protégé Nicholas Trist, who was married to one of Jefferson's granddaughters, conceived the idea of having Congress purchase the papers. Trist presented the idea to Rives, who advocated it to Van Buren in an August 29 letter. Rives wrote that the transaction could be justified by precedent, since Congress had purchased papers of George Washington in 1833-34 for $25,000.[33] Van Buren conveyed his approval, which Rives forwarded to Dolley in October when Trist had presented his idea to her.[34]

Dolley appealed to her friends in Washington including President Jackson, Rives, and Henry Clay. Though they and others wanted to help, the nation's finances were precarious, and Congress was confronting a number of other issues including fiscal policy, debates about slavery, and recognition of Texas independence. The main obstacle was the $100,000 asking price. Rives had to break the news to Dolley that the most Congress would be willing to pay was $30,000, and that he advised her to accept it. With no promising alternative, Dolley agreed.[35]

Senators debated purchase of the Madison papers February 20, 1837. The most vocal opponent was John C. Calhoun. Calhoun had resented Madison's opposition to nullification. Calhoun also mentioned Madison's bequest to the American Colonization Society and argued that it was unconstitutional for Congress to be funding such an organization. Calhoun claimed that he revered Madison, and because Madison opposed action by Congress that was unauthorized by the Constitution, such as this purchase, Calhoun was actually being faithful to Madison by opposing the measure. He also said that the proposal was made only because Mrs. Madison could not find a private buyer for the papers.

Calhoun's fellow South Carolina Senator William Preston spoke in support of the purchase. He argued the measure was constitutional because these papers were an important part of the Constitution. Though he did not necessarily approve of Madison's bequests, the debate was about a transaction with Mrs. Madison, not what she did with the proceeds. Daniel Webster also spoke in favor, pointing out that Congress annually purchased many books.

Senator John Niles of Connecticut opposed the measure because, he said, buying material with intent to publish was a new and potentially dangerous power for Congress to assume. Senator John J. Crittenden of Kentucky stressed the importance of the papers in expressing his support. As for constitutional objections, he asked under what authority Congress had built the Capitol.

Calhoun said that Mrs. Madison had been offered $5,000 by a private publisher, and suggested she should have accepted the offer. Crittenden retorted that Mrs. Madison's reverence for her husband's memory would induce her to prefer a sale to the government rather than a private bookseller. Crittenden claimed that if he personally owned the manuscripts in question, he would demand more than $30,000 for them. Calhoun replied that, "Mr. Madison had died childless and had left his wife in easy circumstances," adding that he should have left the papers to the American people for free.

Rives rose in reply to Calhoun. The measure, he said, ". . . is directed to the preservation of the monuments of our creation and organized existence as a nation and a Government." Addressing Niles' objection, Rives said the resolution only called for purchase of the manuscripts and the matter of publication could be debated separately. As for Madison's controversial bequests, Rives pointed out that Madison had bequeathed the Constitution itself to the country. Rives expressed regret that Calhoun had questioned the motives of the dead Madison, and implied that Calhoun had slandered the beloved Dolley:

> Let me in conclusion say, and I regret that the remark is called for by the allusions of the Senator from South Carolina, that the amiable and distinguished lady who is the proprietor of this manuscript is here as no petitioner for charity. She has done what it became her to do as the relict of that great man whose papers were bequeathed to her to enshrine and imbody among the treasures of our country an authentic record of those solemn debates which issued in the formation of our happy and glorious form of government.

Calhoun protested that he "had cast no censure on Mr. Madison," and that he had not said "any thing which any friend of Mrs. Madison had the least right to take exception to." Henry Clay spoke briefly in support of the measure, but observed time was limited and the Senate faced many other pressing matters. The measure passed by a vote of 32 to 14.[36]

Rives wrote Dolley that the measure had passed in the Senate, and that he would do everything in his power to secure its passage by the House. Judith also wrote Dolley, declaring that Calhoun's performance had been "ungenerous and disingenuous," an attempt at revenge for Madison's rejection of nullification.[37]

The House of Representatives never took up the resolution to purchase the Madison papers. Jackson's term in office was about to end, along with the 24th Congress. With time running out, Rives used his mastery of Senate rules to secure the money for Dolley and the papers for posterity. Rives had his fellow Virginia Senator Richard Elliot Parker, who had replaced Benjamin Watkins Leigh, move to insert $30,000 for the purchase of the manuscripts as an earmark into a General Appropriation Bill. Rives relied on the less well known Parker in order to attract less attention, even though the $30,000 was by far the largest item in the bill. Perhaps distracted by the transition of administrations or else too pressed for time to argue, the Senate and House quickly passed the Appropriations Bill.[38]

Apologizing for not writing sooner because of "the constant hurly-burly . . . [of] the last three or four weeks," Rives wrote Dolley Madison March 28 to inform her that the bill had passed and that Congress would pay her the money. Though the process had been difficult, and the money was far below her initial request, Rives wrote, "I think we have reason to congratulate ourselves on our good fortune in getting along, as well as we did."[39] Rives was able to secure unanimous approval of a motion October 14, 1837 that granted Dolley the right to publish the manuscripts in foreign countries. Congress first published the Madison papers in 1840. They were an immediate success and remain a valuable source for understanding the Constitution and Madison's role in its creation.[40]

* * *

1 Gales & Seaton's Register of Debates in Congress Twenty-Third Congress, First Session Dec. 2, 1833 to June 30, 1834, Debates in the Senate 1187.

2 Henry H. Simms, *The Rise of the Whigs in Virginia 1824-1840*, Richmond, The William Byrd Press, Inc. 1929, 84-87.

3 Ibid. 89.

4 Ibid. 92.

5 Ibid, 106. Simms' quote came from the newspaper *Niles Register*, Vol. L, p. 48, which described an 1836 Whig dinner in Richmond in honor of Leigh and Tyler.

6 Ibid. 94.

7 Marquis James, *The Life of Andrew Jackson*, Indianapolis, New York, The Bobbs-Merrill Company, 1938, 685-686.

8 W. C. Rives to Van Buren, April 10, 1835, Rives MSS, LOC, quoted in Richard B. Latner, *The Presidency of Andrew Jackson*, Athens, University of Georgia Press, 1979, 200, also quoted Simms, Ibid, 101.

9 Arthur M. Schlesinger, Jr., *The Age of Jackson*, Boston, Little Brown & Co. 1953, 212.

10 Ibid. 213.

11 Simms, Ibid. 102, quote from the *Lexington Union*, May 29, 1835.

12 Ibid. 99, cites Slaughter letter to Rives May 24, 1835, Rives MSS, LOC.

13 Ibid.

14 Robert J. Remini, *Andrew Jackson and the Course of American Democracy*, Vol. III, New York, Harper and Row, 1984, 373-376.

15 Simms, Ibid, 99, cites Van Buren to Rives, May 23, 1835, Rives MSS, LOC.

16 Ibid, 99, cites Rives to Van Buren, June 2, 1835, Van Buren papers, Library of Congress.

17 Jon Meacham, *American Lion, Andrew Jackson in the White House*, New York, Random House, 2008, 566 quotes Rives to Van Buren, June 2, 1835, Van Buren papers, Library of Congress.

18 Simms, Ibid, 105, cites *Lynchburg Virginian*, December 21, 1835 and *Richmond Whig*, January 9, 1836.

19 Marquis James, *The Life of Andrew Jackson*, Indianapolis, New York, Bobbs-Merrill, 1938, 152-153.

20 Ibid, 382.

21 Senator Benton's speech on the Expunging Resolution, Gales & Seaton's Register of Debates, Senate, 24th Congress, 1st Session, 877-933.

22 Simms, Ibid, 106, Tyler's letter of resignation appears in Register of Debates, Ibid, 636.

23 Raymond L. Dingledine, Jr., The Political Career of William C. Rives, University of Virginia PhD dissertation, 1947, 248.

24 William C. Rives speech on the Expunging Resolution, March 28, 1836, Register of Debates, Ibid, 981-999.

25 Benjamin Watkins Leigh speech on the Expunging Resolution, April 4, 1836, Register of Debates, Ibid, 1058-1089.

26 Madison to Rives, April 19, 1836 and Madison to Leigh, May 1, 1836, *Letters and Other Writings of James Madison*, [edited by Rives and Fendall], Philadelphia, J. B. Lippincott and Company, 1865, Vol. IV, 432-433.

27 Madison to Rives, June 22, 1836 (http://hdl.loc.gov/loc.mss/mjm.24 0996 0996) In the letter Madison acknowledges receipt of an Honorary Membership in the U.S. Naval Lyceum, mentions his poor health, and hopes for a visit from Rives and Judith. Madison wrote his final letter to George Tucker June 27, thanking Tucker for dedicating his life of Jefferson to Madison, and summarizing his life's work to provide "permanent liberty and happiness" to the country. *Letters and Other Writings of James Madison*, Ibid, 435.

28 Rives' Senate remarks, June 30, 1836, Register of Debates, Ibid, 1912.

29 Ibid, 1914.

30 See David W. Houpt, "Securing a Legacy: The Publication of James Madison's Notes from the Constitutional Convention," and Holly C. Shulman, "'A Constant Attention': Dolley Madison and the Publication of the Papers of James Madison, 1836-1837," both articles appear in *Virginia Magazine of History and Biography*, Vol. 118, No. 1 (2010).

31 Shulman, Ibid. 43.

32 Houpt, Ibid, 10-11.

33 Rives to Van Buren, August 29, 1836, Dolley Madison Digital Edition, http://rotunda.upress.virginia.edu/dmde/DPM2840, (DMDE), quoted in Houpt, Ibid, 15.

34 Rives to Dolley Madison, October 18, 1836, DMDE, quoted in Houpt, Ibid, 22.

35 Rives to Dolley Madison, December 31, 1836 and Dolley Madison to Rives, January 15, 1837, DMDE, cited in Houpt, Ibid, 25.

36 Senate Debate on Joint Resolution to Purchase the Copy-right of Madison's Manuscript Works, February 20, 1837, Register of Debates, Senate, 24th Congress, 2nd Session, 858-871.

37 Rives to Dolley Madison, February 20, 1837 and Judith Rives to Dolley Madison, February 23, 1837, DMDE, quoted in Houpt, Ibid, 30.

38 Register of Debates, Ibid, 1015, Houpt, Ibid, 31, Shulman, Ibid, 61-62.

39 Rives to Dolley Madison, March 28, 1837, DMDE, quoted in Houpt, Ibid, 32.

40 Houpt, Ibid, 32-34.

CHAPTER ELEVEN

A Country to Serve

THE MONTH BEFORE THEIR CLASH over Dolley Madison's manuscripts and honor, Rives and Calhoun had fought each other in the Expunging debate. The climax of Senator Benton's Expunging fight provoked some of the lengthiest and most hyperbolic speeches of the Twenty-fourth Congress, which experienced no shortage of extended oratory. Benton knew he had a majority of supporters and brought the matter forward January 14, 1837.

Calhoun expressed his opposition:

> The gentleman from Virginia [Mr. Rives] says that the argument in favor of this expunging resolution has not been answered. Sir, there are some questions so plain that they cannot be argued. [He charged,] No one, not blinded by party zeal, can possibly be insensible that the measure proposed is a violation of the Constitution. . . .[1]

Clay called the expunging a foul deed, "which like the bloodstained hands of the guilty Macbeth, all ocean's waters will never wash out.[2]

Rives, along with Buchanan, Niles, and Benton, spoke in favor of the expunging "with an air of ease and satisfaction that bespoke a quiet determination and a consciousness of victory."[3] Benton declared that Jackson "came into office the first of generals; he goes out the first of statesmen."[4] Anticipating a long and bitter debate, Benton had ordered a committee room stocked with provisions to sustain his allies, including hams, turkeys, rounds of beef, wine and coffee.

The vote, taken near midnight, favored expunging by a margin of 24 to 19. The Senate Secretary opened the original manuscript journal of the Senate, which contained Clay's March 28, 1834 resolution condemning the President. He drew a black line around Clay's words with the notation "Expunged by order of the Senate January 16, 1837." This brief work of penmanship provoked jeers and hisses from the gallery, general chaos on the Senate floor, and lingering bitter resentment from members of the losing faction. Shouting matches prolonged the session before the motion for adjournment was finally heard and approved. Benton reported that Jackson was pleased by the expunging vote and later gave a grand dinner to the expungers and their wives. The next day the Senate took up "Abolition in the District of Columbia."[5]

Rives had loyally supported Jackson against the nullifiers and the Bank, and for the expunging, but he finally broke with the administration over economic policy. Sale of government land and revenue from the 1833 tariff allowed the government to pay off all debt and register a surplus 1835-1837, the only time in its history. Congress passed and Jackson signed an 1836 distribution act sending the approximately $40 million surplus back to the states. Jackson had done away with the National Bank, and so the government money lay in various state banks, called "pet banks" by Jackson's critics. The western banks, which made reckless land purchase loans, were characterized as "wildcat banks." Distribution of the surplus federal funds drained the reserves of the state banks, undermining the value of their bank notes, which speculators were using to pay for land.[6] Senator Benton proposed a measure to stop the "conversion of land into inconvertible paper."[7] The government would henceforth accept only gold and silver in payment for public lands. Benton's measure was defeated in Congress and opposed by the majority of Jackson's cabinet. While Congress was in recess in July 1836, Jackson, with Benton's assistance, issued an Executive Order embodying Benton's idea, which was called the Specie Circular.⁸ Since government land could only be bought with hard cash, land buyers made a run on the banks to redeem their bank notes. The economy contracted.

Rives was still firmly behind Jackson and Van Buren through the 1836 election. Van Buren wrote Rives in April 1836 that he was growing tired of questions about his views on slavery. "God knows I have suffered enough for my Southern partialities. . . . Since I was a boy, I have been stigmatized as the apologist of Southern institutions, and now your good people have it that I am an abolitionist." Rives answered reassuringly. Van Buren's stated view that Congress had no right to interfere with slavery in any state satisfied influential *Richmond Enquirer* editor Thomas Ritchie.⁹ Van Buren would campaign in 1848 as the presidential candidate of the Free Soil Party, whose platform called for forbidding slavery in the territories.

After Van Buren's election in 1836, he offered Rives a position in his Cabinet as Secretary of War. Hoping to be named Secretary of State, Rives reminded Van Buren of his diplomatic experience. Jackson's Secretary of State John Forsyth wished to remain in office, and Van Buren was unwilling to risk offending Jackson by replacing him with Rives. Rives declined Van Buren's offer, with the excuse that being Secretary of War would require him to stay in Washington year round. The Senate schedule allowed periodic escape to Castle Hill.¹⁰ Disappointment over losing the vice presidency and the State Department likely influenced his decision to oppose Jackson and Van Buren over the Specie Circular.

Senator Ewing of Ohio offered a resolution to rescind the Specie Circular. Rives supported Ewing's bill while offering an amendment, which would gradually eliminate bank notes for amounts less than $20. Rives advocated requiring all debts owned by the government to be paid in specie or, significantly, in notes from specie paying banks. In a January 10, 1837 speech, he took great pains to praise Jackson's performance in office, but he stated that the Specie Circular (called the Treasury Circular in Senate debates) had accomplished its purpose and was never intended to be permanent. Rives stated that the process of reducing the currency available to the country and deflating prices was delicate business. He argued that total elimination of bank notes was neither desirable nor practical. There was simply not enough gold and silver in circulation to transact all of the country's business. The Secretary of the Treasury estimated that the total specie in circulation amounted to approximately $28 million. Rives pointed out that government revenue of the previous year was $47 million. Rives quoted British economist Adam Smith's *Wealth of Nations* as a model for his proposal.

Rives concluded:

> I repeat, then, there is nothing in our present situation to excite alarm or despondency, whatever occasion there may be for vigilance and caution. Let us look our dangers steadily in the face, but let us not be dismayed by them. Let us grapple with the difficulties which may oppose us in a spirit of strenuous and determined patriotism, and we shall triumph over and subdue them. In conclusion, let me say to the political friends with whom I have had the honor to act in trying times, that, after having successfully dissipated so many panics raised under other auspices, we shall not, I trust at last become the victims of a panic of our own creation.[11]

Despite Rives' effort and counsel to avoid panic, the Panic of 1837 threw the country into depression soon after Van Buren's inauguration. Although Rives delivered mollifying words of praise for him, President Jackson was furious when he heard of the speech and bill. He felt it empowered Congress to recognize state bank notes as legitimate U.S. currency. This was "soft money" heresy in his eyes. Jackson wrote his nephew A. J. Donelson, "Mr. Rives' course is a strange one . . ." that had split "our friends in the Senate. . . . I fear it springs out of jealousy." Jackson implied Rives was acting out of anger over losing the vice presidential nomination. Jackson felt these amendments were not consistent with Rives' professed belief in hard money and strict construction. "I would yield much to my friends and particularly now as I am going out of office and I may say out of life, but I have the great republican principles to sustain."[12]

The Ewing/Rives proposal passed 41 to 5 in the Senate and 143 to 59 in the House. Jackson refused to sign it, administering a pocket veto to the measure that reached his desk two days before the conclusion of his presidency. Even though his party held a majority in both houses, Jackson had delivered a farewell slap to Congress. Old Hickory reportedly confessed two regrets to Washington newspaperman Francis Blair, Benton and others: that he had been unable to shoot Henry Clay or to hang John C. Calhoun.[13]

Causes of the Panic of 1837 included the loss of the restraining influence of the National Bank on land speculation, reckless banking practices by the state banks, and bad crops. Furthermore, western European countries also were experiencing depression. Many believed the distribution of the revenue surplus and the Specie Circular were also to blame. Van Buren discussed the dire situation in an April 10 letter to Rives. "The situation of the Western and Southwestern Banks, and their relation to the government, presents matters of gravest consideration. . . . We must take care that we are not obliged to meet Congress and the advocates of a United States Bank, with broken Deposit Banks and unavailable funds." Speaking more frankly and persuasively than he would have dared speak to Jackson, Rives recommended revoking the Specie Circular, which was harmful politically and without merit as financial policy. Van Buren asked Rives to confer with fellow democrats including the future president James Buchanan, and New York Senators Nathaniel Tallmadge and Silas Wright to maintain party unity on financial and other issues. Rives wrote Van Buren in June, agreeing with the new president that there were three possible solutions: a National Bank; maintaining and improving the present system of state Deposit Banks; or separating the government from all state banks and bank notes. Rives favored the second solution. Van Buren preferred the third scheme, a bank network called the Independent Treasury or Sub Treasury that would handle government revenue and payment, divorcing government from private business.[14]

Rives opposed the Sub Treasury scheme, and during the summer of 1837 a majority of Virginia Democrats declared their agreement with him.[15] This opposition to Van Buren became known as the Conservative Revolt. Conservative on this issue meant adherence to traditional financial arrangements in banking and collecting government revenue as opposed to the "radical" Sub Treasury scheme. Rives wrote Van Buren that the Panic was a temporary difficulty from which state banks would recover. If the state bank system, he wrote, "has been temporarily thrown out of gear, it is owing to disturbing causes of a very peculiar character, which are not likely to occur, or may be guarded against in the future."[16] Whigs were happy to see dissension in the ranks of the opposing party. They denounced the Sub Treasury plan while calculatingly refusing to submit a plan of their own. Van Buren called Congress into extra session in September to address the financial situation. He issued a special message on September 4, 1837 advocating separation of the government from banks.[17]

Rives delivered a Senate speech September 19 that repeated many of the points of his January 10 speech. He referred to the proposal of the prior speech that received overwhelming Congressional approval. He said he would not speak of the circumstances that prevented it from becoming law (Jackson's veto). Rives observed that Van Buren recommended that all U.S. revenues be collected exclusively in gold and silver. "It is my misfortune to differ with the President in his views of the expediency of this proposition." If the government accepted only specie, specie would command a premium and bank notes would lose more of their value. Rives reminded his critics that contrary to their charges, he did not own stock in any state banks. He modified the proposal he made in January to include "the public dues may be collected in any other medium specially authorized by law." Rives noted that land, labor and capital were in their accustomed fertility and abundance, yet industry was paralyzed, commerce at a standstill, currency degraded and deranged, precious metals fled from circulation. The remedy was simple: restoration of confidence. Expanding the money supply by allowing government to accept payment in notes of specie paying banks would help restore that confidence. "We shall soon see our youthful and vigorous country rising from her monetary prostration and Antaeus-like, gathering strength from her fall."[18]

Van Buren considered Rives' plan inflationary.[19] Rives would continue to point out that the Sub Treasury was originally a Whig idea proposed by Congressman William F. Gordon of Virginia that was denounced by Democrats in 1835. The proposal recommended locating sub treasuries in port city customhouses with separate branches in large interior cities.[20] When Van Buren first requested that Rives examine his Sub Treasury proposal along with Senators Silas Wright of New York and John Niles of Connecticut, none of the three were in favor. Wright wrote that few votes could be mustered in its support.[21] When Van Buren

applied pressure to adhere to his designated party policy, Wright
and Niles obeyed. Rives refused to submit. Wright wrote Van
Buren, criticizing Rives' recalcitrance and suggested Rives had
ulterior motives.[22]

John C. Calhoun of South Carolina had recently rejoined
the Democrats. He supported the Sub Treasury Bill along with
his amendment requiring the government to accept only gold
and silver in payments. This was designated the "Specie Clause."
Calhoun's principal cause was states rights, and his biographers
have attributed his position on this issue to his belief that it promoted states rights and southern power.[23] Calhoun's amendment
only strengthened Rives' opposition to the bill. Rives had no
reluctance to oppose Calhoun on any issue.

The Senate approved Calhoun's Specie Clause 24 to 23 and the
Sub Treasury Bill by a vote of 25 to 23 on October 3, 1837. Rives'
bill lost by four votes.[24] However, in the House, Conservatives
joined with the Whig opposition to form a majority voting to
postpone the bill till the regular session, which would begin in
December.

Rives' letter to Judith revealed an image of a president taking a
solitary ride through the streets of Washington which contrasts
with 21st century security procedures. Also travel time between
the capital and Castle Hill had been shortened to two days, by
road improvements:

Washington Oct 7th,'37
My dearest wife,

Rejoice with me that the dreadful affair of the speech
is over. It is not only written out, but printed, a copy of
which I send you. I hope you will not find it altogether
unworthy of one who has the honor to call himself
your husband. I will send Francis and Will a copy, as

well as Mr. Provost, when I am supplied with more.

To-day I fell in with the President in taking my ride on horseback. He was also on horseback, all alone, and looking very badly. He is wasted away to a lath, and sallow and bilious in the extreme. I really pitied him. I thought he spelt again for an invitation to Castle Hill, but this would be so evidently a political maneuver that I could not indulge him in it. As he has made a poor return for past civilities, I did not wish to get him any further in my debt.

Congress will adjourn on Monday the 16th instant, and on that night or the following, I expect to take my flight for my loved home. We arrive, you know, the second day after departure from here. I shall expect to receive letters from you to the last moment, and assuring you that, so far from little Ella being a prophetess on the subject of my health, the President said to-day he never saw me look better. I remain, with warmest love to all our dear children, including her little lady-ship, your own devoted and doting husband,

WC Rives[25]

Rives need not have felt sorry for Van Buren. The President continued to press for his Sub Treasury and a separation between government money and state banks in his December message to Congress. Silas Wright introduced a new Sub Treasury Bill in January that included a Specie Clause. Rives offered a substitute bill which would authorize Congress to select and oversee 25 state banks as depositories for government funds. In the lengthy series of speeches on the subject, John C. Calhoun argued in favor of the Sub Treasury and alleged that Rives' plan would enable a league of state banks to gain control of the country's financial resources.[26]

Henry Clay delivered a speech with the lengthy title that summarizes its lengthy content:

> Establishing a Deliberate Design on the Part of the Late and Present Executive of the United States to Break Down the Whole Banking System of the United States Commencing with the Bank of the United States and Terminating with the State Banks and to Create on Their Ruins a Government Treasury Bank Under the Exclusive Control of the Executive and in Reply to the Speech of the Hon. J. C. Calhoun of South Carolina Supporting that Treasury Bank.[27]

Daniel Webster also delivered a reply to Calhoun. In his speech Webster argued that a mixed system of paper and metal currency had prevailed since the beginning of the country. Maintaining a specie only system, in his opinion, would have required excessively time-consuming counting of currency. Like his fellow Whig Clay, Webster blamed Jackson's 1832 veto of the Bank Re-Charter as the "true source of all the disorders of the currency." Webster said that he had known Calhoun for 25 years. After years of agreements and disagreements, "Here we part, unlikely to reconcile, I say with regret." Webster had disagreed with Calhoun's nullification doctrine and he declared, "nullification embraces the Sub Treasuries." Webster pointed out that Calhoun voted for the Bank Bill of 1816 that authorized notes of specie paying banks as acceptable U.S. revenue payment. Webster concluded: "Calhoun will march off under the banner of states rights, to Where? He will never hear me trying to 'rally the North' as he calls for rallying the entire South. Let him go. I remain here standing on the platform of general constitution. I serve no other master but the United States."[28]

Rives' fellow Conservative Nathaniel P. Tallmadge entitled his speech "In Defense of the People of New York Against the Charge of Bank Influence in the Result of Their Election." Tallmadge called on Van Buren to abandon the Sub Treasury and revive the state banking system. He also criticized the present system of party discipline and Executive intimidation. Tallmadge said he was proud to be a Conservative as opposed to the "subservatives" who abandoned their principles for party loyalty.[29]

In his speech on February 5 and 6, 1838, Rives repeated his objection that the Sub Treasury scheme created two currencies: a better one for the government and an inferior one for the people. The Sub Treasury "would be a National Bank under the worst possible form." While proposing that 25 state banks be selected and supervised by Congress for receiving government deposits, Rives declared, "I stand here as no advocate of the banks. I have not the slightest interest in nor connection with them, direct or indirect. . . . I am as sensible as any man to the dangers and abuses to which they are liable. . . . But as a practical legislator and patriot I am bound to look to the actual interest of society."

Rives reminded his fellow Democrats that they opposed the Sub Treasury three years earlier. His ringing words about having a country to serve as well as a party to obey were an attack on Van Buren, Silas Wright, and others who felt that obeying the party was the best way to serve their country.

> In offering the measure I have submitted to the Senate I have discharged what I consider to be my duty to the country. That country is now in a state of suffering and distress aggravated by deep anxieties and apprehension in regard to the future. The measure I propose would,

I firmly believe, give relief for the present and hope for the future. It could not fail to restore confidence and, in doing that, to revive the languishing energies of trade, to quicken the labors and hopes of the husbandman, the manufacturer and the mechanic to raise enterprise again upon its feet and above all to put an end to that unnatural and suicidal war which in the last 18 months has grown up between the Government of the country and its business and industry. In presenting such a measure I cannot but regret that I shall be deprived of the support of many members of this body with whom I have lately stood side by side in upholding and defending the principles on which it rests. My consolation however is that I stand now where I stood then. On the other hand the measure they bring forward and patronize is one which, three years ago, we all united in opposing, and which was then denounced, in the name of the Administration and its friends, as a 'dangerous enlargement of Executive power, and putting into its hands the means of corruption.' This measure cannot have changed its character by mere efflux of time, and thinking of it now as I thought of it then I still oppose it.

In taking this course, I know full well, Mr. President, I am to incur the anathemas of party. But I can never forget that I have a country to serve as well as a party to obey....[30]

Rives' bill was rejected in a 29 to 20 vote. The Sub Treasury Bill narrowly passed the Senate only to be defeated in the House, where Conservatives led by James Garland of Virginia joined with Whig opposition.[31] Rives did receive expected criticism from Van Buren supporters as well as endorsement from around the

Willam C. Rives, 1839 lithograph by Charles Fenderich.

country. Copies of his portrait were printed with the "country to serve" quotation appearing below. A February 20 Democratic Party meeting in Nashua, New Hampshire published an endorsement of Rives' measure declaring, "that it will have a tendency to bring immediate relief to the country and that if its details are carried into effect it will produce a uniform currency, facilitate exchanges and supercede the necessity of a National Bank."[32]

Rives' fight against the Sub Treasury brought attention and approval from a thirty-year old Illinois Whig state representative named Abraham Lincoln. In a speech delivered December 20, 1839 in Springfield, Lincoln included among his arguments against the Sub Treasury the unnecessary cost of the system. Lincoln said Treasury Secretary Levi Woodbury estimated the

Sub Treasury would cost the government $60,000 to act as its fiscal agent. "Mr. Rives who, to say the least, is equally talented and honest, estimates that these services under the Sub Treasury system cannot cost less than $600,000."[33]

The Conservative newspaper *The Madisonian* lavished praise on Rives two days after his speech. The "nullifier" refers to Calhoun.

> After the glorious effort made by Mr. Rives in the United States Senate on Monday and Tuesday, the poisoned shafts of his enemies, hurled from every quarter with so much bitterness and violence, will fall far short of the proud eminence to which he has arisen. . . . The impotent efforts of a nullifier cannot sully the character he envies but cannot emulate, nor avert the destinies of a cause he fears, but cannot resist. . . . Whatever effect the course of recent events may have had upon the friendship and confidence hitherto existing between the present Chief Magistrate and Mr. Rives, we are certain that Mr. Van Buren expected no other course from him, and that he regards his present position as the evidence, at least, of his consistency.[34]

Rives' defiance of Van Buren further wounded a friendship that had been damaged by the 1835 vice presidential contest and the 1836 non-offer of the Secretary of State position. The friendship reached a breaking point in 1839, after which the two did not meet until 1857 when they dined together at the home of retired New York businessman George Barclay.[35] Van Buren was a formidable adversary. He earned his nicknames "the Little Magician" and "the Little Fox" for his political cunning and maneuvering. Historians have called him the "American Talleyrand," after the legendary French statesman, who "swore fidelity to eight different governments," as Judith Page Rives noted at Louis Philippe's coronation in 1830. Breaking with Van Buren and fellow Democratic Republicans greatly diminished Rives' chances for a future cabinet position or other higher office. His Senate seat was also in jeopardy. Van Buren would be a one term President.

★ ★ ★

1 Gales & Seaton's Register of Debates in Congress, Senate, 24th Congress, 2nd Session. 417.

2 Ibid, January 16, 1837, 439.

3 Thomas Hart Benton, *Thirty Years View*, Vol. I, New York, D. Appleton & Co., 1854, 728. Gales & Seaton's Register notes that Rives made a speech, but the speech was not reported. Likely it was similar to his March 28, 1836 speech on the same topic.

4 Ibid. 725.

5 Gales & Seaton's Register, Ibid, 505-506, and Benton, Ibid, 730-731.

6 Richard N. Current, T. Harry Williams, Frank Friedel, W. Elliot Brownlee, *The Essentials of American History*, Third Edition, New York, Alfred A. Knopf, 1980.

7 Benton, Ibid. 677.

8 Ibid.

9 Van Buren to Rives, April 1, 1835, Rives MSS, LOC, Rives to Van Buren, April 10, 1835, Van Buren papers, Library of Congress, quoted in Henry H. Simms, *The Rise of the Whigs in Virginia 1824-1840*, Richmond, William Byrd Press, Inc. 1929, 101.

10 John Niven, *Martin Van Buren The Romantic Age of American Politics*, New York, Oxford, Oxford University Press, 1983, 406.

11 "Mr. Rives On the Currency of the U.S and Collection of the Public Revenue," Register of Debates, Ibid, January 10, 1837, 343-359.

12 Andrew Jackson to A. J. Donelson, January 11, 1837, Donelson papers Library of Congress, quoted in Robert J. Remini, *Andrew Jackson and the Course of American Democracy*, Vol. III, New York, Harper and Row, 1984, 409-410.

13 Marquis James, *The Life of Andrew Jackson*, Indianapolis, New York, The Bobbs Merrill Company, 1938, 723-724.

14 Van Buren to Rives April 10, 1837, Rives MSS, LOC, Rives to Van Buren, April 17, 1837, Ibid, Van Buren to Rives, Ibid, Rives to Van Buren, June 3, 1837, Van Buren papers, Library of Congress, quoted in Simms, *Rise of the Whigs*, 118-120.

15 Simms, Ibid, 123.

16 William C. Rives to Martin Van Buren, June 3, 1837, Rives MSS, LOC, quoted Jean E. Friedman, *The Revolt of the Conservative Democrats*, UMI Research Press, 1976, 61.

17 Simms, Ibid, 124.

18 Gales and Seaton's Register of Debates, 25th Congress, Senate, 1st Session, September 4-October 16, 1837. 77-104.

19 Niven, Ibid, 421.

20 Friedman, Ibid, 23.

21 Ibid. Notes letter from Silas Wright to Azariah Flagg, September 18, 1837, Flagg Papers, New York Public Library.

22 Silas Wright to Martin Van Buren, June 22, 1837, Martin Van Buren Papers, Library of Congress, noted in Friedman, Ibid, 62.

23 Friedman, Ibid, 68.

24 *Congressional Globe*, 25th Congress, First Session 5:96, cited in Friedman, Ibid, 70-71.

25 William C. Rives to Judith Page Rives, October 7, 1837, Rives MSS, LOC, box 23.

26 *Congressional Globe*, 25th Congress, 2nd session Appendix 188-195.

27 Henry Clay Senate Speech February 19, 1838, Washington, printed by Gales & Seaton, 1838.

28 Daniel Webster Speech of March 12, 1838 in Answer to Mr. Calhoun, Boston, John H. Eastburn, 1838.

29 Nathaniel P. Tallmadge, Senate Speech February 8, 1838, Washington, Printed at the Madisonian Office, 1838.

30 William C. Rives, February 5 & 6, 1838, *Congressional Globe*, Senate, 25th Congress 2nd Session Appendix 608-614.

31 Friedman, Ibid, 82-84.

32 "To the Democratic Republicans of Nashua: Let the Currency of the People Be the Currency of Government," Proceedings and Address of Democratic Party Meeting Held February 20, 1838, American Broadsides and Ephemera, New York Public Library Catalogue, 1st Series #5288.

33 Abraham Lincoln, December 20, 1839 Speech at a Political Discussion in the Hall of the House of Representatives at Springfield Illinois, *Complete Works of Abraham Lincoln*, edited by John Nicolay and John Hay, New York, Francis D. Tandy Company, 1922, Vol. I, 25.

34 *The Madisonian*, Washington, Thursday February 8, 1838.

35 WCR, Jr., Rives MSS, LOC, Box 103, 40. George Barclay's daughter Matilda was the wife of Rives' eldest son Francis. The Barclay home was at No. 8 Washington Place, adjoining the house of "Commodore" Cornelius Vanderbilt. (See George Lockhart Rives, *Genealogical Notes*, 44).

CHAPTER TWELVE

Armed Neutrality

ALTHOUGH HE WAS NO LONGER IN OFFICE, Andrew Jackson continued to exert political power and influence until his death in 1845. He wrote letters to Van Buren and other allies freely expressing his opinions. In a letter to Francis Preston Blair, Jackson called the Conservative wing of the party headed by Rives and New York Senator Nathaniel P. Tallmadge the "no party party." Jackson also implied that Conservative support for state banks was the same as Whig support for the Bank of the United States. They were all "Bankites."[1]

Rives and Tallmadge had been faithful Jackson supporters and saw themselves as maintaining Jackson's 1835 policy of using state banks as government depositories. Like Rives, Tallmadge had been a Van Buren friend and supporter, and had worked hard to secure his Vice Presidential nomination. Van Buren was in England during the 1832 Democratic Republican convention, and Tallmadge was then a New York State Senator from Dutchess County.[2]

New York politics in 1838 were further complicated for Tallmadge by the radical "Locofoco" wing of the Democratic Party. The Locofocos got their name at a Tammany Hall Democratic party meeting when party regulars turned off the gaslights to silence them. The radicals responded by lighting friction matches called "locofocos." The Locofocos favored the Sub Treasury and opposed state banks, paper money, and tariffs as well as extreme economic inequality.

Rives based his aversion to party politics on an idealized concept of government envisioned by the framers. Jefferson and Madison had both considered political parties evil, though Madison conceded they were a necessary evil.[3] Despite those ideals, Madison and Jefferson had organized the country's first opposition party, the Republican Party (ancestor of the Democratic Party), to battle Adams and the Federalists. However, those early parties were not organized down to the state and local level.

Rives' opposition to Van Buren's use of Executive power seems inconsistent with his previous support of Jackson's aggressive measures against the Bank, the nullifiers and the Whigs. Perhaps Rives did not like Van Buren's style of leadership, which differed from Jackson's. Jackson was a unique forceful and forthright leader. Lacking Old Hickory's magnetism, Van Buren was an organizer and negotiator. The astute John Randolph said that Van Buren "rowed to his objective with muffled oars."[4] Van Buren is credited with organizing the modern Democratic Party.[5] Before 1840, section was a greater influence than party on voting. Emphasis on party discipline brought a degree of power to a greater number of voters. For Rives this was poor reward for suppression of individual thought and action. Van Buren's determination to enforce party unity and discipline had the effect of increasing Rives' resistance.

Rives wrote: "It is principle alone which constitutes the legitimate distinction of party. When a party abandons its principles and is held together only by some common interest of power or office, it loses every thing which sanctions and dignifies political association, and it degenerates at once into faction."[6]

Van Buren expressed his contempt for Rives in a letter to Jackson a month before Rives' "country to serve" speech. "Mr. Rives has relieved us of all uncertainty as to his intentions. There is an end of that."[7] However, Van Buren apparently encouraged a flattering article about Rives in the *United States Magazine and Democratic Review*. The article said Rives was "one of the most accomplished men of the day" who would not allow a "minor diversity" of opinion to set him in opposition to the Democratic party."[8] Jackson wrote Van Buren about Rives' "treachery," and predicted he would join with the Whigs.[9]

Virginia newspapers carried articles about the possibility of an alliance between Whigs and Conservatives, particularly in the case of Rives, whose Senate term was due to expire March 4, 1839. According to historian Jean Friedman, "Fear of a permanent Conservative-Whig coalition" prompted Van Buren to visit Rives at Castle Hill and his neighbor Thomas Jefferson Randolph at Edgehill in July, 1838.[10] A September 2 letter to Rives from Benjamin Lewis Bogan may indicate that Van Buren offered Rives the Vice Presidency in exchange for his return to the party fold. Bogan was a Washington government clerk and former editor of the Shenandoah County *Woodstock Herald*.[11] Bogan wrote:

> Your letter afforded me real delight. . . . I could not help expressing my joy that you were not approachable with the offer of the Vice Presidency at this time. . . time was when such a consummation was the first wish of my heart. . . . Clouds, my good sir, may hover over the political horizon, but do not fear the storm. . You may rest assured when the storm abates, a sunshine will follow, and then the mist of party will disappear, and justice will be done to your efforts by the People of this Country for your patriotism.[12]

The letter is not conclusive proof of an offer. The subject may have been a hypothetical discussion only between Rives and Bogan. Van Buren wrote a terse note to Rives in September:

My dear sir,

I send you enclosed the proceedings of your friends here. With prudence & moderation on the part of those who have the good of the country at heart this excitement may be made to strengthen & improve the relations between the North & the South & greatly fortify the Union. I returned a day or two since from a succession of general work & like locations throughout our State. I hope Mrs. Rives' health is good. Remember me affectionately to her & believe me to be

Very truly yours
M. Van Buren
Albany Sept 18, '38[13]

Van Buren had enclosed with the letter a pamphlet from a New York anti-abolition society meeting. The reference to "prudence and moderation" and "those who have the good of the country at heart," likely were appeals for conciliation from Rives. By attending an anti-abolition meeting, Van Buren was standing up for Southern interests. This seemed to invite some reciprocal gesture.

R. Wallace, a loyal friend of Rives in Warrenton, Virginia, counseled Rives that he should not expect any support from Virginia Whigs who would destroy him if given the opportunity. Wallace said the majority of (Democratic) Republicans were for Rives. Rives could vote against the Sub Treasury if he must, but Wallace advised that the best thing he could do to ensure his re-election would be to stop talking about the issue so much.[14] If he knew his man, Wallace should have realized that plea was futile. Rives did not row with muffled oars. He would not change his actions for political gain or even political survival. Once decided, he committed himself to a cause with full force, which gained him admirers as well as enemies.

Rives published in the *Charlottesville Jeffersonian Republican* in September three lengthy articles explaining "Principles and Policy of the Conservatives." The articles later appeared in other papers, including the *Richmond Enquirer*. Covering the same ground as his speeches, the articles told of Jackson's transfer of government deposits from the Bank of the United States to the state banks, and how Democrats, including Van Buren, had condemned the initial Whig proposal for a Sub Treasury. Democratic Republicans, at the time, agreed the scheme was an enlargement of Executive power, because it placed all government money under the control of the President. "The whole Republican party was in favor of the State Bank system and stood firmly and inflexibly opposed to the Sub Treasury scheme." He maintained that the Conservative position was the consistent and true Republican position. Invoking lessons of history, as Rives was fond of doing, he told of how Russia and other European countries adopted a position of "armed neutrality" during struggles between England and France in the 1700s. The Conservatives, Rives suggested, would adopt similar "armed neutrality," in order "to protect the rights and interests of the people from the encroachments of both belligerents [Whigs and Republicans] whichever of them may in their turn endanger the general security." Conservatives were neutral on the matter of the presidential election, which would take place in two years. He concluded:

> Let them [Conservatives], then, stand firm and unmoved on their principles. Let them resist every attempt, open or disguised, to extend Executive power; let them ward off every hostile blow which may be aimed at the institutions or rights of the States; let them rebuke the wild and disorganizing doctrines with which the public mind has of late, been vainly attempted to be poisoned; let them hold the Republican faith in the purity of their

fathers, and with the blessing of Providence on their courage and constancy, they will be the chosen instruments of the most lasting benefits to their country. By their means, the Government will be brought back to its true "Republican tack," the Republican party itself will be re-organised, and restored to its original principles, such as they were in the days of Jefferson and Madison, and a long career of usefulness and honor will be again opened before it in the re-animated confidence and strengthened affections of an united people.[15]

The editor of the *Madisonian* Thomas Allen praised Rives' articles in a September 30 letter and promised to reprint them in his own paper. Allen also criticized his fellow editor Thomas Ritchie of the *Richmond Enquirer* for switching sides on the Sub Treasury issue. Ritchie supported Rives' position until Democratic Republican Party leaders threatened to establish a rival newspaper in Richmond.[16] Allen wrote that Ritchie "seems to be controlled by men rather than principles, and his paper indicates anything but consistency and good sense." Allen lamented that consistency was also lacking within Conservative ranks. "In all the states except Virginia, they appear to have forgotten what made them Conservatives."[17] Conservatives could not seem to agree with themselves, making any formal alliance with the Whigs unlikely.

Rives' actions and speech in December 1838 made reconciliation with Democrats and Van Buren even more unlikely. Rives revealed that Treasury Secretary Levi Woodbury sold bonds of the Bank of the United States and deposited the proceeds in the Bank of the United States. Rives charged Wright, Benton and Calhoun with hypocrisy for supporting this paper money transaction while claiming to be advocates of hard money, and foes of the Bank. Rives asked if these transactions were part of a "scheme to re-instate the bank in its character of fiscal agent of the Government?" Senator Wright had known of the transactions and had warned Woodbury to transfer the accounts away from the Bank of the United States. However, Wright accused Rives of politically motivated attack, which was not the action of an armed neutral but of a belligerent.[18]

Rives replied:

> The honorable Senator from New York [Mr. Wright] expresses his surprise that, standing as I do, holding the relations that I do with the President I should have taken the course I have on this subject. That gentleman perhaps knows those relations better than I do. But the gentleman mistakes me, if he thinks any intimations of the displeasure of the Executive shall terrify me from denouncing that course against which I warned him. I owe no responsibility to the President for words I utter here. I am responsible and responsible alone, to that old and unterrified Commonwealth which I have the honor, in part, to represent in this body.[19]

The Virginia General Assembly would soon decide whether Rives would continue to represent that Commonwealth. Although some Whigs spoke favorably of Rives, the *Richmond Whig* denounced him in 1838, and called Conservatives "That forlorn and terror-stricken squad of *tertium quids*."[20] As the election drew near, the *Richmond Whig* reconsidered Rives, because it claimed he had served the Whig cause by doing more than any man in Virginia to break up the Jackson party.[21]

Balloting for the Senate election began February 15, 1839. The Conservatives nominated Rives, the Whigs nominated John Tyler, and the Democrats nominated John Y. Mason. Tallies on the first ballot were Mason 66, Tyler 62, and Rives 29. 83 votes were needed for a majority. Because Rives' total was greater than the number of Conservatives in the legislature, he had received some Whig votes. As balloting continued, Chapman Johnson was brought forward as a compromise candidate, but his highest total was 77, while Rives' best showing was 78 votes, both short of the needed 83. The election was indefinitely postponed on February 23. The stalemate was attributed to unwillingness to concede on the part of Rives' "Spartan Band" of 14 Conservatives who prevented the election of a Democrat, as well as 13 "Impracticable Whigs" who would not support Rives. These Whigs despised Rives for his support of Jackson's Force Bill and the Expunging of the Senate Journal.[22]

Rives' friend John M. Patton wrote him that the contest generated much excitement, with Rives being the main topic of debate. "Christian, Jew and Turk alike are upon you."[23] A surprising advocate for Whig support of Rives was his longtime opponent in debate, Kentucky Senator Henry Clay. Clay wrote Virginia Whig leader Judge Francis Brooke that he believed Rives had broken completely with the Administration, which presented an opportunity. Clay suggested Whigs could use Rives to help create a Virginia majority opposing the Van Buren administration. Clay advised forgiveness of Rives' past support of Jackson's policies. He observed, "It is manifest that if we repel the advances of all the former members of the Jackson party to unite with us, under whatever name they may adopt, we must remain in a perpetual and hopeless minority." Clay said Whigs should extend the same forgiveness "to the repentant in politics . . . which the Christian religion promises to the contrite even in the eleventh hour. The difference between Mr. Rives and some others now incorporated in our party is that their watches did not run together"[24]

Rives was out of office, but he was not out of politics. He issued an "Address to the People of Virginia" in March. Rives stated that he had to respond to his critics "at the moment of passing from his second term of office as Senator to the quiet and not unwelcome scenes of private life."

Rives noted that within the last few months:

> The Robespierrean Press at Washington, under the immediate control of the administration, has daily exerted all its diabolical resources of falsehood and defamation to blacken my character, assail my motives, and misrepresent my conduct. It has culled from its vocabulary of abuse all its most hacknied terms of political vituperation, such as Federalist, renegade, deserter, Traitor, and by attaching them to my name, has sought to make it the object of general odium and reprobation.

Rives said these attacks have been launched because he had not been willing to sacrifice his principles "to the mandates of party discipline and the influences of official power." He responded to charges of acting out of malice toward Van Buren and out of ambition, saying he had been Van Buren's friend, and that ambition would have made him stay within the party by following orders in order to rise within its ranks. Narrating once again the issues described in previous speeches, Rives summarized, "I have not abandoned my party; they have abandoned me." Accused of joining with the Whigs, Rives says Whigs and Conservatives made no arrangement. Both groups happened to oppose the Sub Treasury.

Rives concluded:

> Every reflecting mind must have observed with painful anxiety the rapid growth of Executive influence within the last few years, sustained by a system of party discipline, and of organized denunciation through the press,

such as has never existed in any country, pretending to freedom, under the sun. . . . If I am to fall victim to power, the cause of liberty and truth will fall with me, and he, who is buried in their ruins, is happier, far than he who survives them.[25]

Rives never wavered in his opposition to the Sub Treasury, or to the National Bank, which he believed it resembled. His opposition to Van Buren and his Democratic Party politics began to assume a personal tone. With the exceptional zeal of a convert, Rives had become a dedicated enemy of his former friend. He would not quiet his denunciations even if his rhetoric made him new enemies among political leaders and the electorate. Rives would not sacrifice principle for political gain.

During the Virginia 1839 spring campaign for Congress and the General Assembly, Conservatives insisted the main issue was Rives and his now empty Senate seat. Results left the Virginia House of Delegates with a Whig majority and the Virginia Senate with an Administration Democratic majority. Both houses also had a handful of Conservatives. The numbers indicated Rives' prospects for returning to the Senate were uncertain.[26]

Conservatives were defeated in 1839 Congressional contests in other states, which enabled Van Buren to win approval for his Sub Treasury Bill from both the House and Senate. He signed the bill into law July 4, 1840. 1840 was a Presidential election year.

✶ ✶ ✶

1 Andrew Jackson to Blair, September 6, 1837, *Correspondence of Andrew Jackson*, edited by John Spencer Bassett, Washington DC, Carnegie Institution of Washington, 1926-35, Vol. 5, 508-509.

2 John Niven, *Martin Van Buren The Romantic Age of American Politics*, New York, Oxford, Oxford University Press, 1983, 301.

3 Jean E. Friedman, *The Revolt of the Conservative Democrats*, UMI Research Press, 1979.

4 William Cabell Bruce, *John Randolph of Roanoke 1773-1833*, Vol. II, New York, G. P. Putnam's Sons, 1922, 203.

5 Friedman, Ibid, 10.

6 "Address of W C Rives to the People of Virginia," March 18, 1839, Charlottesville, Printed by James Alexander, University of Virginia Special Collections, E390.R62 1839, 13.

7 Martin Van Buren to Andrew Jackson, January 8, 1838, Martin Van Buren Papers, Library of Congress, quoted in Friedman, Ibid, 82.

8 Friedman, Ibid, 82.

9 Andrew Jackson to Martin Van Buren, April 4, May 8, 1838, Martin Van Buren Papers, Library of Congress, cited by Friedman, Ibid, 85.

10 Friedman, Ibid, 85.

11 http://www.zaring.name/MathiasA.pdf.

12 B. L. Bogan to William C. Rives, September 2, 1838, Rives MSS, LOC, box 58.

13 Martin Van Buren to William C. Rives, September 18, 1838, Rives MSS, LOC, box 58.

14 R. Wallace to William C. Rives, October 21, 1838, Rives MSS, ibid, quoted in Henry H. Simms, *The Rise of the Whigs in Virginia 1824-1840*, Richmond, Virginia, The William Byrd Press, Inc., 1929, 130.

15 William C. Rives, "Principles and Policy of the Conservatives," *Richmond Enquirer*, January 17, 1839, reprinted from the Charlottesville Jeffersonian Republican.

16 Friedman, Ibid, 38.

17 Thomas Allen to William C. Rives, September 30, 1838, Rives MSS, LOC, box 58.

18 Friedman, Ibid, 88-89.

19 William C. Rives, Senate Speech Friday, December 28, 1838, *The Congressional Globe*, 25th Congress, 3rd Session 49-50.

20 *Richmond Whig*, October 13, 1837 and February 2, 1838, quoted in Simms, Ibid, 128, "*tertium quid*" literally the third something, means a nondescript, a meaningless thing.

21 *Richmond Whig*, January 29, February 1, 1839, cited in Simms, Ibid, 132.

22 Simms, Ibid, 132-33.

23 John M. Patton to William C. Rives, February 15, 1839, Rives MSS, LOC, quoted in Simms, Ibid, 133.

24 Henry Clay to Francis Brooke, December 26, 1838, Private Correspondence of Henry Clay, edited by Calvin Colton, Boston, Frederick Parker, 1856, 434.

25 "Address of W C Rives To the People of Virginia," March 18, 1839, Charlottesville, Printed by James Alexander, University of Virginia Special Collections E390.R62 1839.

26 Simms, Ibid, 137-138.

CHAPTER THIRTEEN

Independent Whig

RIVES WAS NOT LIKELY to support Van Buren's campaign for re-election. In a speech at a public dinner given for him at Louisa Courthouse, September 7, 1839, Rives continued to denounce Van Buren's rule:

> Who and What are the Party? The President and the President alone is the party. He determines measures to propose and what the party is to support. . . . No one can object . . . to do so . . . threatens the President and the unity of Party. As Legare [Congressman Hugh S. Legare of S.C.] said, the whole body is doing what almost every member of it disapproves.[1]

Rives repeatedly refused to endorse any presidential candidate in 1839. Henry Clay had been the perennial Whig candidate, and Rives did not agree with his pro-Bank, pro-tariff positions. Virginia Whigs endorsed a ticket of Clay with the Conservative Nathaniel P. Tallmadge as candidate for Vice President. The Virginians thought this would create a winning coalition of Whigs and Conservatives. Some of his fellow Conservatives urged Rives to support the candidacy of General Winfield Scott. The fall 1839 Whig Convention in Harrisburg, Pennsylvania nominated General William Henry Harrison for President. Though he was born in Virginia, Harrison lived in Ohio and was therefore a western candidate. Whigs decided a southerner was needed to provide sectional balance and chose former Virginia Senator John Tyler.

Harrison wrote Rives a letter declaring that he would not oppose the interests of southern slaveholders, and that he believed in limited Executive power. He would use the veto only for matters he considered unconstitutional.[2] Harrison had made a speech in Ohio in 1833 in which he advocated using surplus national revenue for emancipation purposes. Democrats during the campaign referred to this speech to portray Harrison as an abolitionist, but Virginia Whigs declared that was impossible because Harrison was a native Virginian whose father had been a slaveholder.[3] Satisfied with Harrison's positions, Rives sent a statement of his endorsement to the Richmond Whig declaring that Harrison was the true Republican, superior to Van Buren in every way.[4] Rives and fellow Conservative Nathaniel Tallmadge campaigned for Harrison in New York and Pennsylvania. According to historian Jean Friedman, they delivered "nineteenth century, long-winded speeches, remarkable more for endurance of the speaker and audience rather than for their substance."[5]

Rives had his doubts about Tyler, who had opposed him in the inconclusive Senate contest, and had replaced him after his forced resignation in 1834. However the Vice Presidency had not been a powerful office up to that time. John Quincy Adams wrote that the possibility of Tyler becoming President "was never thought of . . . by anybody."[6]

With Tyler out of the Senate contest, Rives appeared likely to regain his seat. The General Assembly voted January 29, 1840, but neither Rives nor his Democratic opponent J. Y. Mason received a majority of votes in two days of balloting. Three obstructionist Whigs kept Rives from winning by refusing to vote for him.[7] Rives had probably lessened his chances by withholding his endorsement of Harrison until after the Senate voting was over.

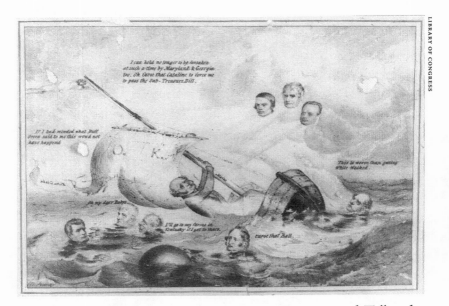

A Whig view of the election of 1840. Rives, Harrison and Tallmadge create a storm from above that sinks Van Buren (clinging to the mast) along with Calhoun, Woodbury, Benton and others.

He did not want to be elected Senator on the basis of which presidential candidate he preferred. The election was again postponed for another year. Democrats and Whigs traded accusations in the papers about who was responsible for Virginia's empty Senate seat. Rives was called a "renegade" and "the armed Neutral who has joined in the battle under the Federal flag."[8] Rives delivered a public speech declaring the *Richmond Enquirer* to be "the libeler of every prominent man who had been on the stage for the last quarter of a century." He promised that after the election, "It shall never defile my portals," which prompted editor Thomas Ritchie to report the paper would immediately strike Rives from its lists.[9]

The campaign of 1840 was famous for its slogan "Tippecanoe and Tyler Too." Tippecanoe refers to a famous victory over Indians won by General William Henry Harrison. Another

Whig campaign slogan was "Van Van is a used up man." When Whig campaigners charged Van Buren with being an aristocrat who drank champagne, a Democratic newspaper unwisely answered that Harrison would be content in a log cabin drinking hard cider. The Whigs pounced on the idea, proclaiming their candidate was a humble man of the people, though Harrison was actually a wealthy man who lived in a large house. Harrison rallies featured model log cabins and plenty of hard cider.[10]

Rives spoke at rallies throughout Virginia and was the principal speaker at a huge Harrison rally in Winchester:

> It was the most imposing occasion of its kind ever held in the Valley of Virginia. Early in the day, about 8 a.m., a large number of our citizens formed in procession, and marched out of town to meet our Berkeley friends, [then Berkeley, Virginia; now in West Virginia] about 400 in number. The whole line of procession entered the town about 10 o'clock, with bands of music, the log cabin drawn by ten horses, streamers and ensigns, and banners flying, on one of which was observed in large capitals, 'I cannot forget I have a country to serve, as well as a party to obey.'[11]

Another large banner read "William C. Rives: Honor to the man who was prepared to sacrifice himself for the good of his country." The crowd swelled to an estimated 5,000 as Rives spoke for two and a half hours. His "high pitched voice could be heard at the edges of the crowd, as with dilated nostrils, flashing eyes, and impassionate gesticulations, he worked his audience into pitches of enthusiasm, distillating his s's and rolling his r's."[12]

Rives attended an October 1840 Whig convention in Richmond. The featured speaker from another state was Daniel

Webster. He spoke of how the Whig party, which included men with differing opinions on some issues, was united against a common enemy. Some Whigs, including Tyler, were adamantly for states rights while others were national Whigs like Henry Clay, favoring National Bank and higher tariffs. Webster denounced the common Administration enemy, including the Sub Treasury, the increasing power of the Executive, and Secretary of War Poinsett's plan to expand the size of the standing army. Echoing charges Whigs had made against Jackson, Webster and others said Poinsett's plan gave the President power of the purse and sword. Rives suggested Van Buren might use his 200,000 man army like Cromwell to suppress dissent.[13] Webster assured southern states their institutions (code for slavery) would not be interfered with.[14]

Virginia Democrats tried to break up the Whig coalition by pointing out how its members had opposed each other. Before the big spring Whig rally in Winchester, the Democratic Winchester Virginian suggested that the participants should wear masks so that Tyler, "the gaunt Nullifier" would not have to look at the face of Rives, "the Little Expunger," applauder of Jackson's Proclamation and Force Bill, who had taken Tyler's Senate seat.[15] Democrats were also incensed that the Whigs had managed with the log cabins and hard cider to overturn their usual charge that the Whigs represented moneyed aristocratic interests.[16]

Harrison and Tyler won a decisive Electoral College victory of 234 to 60 over Van Buren. Van Buren lost New York, but carried Virginia, and the vote margins in several states were small. A Whig cartoon of Van Buren's defeat portrayed Rives, Harrison, and Tallmadge creating a gale, which wrecked the ship of Van Buren. The defeated president was shown lamenting his Sub Treasury bill as he floundered in the water with Calhoun, Benton and other allies.[17] While enjoying Van Buren's defeat that he had energetically sought, Rives was returned to the Senate by the Virginia Legislature January 18, 1841. William Henry Harrison was inaugurated March 4, 1841, the first Whig President. The Whigs had been united against the common enemy, Van Buren. Now they were in control, their differences would erupt.

Rives wrote Judith February 15 that he had met with President-elect Harrison. Rives claimed that he was not ambitious about gaining higher office, but Harrison's mention of the top cabinet post seemed to tantalize him:

> When he came here, he told me with all possible naïveté that he wanted to make me his Secretary of the Treasury, by far the most important post, at present, in the Government, but that they (his Whig advisors) would not let him. He also informed Mr. Allen and other friends of mine that, as soon as he found he was elected President, he determined to offer me the Department of State, (that being nominally the highest place in the Cabinet), but in that also he was overruled by the same influence. These things seem to shew a singular infirmity of purpose. . . . After expressing a wish that I would give him my views unreservedly on all subjects, he told me (because he said I ought to know it), that the conservatives, and myself particularly, were viewed with a very jaundiced eye by the Whigs; but he begged me to be assured that he neither participated in, nor respected, those feelings.[18]

Harrison certainly had infirmity of health, if not of purpose, because he died one month after his inauguration. The Constitution was not clear about whether the Vice-President should become President in such a case. Some felt the Vice

President should be a caretaker until a new President could be elected. John Tyler took decisive steps to assume the Presidency. In Williamsburg when he learned of Harrison's death, he hastened to Washington, taking a boat to Richmond and a train from there to the capital. He met with members of Harrison's Cabinet and offered to let them remain in their positions. He had a federal judge administer a presidential oath. Tyler also issued an inaugural address. Some called Tyler "His Accidency." During his ensuing administration, Tyler received letters from enemies and critics addressed to him as "Vice-President-Acting President." He would return these letters unopened.[19]

On April 9, the day he released his inaugural address, Tyler wrote Rives and thanked him for his April 6 letter expressing support and encouragement. He confessed that he felt pain and anxiety about being "the instrument of a new test" of government under the Constitution. "The experiment is to be made at the moment when the country is agitated by conflicting views of public policy, and when the spirit of faction is most likely to exist." Tyler promised:

> In the administration of the government, I shall act upon the principles which I have all along espoused, and which you and myself have derived from the teachings of Jefferson and Madison, and other of our distinguished countrymen, and my reliance will be placed on the virtue and intelligence of the people. From yourself, my dear sir, I shall always be gratified to receive suggestions, and to be afforded an opportunity of profiting by your views. . . ."[20]

The words Jefferson and Madison were magic to Rives. Though they had been political rivals and opponents, Rives would be President Tyler's only consistent supporter in the Senate. However, Rives confided doubts about Tyler in letters to Judith. In one he said he feared that Tyler had neither "energy or intellectual scope enough for his high station." Another letter to Judith described Tyler as "direct and well-intentioned, I believe, but his own indecision has harassed him, till he is almost worn down both in mind and body. This, however, is altogether *entre nous* [between us]."[21]

Tyler called a Special Session of Congress beginning May 31, 1841. Henry Clay originally suggested this session to Harrison for the purpose of solving the country's financial problems. Clay's solution was a National Bank, which Tyler and Rives opposed. Tyler had become a Whig in 1834 because he opposed Jackson, not because he supported Clay. Tyler sent a message asking Congress to devise a "suitable fiscal agent" to collect and disburse public funds. He noted the Sub Treasury had been unsatisfactory, and warned that if Congress devised a solution inconsistent with his states rights principles, he would veto it.

Clay introduced a measure to repeal the Sub Treasury and establish a National Bank, which Clay pronounced the only alternative. Rives replied to Clay that the Bank was not the only alternative and that Tyler's message had indicated other alternatives, including state banks. "The Senator from Kentucky seems to desire not only to put down the Sub Treasury law, but by the same blow to prostrate the State banks, and any other fiscal agent so that nothing should remain to be adopted but a Bank of the United States."[22]

The Sub Treasury was repealed August 9, 1841, but devising its replacement proved more complicated. Treasury Secretary Thomas Ewing, following a plan suggested by Rives, proposed establishing a bank in Washington overseen by Congress with branches in states which consented to their establishment. The plan was taken up by the Senate Banking Committee, of which Clay was Chairman. Clay removed the provision that required consent from states where branches would be located. Rives attacked Clay's bill, saying the lack of required state approval turned the scheme into a National Bank proposal. Rives offered an amendment reinstating the state consent requirement. Rives' amendment failed, but Whig Congressman John Minor Botts offered a compromise solution: establishment of branch banks in the state would be voluntary, but state permission would be assumed unless state legislatures formally objected. Botts' amendment carried.[23]

Rives' companion in the Conservative Revolt, New York Senator Nathaniel Tallmadge, was now firmly in the Clay pro-Bank faction, opposing Rives, who stood with the President. Tallmadge, reacting to a rumor that Tyler might veto the compromise bank bill, sent Tyler an angry eleven page letter complaining that the compromise had been difficult to achieve because of Tyler's constitutional scruples. Tallmadge warned Tyler that a veto would destroy Clay, the Whig party and his entire administration.[24] Tyler did not care for Tallmadge's bullying tactics and vetoed the bill August 16, 1841.

Henry Clay turned apoplectic. He denounced Tyler, suggested he should resign, and said that if it had been foreseen at the Harrisburg Whig Convention that Harrison would die in office and that Tyler would succeed him and veto this Bank Bill, nobody would have voted for him.

When Clay concluded his remarks, Rives rose to defend the President. In his speech he stated that Clay, veiling his "open and violent attack" with professions of great regard, had charged Tyler with perjury, faithlessness to party and country. Rives said that Tyler considered a Bank of the United States unconstitutional, as did Jefferson. Rives referred to a speech against the Bank made by Madison in 1791. Rives said that Tyler had always openly opposed a National Bank. He asked, if the Bank was the most important issue for Whigs, why did they nominate him? Rives also pointed out that General Harrison thought the National Bank was unconstitutional.

Rives concluded:

> Let us call in the aid of practical men. Let us not attempt to arrange in haste the details of such an institution on mere theoretical or party principles, but let us build up, with cautious deliberation, a system which will stand the test of scrutiny and time, and be worthy of the Administration and the country. All previous systems have been rejected and condemned: the Sub Treasury, the pet banks, an old fashioned Bank of the United States, a new fashioned fiscal agent. We have before us a complete tabula rasa, appealing emphatically to all parties to lay down, so far as this question is concerned, former prepossessions on the altar of the country, and to unite in, an honest and patriotic effort to build up a permanent system for the common good.

Rives' suggestion for a creative new solution stoked even greater fury from Clay, who lashed Rives with the full force of his legendary verbal might. Clay called the use of state banks as government depositories a "half way house" to a National Bank. Clay replied to Rives:

> I have no desire to prolong this unpleasant discussion, but I must say that I heard with great surprise and regret the closing remark, especially, of the honorable gentleman from Virginia as, indeed, I did many of those which preceded it.

The gentleman stands in a peculiar situation. I found him several years ago in the half way house, where he seemed afraid to remain, and from which he is yet unwilling to go. I had thought after the thorough riddling which the roof of the house had received in the breaking up of the pet bank system, he would have fled somewhere else for refuge, but there he still stands, solitary and alone, shivering and pelted by the pitiless storm. The Sub Treasury is repealed, the pet bank system is abandoned, the United States Bank Bill is vetoed, and now, when there is as complete and perfect a reunion of the purse and the sword as there ever was under General Jackson or Mr. Van Buren, the Senator is for doing nothing!

... There is a rumor that a cabal exists ... whose object is the dissolution of the regular cabinet, the dissolution of the Whig Party, the dispersion of Congress. . . . The great error . . . of the honorable Senator is in thinking that the sentiments of a particular party in Virginia are always a fair exponent of the sentiments of the whole Union. . . .

Rives responded forcefully to Clay's attack:

The Senator from Kentucky has reminded me, rather ungraciously I think, considering how long he took shelter with me under the same roof of the horrible half way house for which he supposes me to retain a preference. For four long years did the honorable Senator himself inhabit this half way house, valiantly defending it with all the vigor of his prowess and eloquence against the fierce assaults of the forces of the late Administration. . . ."

Rives denied he had any special relationship with the President and said that he would defend a President from any other State who was attacked for upholding the Constitution. He also denied wanting to form a third party:

> I have shown myself at all times restive, under mere party influence and control from any quarter. All party, in my humble judgment, tends, in its modern degeneracy, to tyranny, and is attended with serious hazard of sacrificing an honest sense of duty, and the great interests of the country, to an arbitrary lead, directed by other aims. I desire, therefore, to take upon myself no new party bonds, while I am anxious to fulfill, to the fullest extent that a sense of duty to the country will permit, every honorable engagement implied in existing ones. In regard to the breaking up of the Cabinet ... he may rest assured that he will never see me in any Cabinet, under this or any other Administration. During the brief remnant of my public life, the measure of my ambition will be filled by the humble, but honest, part I may be permitted to take on this floor in consultations for the common good. . . .

Rives hurled a counter-accusation at Clay, saying he had heard "rumors of an organized legislative dictatorship, sending deputations from this Capitol to the President of the United States to bring him to terms, and teach him his duty." [25]

Author and son of the President, Lyon Gardiner Tyler, in Letters and Times of the Tylers, offers a biased account of the exchange. "Mr. Rives as a debater was immeasurably superior to Mr. Clay. . . . He addressed himself chiefly to the judgment of his hearers and wielded the weapons of argument with telling power and force. . . . Never before had Mr. Rives shown to better advantage. . . ." Lyon Tyler also cited an eyewitness report of Honorable R. Barnwell Rhett of South Carolina:

> . . . imposing and great as Mr. Clay always was in the Senate, he was more than matched by the dauntless energy and ability displayed by my honorable friend [Mr. Rives]; and Mr. Clay seemed to be conscious of it. The truth was, the Senator from Virginia had the right, I think, on his side, and wielded its weapons with a courage and force which won for him the admiration of all spectators.[26]

The fight over government banking issues continued. Tyler sent Secretary of State Webster and Treasury Secretary Thomas Ewing to the Congress to negotiate a compromise, which was called the "Fiscal Corporation Bill." Stormy debates in Congress included more attacks on Tyler by Clay. A freely circulated letter by John Minor Botts accused Tyler of being a Locofoco. This was a preposterous charge that Tyler, a Virginia plantation owner and slaveholder, would sympathize with a group that opposed such privilege. The bill reached Tyler's desk on September 9. Tyler vetoed the bill and confided to his fellow Virginian Littleton W. Tazewell that Clay had forced him to do so. The issue was personal. Tyler and Clay were in a struggle for control of the Whig Party.[27]

Tyler lost. Two days later his entire cabinet resigned, except for Secretary of State Webster. Whigs expected this would provoke Tyler to resign. Instead, he swiftly appointed new Cabinet members. On September 13, a group of Whigs gathered on the Capitol steps and declared Tyler was no longer a member of the Whig party. A Whig Convention in Syracuse in October 1841 recertified the expulsion.[28] Tyler was President without party, the only president ever expelled from his political party. Rives was also facing dwindling party support from the Whigs, and he knew his political days were numbered, having mentioned "the brief remnant of my public life" in his rejoinder to Clay.

Tyler's fellow Virginian Littleton Tazewell helped him create the Exchequer Plan, which was based on a banking proposal made by Andrew Jackson in 1830. The plan called for a bank based in Washington with branches in various states. The bank would operate under a nonpartisan Board of Control. Unlike the former Bank of the United States, there would be no private shareholders. The bank would hold government revenue and deal in both specie and paper money. Tyler hoped that he could win enough support from moderates of both parties to implement the plan. This hope was futile because of increasingly divisive partisan politics. Clay was determined to oppose Tyler at every opportunity and Democrats were uninterested in coming to his aid. Virginia Whig Congressman Botts even proposed impeaching Tyler for high crimes and misdemeanors, making Tyler the first president to face impeachment charges, though the House rejected the measure.[29] The Exchequer Plan was defeated even though Tallmadge decided to endorse the plan in the Senate. Tallmadge knew that this disobedience to Clay would doom his political future. Tyler rewarded Tallmadge's effort by making him Governor of the Wisconsin Territory.[30]

Clay was able to push through a Tariff Bill of 1842 that raised tariff rates to approximately the same levels as the 1832 Tariff of Abominations. Rives opposed the bill. He delivered a three-hour speech arguing against higher tariffs as well as Clay's proposal to distribute proceeds from sale of public lands to the states. Afterwards, Senator Crittenden of Kentucky said he regretted the "loss of time occasioned by the very eloquent dissertation of the Senator from Virginia on such a variety of subjects." Crittenden cuttingly remarked that opposing views were available in the form of Rives' previous speeches on these issues.[31]

Rives had supported Jackson's distribution of land sales proceeds to the states, but stressed that there was a Treasury surplus during Jackson's administration unlike the present deficit. Clay's 1842 tariff resulted in increased government revenues, reduction of government debt, a surplus of foreign specie, and higher cotton prices for southern planters.[32] Realizing its beneficial effect, Rives would defend the 1842 tariff, called the Black Tariff by its critics, against a motion for its repeal in 1844.

As Chairman of the Senate Foreign Relations Committee, Rives helped guide the Senate toward ratification of a treaty with England known as the Webster-Ashburton Treaty. Secretary of State Daniel Webster negotiated the agreement with British Lord Ashburton. The treaty fixed a border between Maine and Canada that had been in dispute since the revolution. It also settled other matters between the two countries.

During an 1837 rebellion in Canada, an American ship *Caroline* had been used to ferry arms to the rebels on the Niagara River. Canadian loyalists sent a force across the river that cut the *Caroline* from her moorings and let her drift over Niagara Falls. An American was killed and Canadian Alexander McLeod was arrested and put on trial for his part in the raid. He was acquitted. Outrage swelled on both sides of the border and in the Senate, where future President James Buchanan of Pennsylvania and others accused President Tyler of weakness and said General Harrison would have acted more forcefully. Rives defended Tyler's handling of the situation in a June 10, 1841 speech proclaiming that a great country couples force with wise restraint, and said that Buchanan "may dismiss his apprehension that the honor of the country will be compromised."[33]

Another incident involved the *Creole*, a ship carrying slaves from Virginia to New Orleans. The slaves were able to gain control of the ship at sea, and sailed it to the Bahamas. British authorities there declared they were free, which infuriated southerners. In order to stamp out exportation of slaves from Africa, the British wanted to be able to search merchant ships suspected of carrying newly captured Africans. Search and seizure of its merchant ships was a sensitive topic for Americans.

Ashburton and Webster liked each other and admired each other's countries. Therefore they were able to compromise. The boundary settlement gave the United States most of the territory it desired, including the fertile Aroostook Valley. Both Great Britain and the United States pledged to patrol the African coast to suppress the slave trade. The treaty also included extradition agreements for certain crimes. In letters that were not part of the formal treaty, Ashburton suggested the British should have apologized for attacking the *Caroline*. Webster allowed the raid was in self-defense. Ashburton pledged American ships could not be forced by violence to enter British ports.

Senator Benton and a few others raised objections to the proposed treaty. In a lawyerly speech of August 17 and 19, 1842, Rives delivered a detailed exposition of its features. Early in his remarks he stressed the issue was not about one political party gaining advantage over the other, and not about whose name was on the treaty. Tyler was pleasantly surprised when the Senate approved the treaty by a vote of 39 to 9. The President, Cabinet and Senate had worked together for once to create the greatest success of the Tyler Administration.[34]

* * *

1   Speech of William Cabell Rives at a Public Dinner given him at Louisa Courthouse on 7th September,1839, Charlottesville, James Alexander, 1839. University of Virginia Special Collections Accession #F221. V. 96 v. 226.

2   William Henry Harrison to William C. Rives, January 23, 1840 Rives MSS, LOC, quoted in Henry H. Simms, *The Rise of the Whigs in Virginia 1824-1840*, Richmond, The William Byrd Press, Inc. 1929, 141.

3   Simms, Ibid, 151.

4   Richmond Whig, February 27, 1840, see also "Letter from the Honorable William C. Rives of Virginia, February 15, 1840," Washington, 1840.

5   Jean E Friedman, *The Revolt of the Conservative Democrats*, UMI Research Press, 1979, 105.

6   Charles Francis Adams, ed., *Memoirs of John Quincy Adams, Comprising Portions of his Diary from 1795 to 1848* (12 vols.; Philadelphia 1876), 10:457. quoted in Christopher J. Leahy, "Playing Her Greatest Role, Priscilla Cooper Tyler and the Politics of the White House Social Scene, 1841-44, *Virginia Magazine of History and Biography*, Richmond, Virginia Historical Society, Vol. 120, No. 3, 247.

7   Simms, Ibid, 142.

8   *Richmond Enquirer*, February 25, 1840, Winchester Virginian, March 4, 1840, quoted in Simms, Ibid, 143.

9   *Richmond Enquirer*, April 21, 1840, quoted in Simms, Ibid. 143.

10 T, Harry Williams, Richard N. Current, Frank Friedel, W. Elliot Brownlee, *The Essentials of American History*, New York, Alfred A. Knopf, 1980.

11 *Charlestown Free Press*, April 23, 1840.

12 *Madisonian*, May 28, 1840 and William Cabell Rives, Jr. notes, quoted by Raymond C. Dingledine,Jr., "The Political Career of William C. Rives," University of Virginia Phd. Dissertation, 1947 365-368.

13 Letter from the Honorable William C. Rives, February 15, 1840, Washington, 1840.

14 Simms, Ibid, 149-150.

15 *Winchester Virginian*, April 15, 1840, quoted in Simms, Ibid, 152.

16 Simms, Ibid, 153.

17 "The Shipwreck," painting by Napoleon Sarony, printed and published by H.R. Robinson, 1840, Library of Congress Prints and Photographs online catalogue, Call Number: PC/US- 1840.R661, no. 79, http://www.loc.gov/pictures/item/2008661376/.

18 William C. Rives to Judith Page Rives, February 15, 1841, Rives MSS, LOC, box 24.

19 Edward P. Crapol, *John Tyler The Accidental President*, Chapel Hill, University of North Carolina Press, 2006, 10-12.

20 John Tyler to William C. Rives, April 9, 1841, *The Letters and Times of the Tylers*, Lyon G. Tyler editor 1896, reprinted New York, Da Capo Press, 1970, Vol. II, 20.

21 William C. Rives to Judith Page Rives, July 22, 1841 and August 22, 1841, Rives MSS, LOC, box 24.

22 *The Letters and Times of the Tylers*, Ibid, 42-43.

23 Friedman, Ibid, 107.

24 Nathaniel P. Tallmadge to John Tyler, August 13, 1841, Nathaniel P. Tallmadge Papers, State Historical Society, Madison Wisconsin, cited by Friedman, Ibid, 107.

25 *Congressional Globe*, 27th Congress, 1st Session, Speeches by Henry Clay and William C. Rives, August 19, 1841, Appendix 368-370.

26 *Letters and Times of the Tylers*, Ibid, Vol. II, 83, Remarks of Rhett delivered in Confederate Congress in 1862 on the death of John Tyler.

27 Friedman, Ibid, 108.

28 Ibid, 109.

29 Crapol, Ibid, 106.

30 Friedman, Ibid, 110-113.

31 *Congressional Globe*, 27th Congress, 2nd Session, June 24, 1842, 676.

32 Michael F. Holt, *The Rise and Fall of the American Whig Party: Jacksonian Politics and the Onset of the Civil War*, New York, Oxford, Oxford University Press, 1999, 167.

33 *Congressional Globe*, 27th Congress, 1st Session 113.

34 Norma Lois Peterson, *The Presidencies of William Henry Harrison and John Tyler*, University Press of Kansas 1989, 115-130.

CHAPTER FOURTEEN

Dans les Bras de Monsieur

ALIENATION FROM BOTH Whig and Democratic parties ensured that Rives' Senate term due to expire in 1845 would be his last. However, he did not let his political difficulties detract from his social life. Rives claimed he never sought political office, only agreeing to serve when called upon. However, the Rives clearly enjoyed the way his political office enabled them to mingle with the political and social elite.

In a letter to a Virginia cousin, Judith described an 1842 reception at the home of the Russian Ambassador. "Picture to yourself some eight hundred people in a house that would not hold more than half the number, with any convenience. . . . mirrors and glasses suffered not a little from the contact of men's elbows, and as the dancers turned round and round in the same spot like dervishes or spinning tops, when they attempted to waltz, some of them, in attempting a few parlor capers, damaged the chandeliers. . . ." Judith spoke with General Winfield Scott, who was seeking the presidential nomination. "The General was witty, as he had been dining out, and told us all he meant to do when he was president. . . ." Judith observed that political foes appeared to have set aside their differences for the evening: "To see the reconciliations in society, one would suppose that the millennium had arrived. Lambs and Lions, and all manner of animals were together as quietly as possible."[1]

Judith also wrote of the etiquette that required calls and return visits between members of the government and society. "It is a matter of some consequence to take the rounds once, for all that are neglected, are irreconcilably offended, but after the first time, I don't trouble myself to go again, except to see people whose acquaintance I really wish to cultivate."[2]

In another letter, Judith recounted how she brought her son Will to Washington from the Episcopal School in Alexandria, because he had a fever. She had "breakfasted among a hundred boys without great ceremony ... got into a dirty old Hack, and ... got into a dirtier little old steam boat, and got to Washington ..." Judith tucked Will into bed, "then made a grand toilette for a grand party of *distingués* at the Secretary of State's [Webster], dined there with a large circle of the elite in the most brilliant style." From there, the Rives went to a reception for author Charles Dickens, who was visiting Washington. Judith claimed she had enjoyed the company of the schoolboys more than the "court circle" at the reception. Judith described Dickens and his wife:

> a youthful looking man, even for thirty, and rather handsome, rather short and stout, with features a little coarsish, except his eyes, which are dark, brilliant, and expressive, wears his hair *à la mode*, long and curling on both sides — The Lady equally stout and short, round eyed. . . . In England, both would instantly be pronounced under bred, and here, knowing people say the same thing, but good feeling sometimes has power to make amends for the want of good taste.[3]

Rives and his wife continued to express their mutual affection in letters when they were apart. In July 1842, Rives wrote Judith that he had much work to do, but promised her that soon, "you will find a very snug resting place *dans les bras de monsieur*." [in the arms of monsieur][4] In an 1844 letter, Rives lamented that he missed his "*compagnon de lit*" [bed partner], and that time with her was "an oasis in the desert."[5] Judith replied with similar senti-ments, although an 1843 letter spoke of envy and jealousy that "raised their gorgon heads" when she imagined her husband in the company of "the bright eyes of pretty Mrs. Bayard" or "our quiet pussy cat friend Matilda," before claiming she was only joking.[6] Judith described to her husband an encounter with a dis-solute friend of Payne Todd (Dolley Madison's son) on a railroad car, and said "there should be a separate place for drunken men in our Virginia rail road."[7]

Railroad and steamboat had become the principal means of travel between Washington and Castle Hill. Rives wrote his wife that the cold and wet weather made him glad that Judith had "the accommodations of the fire-side . . . in the steam-boat and rail cars."[8] The railroad reached Gordonsville from Richmond in 1840, and the Cobham station on Rives property was opened in 1848.[9] Gordonsville was approximately seven miles from Castle Hill, while the Cobham depot was about two miles from the Castle Hill house, permitting a relatively easy carriage pick up. Rives was a designated speaker to an assembled crowd at the opening of Cobham Station when, according to an eyewitness, "whiskey flowed freely, to the detriment of many."[10]

In 1844 the Rives enlarged Castle Hill with symmetrical one-story wings. Each contained an enclosed room and adjoining glassed-in conservatory. The project was headed by William B. Phillips, whom Jefferson had praised as the best brick mason to work on the University of Virginia.[11]

John Tyler appointed Rives' former brawling partner Thomas Walker Gilmer Secretary of the Navy in February 1844. Gilmer had previously served as Governor of Virginia. Rives and Gilmer were on speaking terms, having put aside their old feud. The Navy Secretary was joined by the Rives, President Tyler, and scores of other distinguished guests for a celebratory cruise aboard the USS *Princeton* February 28, 1844. The *Princeton* was the first

American warship powered by a steam driven screw propeller instead of paddle wheels. John Ericsson, who later designed the *Monitor*, designed its propulsion system. Ericsson also designed for the ship a huge 15′ gun, the "Oregon," that included three reinforcing iron bands around the breach. Captain John Stockton, for whose hometown the *Princeton* had been named, designed a gun of similar size called the "Peacemaker." However, Stockton's design lacked the reinforcing bands of iron Ericsson had wrapped around the breech end of the Oregon.

President Tyler hosted a White House reception in honor of the *Princeton* the night before the voyage. The venerable and popular Dolley Madison attended the reception and was aboard the vessel as it headed downriver from Washington. The Peacemaker was fired twice with astounding success. A third firing caused the breech to split open. Flying iron fragments instantly killed Gilmer, Secretary of State Abel Parker Upshur, and six others. Twenty were wounded and the deck was covered in blood and body parts.[12]

The following day, Thursday, February 29, 1844, Tyler sent a formal announcement of the tragedy to Congress. Rives rose in the Senate and declared:

> Surely Mr. President, never, in the mysterious ordinances of God, has a day on earth been marked in its progress by such startling and astounding contrasts, opening and advancing with hilarity and joy, mutual congratulation and patriotic pride, and closing in scenes of death and disaster, of lamentation and unutterable woe. . . . It was my sad fortune . . . to be an eye-witness of these never-to-be forgotten events . . . so overwhelming a calamity, which stands almost without a parallel in the records of human misfortune. . . .

Explosion aboard the USS Princeton, *February 28, 1844.*

Rives proposed that the Senate adjourn till the following Monday, that Senators should attend "obsequies" of the cabinet members, and that Senators should wear crape on the left arm for 30 days. He concluded:

> Let the deep sense of common calamity and mutual affliction unite us more closely by the ties of brotherhood and affection. Let us 'put away from us all bitterness and wrath, and evil-speaking,' and when we come together again, under these chastening influences, we shall all feel, I trust, how much better patriots we are, for being better Christians.[13]

Despite Rives' stated wishes, bitterness and wrath remained. Pennsylvania Senator James Buchanan delivered a speech criticizing the Webster-Ashburton treaty, which was ratified by the Senate in 1842. He alleged that Ashburton had concealed old maps that showed the U.S. should have been entitled to more territory. Buchanan had voted against ratification of the treaty.

Rives spoke in defense of the treaty and responded to the implicit criticism of Webster and Ashburton.[14] Webster thanked Rives in the following letter, which Judith claimed revealed Webster's humorous side:

> New York, March 21st, 1844
> My dear Sir,
>
> I pray to tender you both thanks and congratulation for your excellent and admirable speech in reply to Mr. Buchanan. It was read here yesterday by everybody, and praised as universally as it was read. It is to me quite unaccountable that Mr. B. should indulge in such sentiments as he expresses towards England. He talks as if England were still oppressing and grinding us, under a colonial bondage, and as a cruel stepmother &c. a tone quite below the dignity of a government, conscious of its own independence and its own power.
> It is equally marvelous that in speaking on such subjects, and in the face of the world, he should suffer himself to fall into such enormous mistakes. Whoever is about to impute dishonorable conduct to an individual or a government ought to be most careful, one should think, about the accuracy of his facts.
> Mr. B's mistakes brought to my mind a humorous epitaph, which some one proposed for the tombstone of Wraxall. I do not recollect it, but it was something to the following effect, and more and better:
>
> MistakingMiss-dating
> Miss-citingMiss-writing
> Misspelling   Miss-telling
> Ill-sortingDistorting
> ConfusingAbusing

Words, speeches, letters and facts all,
Here lie the bones of Nathaniel Wraxall[15]

Yours truly,
Danl. Webster[16]

Rives made another lengthy speech two months later on South Carolina Senator McDuffie's Proposition to Repeal the Tariff of 1842. Though he had opposed what its opponents called the Black Tariff two years before, Rives now supported it because it had produced revenue and protected domestic industry. Rives argued that a tax on consumption of foreign imports was the least objectionable and least burdensome method of funding the government. He said proposals by McDuffie and Woodbury of New Hampshire for direct taxation on property would inflict tax collectors like a "swarm of locusts" upon the people. A protective tariff passed by the first U.S. Congress on imported cotton had allowed cotton's establishment as a southern staple crop. Rives said the southern states were misguided in preferring to send their cotton to English factories instead of ones in Massachusetts. He referred to Massachusetts businessman and former congressman Nathan Appleton's observation that trade between Boston and New Orleans involved greater tonnage than that between New York and Liverpool. Rives cited words and actions by Washington, Jefferson, Madison, and economist Adam Smith to support his argument. Rives said he had observed with regret the increasing antagonism developing between Massachusetts and South Carolina, and he recounted an important compromise in the framing of the Constitution. South Carolina and Georgia had agreed to empower Congress to regulate commerce (including instituting tariffs) in exchange for being allowed to continue to import slaves until 1808. Rives called for renewed "mutual deference and concession."

The last part of the speech expressed Rives' alarm at McDuffie's hypothetical three-way division of the country according to economic interests. McDuffie had described: a manufacturing confederacy of eastern and middle states, a farming confederacy of western and northwestern states, and a planting confederacy of the south and southwest states. Rives recoiled from McDuffie's assumption that Virginia would gravitate toward the southern planting states. He argued that Virginia had more in common with other middle states Maryland, Pennsylvania, Delaware, and New Jersey than it did with the cotton states. Rives pointed out that Virginia tobacco was charged an exorbitant duty in Great Britain, and its flour was excluded by British Corn Laws. Great Britain had levied a high tariff upon imported sugar produced by slave labor. Rives suggested it might do the same on slave pro-duced cotton.

Rives quoted Adam Smith's observation that every country is necessarily the best market for productions of its own industry. He emphasized that the government and economy were doing well under the present tariff system. In his opinion, those trying to change it were motivated by party allegiance rather than for the good of the entire country. He closed with an appeal to keep our Union, promote internal trade, and to be "true to ourselves, to the memory of our fathers and to the just hopes of our posterity."[17]

The 1842 tariff was repealed in 1846.

The presidential election of 1844 stirred up additional bit-terness and wrath. In January, Rives wrote Judith that he was "shocked and disgusted at the means employed here for put-ting up Mr. Van Buren," which he believed would bring "evil and calamities" upon the country. After much deliberation, Rives decided to endorse Clay, and he hoped that Judith would support his decision, which would be published in the *Richmond Whig*.[18] Apparently Rives did not consider Tyler a viable candidate even though Tyler was seeking re-election. Rives' endorsement of Clay was a blow to Tyler, who had considered Rives his most dependable supporter in the Senate.[19]

Rives' "Reasons for Preferring Mr. Clay to Mr. Van Buren," published in the *Whig* as well as in pamphlet form, was mostly an attack on Van Buren. In it, Rives quoted British historian and statesman Charles James Fox's opinion that "the worst and most dangerous of all revolutions is a restoration." Rives repeated previous criticisms of Van Buren's party politics and the Sub Treasury. Comparing the two candidates, Rives said Clay did not vote for the 1828 tariff of abominations, but Van Buren did. Rives considered Clay's National Bank not as damaging as Van Buren's Sub Treasury. During the War of 1812, Rives said Clay was with Republicans in the House supporting Madison, while Van Buren stood with the Federalists working against Madison. Rives listed issues, including the Oregon and Texas questions, deficient revenue, tariff controversy, abolition, and "collision of sectional interests." He asked which candidate had "power to still the rising tempest," or if that failed, possessed "commanding genius to ride the whirlwind and direct the storm?" The times called for "the highest moral and intellectual qualities of the statesman. . . ." which made Rives prefer Clay.[20]

That Rives would endorse Clay, whose "American System" of National Bank, tariffs and internal improvements he had repeatedly denounced, and whom he had bitterly opposed over expunging and the "Half Way House" state deposit banks, showed how desperate he was to prevent a second Van Buren term. Rives' endorsement of Clay provoked a furious Andrew Jackson to write Van Buren that Rives has "showed his cloven foot. . . . He has no party and no principles."[21] Rives was proud he was not subservient to any party. He detested Van Buren's Democratic Party manipulations, and he never embraced Clay's Whig Party philosophy of activist central government. Rives' guiding principle in this case was his unwavering opposition to the greater foe. Rives would have endorsed a cloven-footed red-caped horned creature before he would have endorsed Van Buren. John Bragg, an enemy of Rives, wrote Van Buren that Rives' actions "ought to be a warning for generations to come."[22] Rives had hoped his letter favoring Clay would appeal to "the independent and patriotic portion of the Democratic party."[23]

The Whig Convention took place in Baltimore at the beginning of May. No other candidate opposed Clay for the nomination, and the platform included a well-regulated currency, tariff, distribution of proceeds from sales of public lands, and a single term presidency. The platform did not mention a National Bank, annexation of Texas, or slavery.[24]

Democrats convened in Baltimore four weeks later. Months earlier, a letter by Van Buren had been published in which he opposed annexation of Texas because it would lead to war with Mexico. This letter generated opposition to Van Buren from pro-annexation southerners who wanted to bring another slave-holding state into the Union by whatever means necessary. Van Buren received a majority of votes on the first ballot, but not the two-thirds majority required in a rule instituted by his opponents. On the second day of balloting, former House Speaker and Tennessee Governor James K. Polk was suggested as an alternative to Van Buren. Polk was for annexation of Texas and he won the nomination.[25]

The Democratic Party had prevented a second Van Buren term, accomplishing Rives' principal goal before he could play an active part. Nevertheless, he had committed his support for Clay and campaigned for him, speaking for three and a half hours in Winchester, August 22. On July 20, Rives addressed a crowd near Mechanicsville in Louisa County, calling Polk a "Duck River Militia Colonel, not one of the best stock for fighting at that. . . . He was dragged out of an obscure hole like Claudius to receive his nomination."[26] This echoed the Clay campaign slogan, "Who is James K. Polk?" With his legislative and executive record, Polk was hardly unknown. The Polk campaign's slogan "Fifty-four forty or fight," referring to the Oregon Boundary dispute with Great Britain, proved more successful. John Tyler had been running as an Independent, but he withdrew from the race and endorsed Polk on August 21.[27] Polk won the election and accomplished a great deal during his single term (1845-49). Success in the Mexican War (1846-48) greatly enlarged the U.S. Southwest, bringing in Texas along with territory that would become California, Arizona and New Mexico.

Rives' last important Senate speech and debate involved the annexation of Texas. John Tyler had favored annexation, but his first Secretary of State Daniel Webster had been opposed, which prevented any progress on the matter. Webster was replaced by Hugh Swinton Legare, who died suddenly in 1843. The next Secretary of State Abel Parker Upshur was killed aboard the *Princeton*. Tyler appointed John C. Calhoun in his place. Calhoun was keenly in favor of annexation; however, Tyler and Calhoun were not universally popular. When they presented an annexation treaty to the Senate in 1844, it failed to receive the required two-thirds majority.[28] In early 1845, Tyler suggested Congress annex Texas by a joint resolution, which would require a majority vote by the Senate and the House, instead of the two-thirds Senate majority the Constitution required for a treaty.

Rives expressed his opposition to the resolution in a February 15, 1845 speech. He stated he was not opposed to the acquisition of Texas if it could be accomplished without violating the Constitution and without disturbing relations between North and South and between the U.S. and other nations. Along with Mexico, Great Britain and France were also wary of U.S. annexation of Texas.[29] Rives observed that annexation proponents were disingenuous in claiming the resolution was not a treaty. He had some fun at Senator Buchanan's expense. Buchanan had spoken in favor of the resolution earlier. Rives pointed out that the language of the resolution was not the language of legislation: "Be it enacted." It was instead, the language of a treaty, which was the same as of a marriage ceremony: "Be it consented." Rives then apologized for making "such an allusion when addressing the honorable gentleman, who was not yet initiated in these mysteries."[30] Buchanan was unmarried, and Rives' remarks produced laughter.

Rives invoked his holy names of Jefferson and Madison in insisting on adherence to the law requiring a two-thirds Senate majority for treaty approval. He warned that use of a simple majority in this case would imperil the rights of the slaveholding states. He counted a 28 to 24 non-slaveholding states majority on the Senate and a 136 to 87 non-slaveholding majority in the House. He argued that the slaveholding states ". . . should be the very last to give up the conservative features of the Constitution. If they were now so blind as to recognize the dispensing power of a mere majority, the time might come when the peculiar interests of the South, involving their rights of property, their domestic peace, the security of their firesides, would be placed at the mercy of such a majority."

He explained that a simple majority might abolish slavery in the District of Columbia, might prohibit interstate transfer of slaves, and might revoke fugitive slave return. Rives addressed the argument made by some that annexation of Texas would raise the value of slaves in Virginia because demand for their labor would bring buyers from Texas. "As a Virginian and a slaveholder who continued to be so far more from considerations of humanity than of interest, he scorned so sordid an appeal."[31] However, Rives continued that the value of slaves was related to the value of cotton, and that cotton production from Texas might lead to

overproduction and a decrease in the value of cotton and slaves.
Rives claimed that he would like to see Texas united with the
Union by constitutional means.

> But, as a nation worthy of our glorious ancestors, we
> could not live or breathe a day except under the shelter
> of our precious and sacred Constitution, the palladium
> of freedom, the hope of the world. . . . Live forever
> our free and glorious Constitution, the sole pledge of
> our peace, of our safety, of our honor, of our blessed
> and happy Union. . . . If we set the precedent of acting
> by simple majority, it will be the 'melancholy office of
> many of us to follow that Constitution to an untimely
> grave.'[32]

Senator Crittenden of Kentucky expressed his agreement
with Rives about the danger of using a simple majority.[33] South
Carolina Senator McDuffie disagreed, saying "If we should lose
Texas by the conduct of this Senate, we would be the jest and
laughing stock of Europe."[34] Rives' plea was in vain, and the bill
passed by simple majority in both houses of Congress.

Rives' oldest son Francis was serving as Secretary of Legation
in London under the American Minister there, Edward Everett.
Francis graduated from the University of Virginia in 1842, and
his father helped him secure the diplomatic appointment from
President Tyler. Francis had decided to return to the U.S., and
Rives instructed him in a letter to call on the new Secretary of
State James Buchanan as well as President Polk. Rives observed,
". . . although my relations with the latter are not of a very friendly
character, that should not prevent you from paying a becoming
mark of respect to the Chief Magistrate of the Nation on your
return from the service of the Government abroad." Rives offered

more political news. He said none of the Cabinet members are well known except Buchanan. "Mr. Calhoun retires with reluctance and in bad humor. . . . Mr. Stevenson of Virginia will be disappointed he is not in the new Cabinet." The letter concluded with important news that the Virginia Legislature adjourned without electing a Senator. Rives' Senate service was at an end. "It is quite a relief to me to be discharged from the bondage of public life and to be restored to the care of my private affairs (which should be very much in need of my attention) and to the cherished affections of my own domestic circle."[35]

Rives hastened to the bedside of his father. Robert Rives died Sunday, March 9 at Oak Ridge. His obituary in the *Richmond Enquirer* praised his business success that placed him in the "first rank of American Merchants." The obituary noted that he dedicated the last thirty years of his life to the improvement of his large estate. "Surrounded by his numerous family, and bestowing his blessing on each and all of them, he was gently gathered, like the Patriarchs of old, to his fathers, in favor with God, and charity with all the world."[36]

Rives was appointed an executor of his father's will.

★ ★ ★

1 Judith Page Rives to Maria L. Gordon, January 7, 1842, and March 16, 1842, "Observations on Washington Society: Mrs. W. C. Rives—Miss Maria L. Gordon Letters, 1842," Raymond B. Clarke, Jr., editor, *Papers of the Albemarle Historical Society*, Charlottesville, Albemarle Historical Society, 1951 Vol. XI, 53-61.

2 Ibid.

3 Ibid.

4 Rives to Judith Page Rives, July 26, 1842, Rives-Barclay Family Papers, 1698-1941. Accession 37776. Personal Papers Collection, The Library of Virginia, Richmond, Va. 23219, box 1, Folder 5.

5 Rives to Judith Page Rives, March 24, 1844, Rives MSS, UVa., Accession #10596, box 1.

6 Judith Page Rives to Rives, January 27, 1843, Rives MSS, UVa., Accession # 2313, box 1.

7 Judith Page Rives to Rives, March 16, 1844, Rives MSS, LOC, box 26.

8 Rives to Judith Page Rives, March 16, 1844, Rives MSS, UVa., #10596, box 1.

9 Edward C. Mead, *Historic Homes of the Southwest Mountains, Virginia*, Philadelphia, 1899, J. B. Lippincott Co., 244.

10 Ibid.

11 K. Edward Lay, Martha Tuzson Stockton, "Castle Hill: The Walker Family Estate, *The Magazine of Albemarle County History*, Vol. 52, Albemarle County Historical Society, Charlottesville, 1994, 47, 54. Lay & Stockton refer to Jefferson's recommendation of Phillips, December 16, 1823, Jefferson Papers, University of Virginia Library, Manuscripts Division.

12 Norma Lois Peterson, *The Presidencies of William Henry Harrison and John Tyler*, 1989, University Press of Kansas, 201-202.

13 *Congressional Globe*, 28th Congress, 1st Session, February 29, 1844, 337-338.

14 Ibid, March 20, 1844, 411-413.

15 Wraxall (1751-1831) was a British historian criticized for his inaccuracies.

16 Autobiography of Judith Page Rives, 76, Also Edith Tunis Sale, *Manors of Virginia in Colonial Times*, Philadelphia, J. B. Lippincott Company, 1909, 240.

17 "Speech of Mr. Rives of Virginia on Mr. McDuffie's Proposition to Repeal the Tariff of 1842," U.S. Senate, May 27, 1844, *Appendix to the Congressional Globe*, 28th Congress, First Session, 727-733.

18 Rives to Judith Page Rives, January 3, 1844, January 26, 1844, Rives MSS, UVa., #10596, box 1.

19 Peterson, Ibid, 198.

20 "Letter of Hon. William C. Rives Giving His Reasons for Preferring Mr. Clay to Mr. Van Buren for Next President," New York, Greeley and McElrath, 1844, University of Virginia Special Collections F221 v.589 no. 4.

21 Jackson to Van Buren, February 7, 1844, Van Buren Papers, Library of Congress, quoted in Jean E. Friedman, *The Revolt of the Conservative Democrats*, UMI Research Press, 1979 113.

22 John Bragg to Van Buren, February 4, 1844, Van Buren Papers, Library of Congress, quoted in Friedman, Ibid, 113, (This was likely Alabama Congressman John Bragg (1806-1878), whose younger brother Braxton Bragg was a Confederate General.

23 Rives to Judith Page Rives, January 26, 1844, Rives MSS, UVa., Accession #10596, box 1.

24 George Lockhart Rives, *The United States and Mexico*, Vol. I, New York, Charles Scribner's Sons, 1913, 627.

25 Ibid, 628-634.

26 WCR, Jr., Biography, Rives MSS, box 103, 104.

27 George Lockhart Rives, Ibid, 643.

28 Ibid, 618.

29 George Lockhart Rives, Ibid, 641.

30 William C. Rives, Speech on the Resolution for the Annexation of Texas, February 15, 1845, Rives-Barclay Papers, Library of Virginia, #37776, box 10.

31 Rives' humanitarian claim was dubious, and his relationship to slavery will be examined in the following chapter.

32 Rives speech, February 15, 1845, Ibid.

33 *Congressional Globe*, 28th Congress, 2nd Session, 359. Other southern Whig Senators agreed with Rives and delivered similar speeches. See Rachel A. Shelden, "Not So Strange Bedfellows: Northern and Southern Whigs and the Texas Annexation Controversy," essay in Gary Gallagher and Rachel A. Shelden, editors, *A Political Nation: New Directions in Mid Nineteenth Century American Political History*, Charlottesville, University of Virginia Press, 2012, 27.

34 Ibid, 334-336.

35 Rives to Francis Robert Rives, February 26, 1845, Rives-Barclay Papers, Library of Virginia, box 1, Folder 9.

36 *Richmond Enquirer*, March 14, 1845.

CHAPTER FIFTEEN

Evil Without Remedy

AT HIS DEATH, Robert Rives owned 8,000 acres and according to one of his grandsons, "an equivalent value of personal estate."[1] An inventory of Robert Rives' personal property included a rosewood piano at Oak Ridge valued at $300, a mahogany bed valued at $50, and a pair of carriage horses valued at $200. However, the most valuable portion of the personal property was human property. A total of 283 slaves located at Oak Ridge and seven other plantations were appraised as worth $76,572. Some individuals were valued as high as $600, and some aged persons were assigned no value. The personal property total, including furniture, livestock, farm equipment, and slaves was $102,820.38. At the end of the inventory was a note from those conducting the appraisal (Lemuel Turner, J. H. Loving and T. S. Whitehead): "It is proper for us to state that we were informed by the Executors that there is a Negro girl named Louisa belonging to the estate of their testator which we have not appraised as she is a runaway."[2]

Rives and his co-executors Mayo Cabell, Robert Rives, Jr., and Alexander Brown were able to settle the estate in slightly over two years. The final accounting of expenses and proceeds was made August 23, 1847.[3] Along with legacies to his ten surviving children, Robert Rives also set aside some of his real estate and human property for the benefit and education of certain grandchildren. One such bequest was 14 slaves willed to the eight children of his daughter Paulina and her husband Richard Pollard. The Pollards agreed among themselves not to separate man and wife among the slaves and to equalize by cash payments to those who received no slaves or slaves worth less than the $673.12 average.[4]

Rives received additional land in Nelson County from his father's estate along with additional slaves. While he was serving in France and in Congress, Rives had mentioned growing indebtedness in letters, though he and his family were living in affluent style. Inheritance from his father strengthened his financial position, though he did not pay off all debts until he sold land and slaves in 1860.

When he was in France in 1831, Rives received letters from his father assuring him that his plantations in Albemarle and Nelson were doing well. Perhaps implying that public service was a distraction from more worthwhile pursuits, Robert Rives wrote, "I shall try to have your plantations there [in Albemarle] and in this county too in such a state of improvement that you will be delighted to spend the balance of your days in the interesting pursuits of Agriculture...."

Rives' boyhood friend Thomas Jefferson Randolph proposed a measure in the General Assembly in 1831 that would emancipate all slaves born after a certain date. Robert Rives vehemently opposed the idea. He accused Randolph of "striking at our lives and property." He estimated slaves in Virginia alone were worth $90 million, and he asked his son, who had expressed support for the measure, how the owners could be compensated without bankrupting the state.[5] Manuscripts in the Virginia Historical Society collection indicate the firm of Brown and Rives acted as agents in sales of enslaved persons.[6]

Nat Turner's rebellion of August 1831 inflamed white imaginations, and rendered slavery debates more complicated. Delegate William Mason Rives of Campbell County wrote Rives in September 1831 that the white population had guns at the ready to suppress any future slave uprising. "The unrelenting cruelty

Union Hill slave cemetery. Dozens of neatly arranged, mostly unmarked field stones.

of the blacks has been retaliated on them fully, and probably on the innocent as well as the guilty, but not on their women and children."[7]

From Paris, Rives wrote Thomas Walker Gilmer, still his trusted friend in 1831, that living in Europe made him aware of "the melancholy anomaly of domestic slavery in our free institutions."[8] Like James Madison, Rives advocated colonization: shipping freed slaves from America to Africa. He served as vice president of the Albemarle chapter of the American Colonization Society, the organization that received money from Madison's will. Rives wrote his father that colonization would rid them of "this consuming cancer of our permanent prosperity."[9] With slaves amounting to three quarters of his net worth, Robert Rives did not share his son's enthusiasm for colonization.

Belief that free blacks and whites could not live together was widely shared by white Americans. Many influential leaders supported colonization, including Henry Clay[10] and Abraham Lincoln. The overwhelming majority of white northerners and southerners of the era viewed blacks as inferior, with what would be considered extreme intolerable racism in 21st century America. One of the country's leading scientists, Harvard Professor Louis Agassiz, gave a speech in Charleston, S.C. in 1850 in which he claimed that the white and black races had originated separately, and that only whites were descended from Adam and Eve.[11] Though Madison and other colonizers noted slaves' reluctance to being shipped to Africa, they rationalized that freed slaves would be better off deported, because they would be hampered by prejudice and limited opportunity in the U.S.[12]

Rives wrote British Secretary of State for the Colonies Earl Grey in 1850 that slaveholders in Virginia would be willing to free slaves for shipment to British islands in the Caribbean to satisfy demand for laborers there. Rives suggested Great Britain should pay for transport expenses and provide the emigrants "a competent allotment of lands and habitation on their arrival." The British did not find the proposal appealing.[13]

Back in the 24th Congress in early 1837, amid disputes over expunging, purchase of Madison's manuscripts, and fiscal policy, Rives took part in a heated slavery debate that also involved his frequent antagonist Calhoun. Monday, February 6, several northern senators, including Tipton of Indiana, Ewing and Morris of Ohio, Buchanan of Pennsylvania, and Webster of Massachusetts presented petitions from their constituents for abolishing slavery within the District of Columbia. Tipton and Ewing claimed they disagreed with the petitions. They were merely submitting them as a service to their constituents. Although both were opposed to slavery, they felt the attempt to abolish it in D.C. would disrupt the peace and unity of the country. Tipton said it would create a haven between two slave states (Maryland and Virginia) for "fanatics, abolitionists and runaway slaves."[14]

The petitions infuriated Calhoun. He protested that the institution of slavery existed when the Constitution was written. He said these abolitionist petitions were the result of Jackson's Force Bill, though he did not explain how they were connected. Senator Southard of New Jersey suggested that the issue of slave trading in Washington was separate from the issue of slavery there. Senator Preston of South Carolina objected to that distinction. Rives tried to intervene between the South Carolinians and the northerners. Similar to his effort to occupy a sensible middle ground in the Sub Treasury debate as a Conservative Democrat, his attempt to mediate drew scornful criticism from both sides.

Rives said he had witnessed the discussion with pain and mortification. He pointed out to the northerners that slavery was supported by the Constitution, and an attack on slavery threatened the Union. However, unlike Calhoun, Rives declared slavery was a great evil, though no remedy for it had been found. Calhoun insisted that slavery was "a great good." Calhoun argued that both races benefitted under the system as measured by population growth, and that slaveholding states were more stable and more resistant to despotism. He also ridiculed Rives' self-contradictory position. If Rives thought slavery evil, then "as a wise and virtuous man," he should work to end its existence, declared Calhoun. Facing criticism from the other side, Rives was advised by Daniel Webster to calm down.

Rives thanked Webster for his "edifying lesson in coolness." However, Rives said northerners could not comprehend the southern predicament. Abolitionist talk increased the danger of slave insurrection and sectional revolt, according to Rives. He told Webster, "If someone is tossing squibs and firebrands about this hall, those sitting on a barrel of gun powder, liable to be blown up, are not quite so calm." Rives brought up a complaint made by Madison and other southerners that slavery had been forced upon the south by "a foreign and unnatural jurisdiction."[15] New

England, English and Dutch traders were to blame.[16] Rives continued that Washington, Jefferson, Madison and John Marshall all lamented the existence of slavery, but could not solve the problem.[17] Rives said slavery was "in the eye of religion, philanthropy and reason an evil." Rives told Calhoun, that by claiming slavery was a great good, "You shock the generous sentiments of human nature . . . you outrage the spirit of the age." In a familiar refrain, Rives proposed that everyone should "stand upon the solemn guarantees of the Constitution."[18]

Rives seemed unable to criticize the founding fathers for evading the issue of slavery, allowing it to become a festering sore upon the Constitution. Madison had often declared slavery was an evil, but had done little to bring about its end beyond promoting colonization, which was unrealistic and impractical. Even most northern politicians evaded the issue of slavery through the 1830s. Perpetuation of the Union and avoidance of Civil War were deemed more important than abolition of slavery. Abolitionists were unpopular even in the North in the 1830s.[19] Though he opposed slavery, Daniel Webster reminded southerners during the February 1837 debate that the "honorable Senator [Rives] had never heard him say more in disapprobation of slavery than had been uttered by the Senator himself this day."[20]

The preacher of Rives' Virginia parish Ebenezer Boyden wrote a pamphlet in 1860 entitled "The Epidemic of the Nineteenth Century." The evil epidemic, according to Boyden, was abolitionism. He claimed that scripture, God and Reason supported the institution of slavery.[21] For the next two decades, as anti-slavery sentiment swelled in the North, Rives argued that abolitionist agitation would only prolong the institution. If northerners would desist from interference, slavery would eventually end "in the free and spontaneous action of the State sovereignties, under the humane influence of a humane and enlightened public opinion . . . the moral and Christian sentiments of the people of the

South."[22] Rives did not specify when this spontaneous action might occur.

Adamant pro-slavery southerners scorned this belief held by Rives and many others that slavery would gradually disappear. Their attempts to solidify and expand slaveholding power helped turn northern public opinion against them. Southern slaveholder demands increased to a point that caused many northerners to view slavery in the South no longer as merely unfortunate, but as intolerable. [23]

Rives initially supported annexation of Texas because he thought it could absorb Virginia's slave population, "facilitating the gradual transfer of our black population further south, & filling their places with the free white population of the north, who will come among us in ten-fold numbers, as soon as the process commences."[24] Rives opposed the Mexican War when he believed its aim was conquest of territory inhabited by racially inferior "mixed and degenerate castes" of Mexicans who might be brought into the U.S. He did not consider Mexicans or blacks as worthy of U.S. citizenship.[25] Unabashed believers in their own superiority, Rives and Judith looked down on a large proportion of white citizens as well. In her autobiography Judith wrote, "Nobody believed the doctrine that 'all men were born free and equal,' though it was repeated everywhere every Fourth of July, nor that even if born free and equal, they could ever remain so."[26]

Edward Coles, like Rives, a native of central Virginia and a protégé of Madison, took the bold step of transporting his slaves to Illinois and granting them their freedom in 1819.[27] Despite Coles' pleas to them, Jefferson and Madison declined to follow his example. Rives freed a small number of his slaves, including two "most important household servants" and sent them to Liberia in 1856.[28] A few years later, Judith was amused by a newspaper article describing how former Virginia slaves in Liberia were described as haughty, considering themselves "the quality" of their new country.[29]

However, Rives sold a greater number than he liberated, including 114 individuals purchased from him in 1860 by Virginia Senator James M. Mason and Congressman James A. Seddon for $70,000.[30] Rives was not inclined to write off that amount of money by freeing the entire group. The 1850 census listed the value of his total real estate at $50,000.[31] Gross annual receipts from all of his farms were between $9,000 and $10,000.[32] Human property was the second most valuable asset in the U.S. in 1860, worth approximately three times the amount invested in manufacturing or railroads in the entire nation. The only asset more valuable than slaves was land.[33] An inventory of Judith's father Francis Walker's estate in 1812 listed 113 slaves appraised at $23,805, out of total property worth $29,670.54.[34]

At Castle Hill, the slaves who waited on the family lived in small wooden dwellings on the western side of the main house. Those who worked on the farm and in the fields lived in more distant log cabins along the base of Walnut Mountain which provided firewood and spring water. Rives' son Will wrote that female slaves toted water from the spring in pails balanced atop their heads, which imparted "erectness and grace to many of the young negro women." Each cabin had its own garden, chicken coop and pigsty. Will claimed that because Castle Hill slaves did not have to pay rent to a landowner, they were better off than European tenant farmers. He described idealized rustic existence in the cabins, the inhabitants relaxing by the fireplace, dining on plentiful bacon, cornbread and buttermilk.[35] Comfort and visual appeal of the slave dwellings was likely a matter of opinion and cultural perspective. A visitor to Monticello during Jefferson's later years wrote that slave cabins there would seem "poor and uncomfortable" only to people with "northern feelings."[36]

When Judith read *Uncle Tom's Cabin*, she wrote her sister that she admired Harriet Beecher Stowe's talent. "The dreadful part it is to be hoped is not of every day occurrence but it is fearful to think that there are such abominations in our land, as I have too often heard from credible sources to doubt."[37] Judith had little reason to dissemble to her sister and probably believed the dreadful did not occur every day at Castle Hill. However, the institution of slavery depended on threatened and actual violence.[38] Judith was delighted that Harriet Beecher Stowe was an advocate of colonization in Africa, "the only reasonable solution of this vexed and troublesome question."[39]

Judith published a less sensational novel in 1857, *Home and the World*, which included scenes from Castle Hill and her European travels. Characters included an "Uncle Tom," based on a Castle Hill slave named Thomas Wilkes who was born at Castle Hill about 1770.[40] In the book, Uncle Tom's wife Betty claimed that she and Tom were better off as slaves than they would be if they were free.[41] Judith may have heard some of her slaves make this claim, and she may have believed it. The story also included a "Mammy," whose "head was wreathed *à la créole* with a Madras kerchief of delicate but varied colors arranged with a degree of skill that a Parisian coiffeur might have envied."[42] Judith had grown weary of the notoriety of "the solemn and awful and lachrymose" *Uncle Tom's Cabin*. She wrote her son Will that her purpose in writing her book was not to counteract Mrs. Stowe, "Truth itself, if portrayed by my humble pen would avail little in opposition to the gloomy fiction so powerfully painted."[43]

Judith described the death of Castle Hill's real life Mammy in an 1856 letter to her son Alfred. As Mammy lay dying,

> . . . she was sufficiently conscious to join in the prayers of High at her bed side, and to express to me her firm faith in a saviour's love and pardon. Every mark

of respect was shown to this good and faithful servant, who I trust, has entered into joy of her Lord. Mr.
Boyden performed the service, and we attended with
the people of the neighboring farms and our own.[44]

Historian Eugene D. Genovese in *Roll Jordan Roll* commented
that Mammies were separated from other blacks and appropri-
ated for white families for raising children and managing the
household. He wrote that the service for the Rives' Mammy was
for whites, and criticized the Rives because they apparently did
not consider whether Mammy's relatives might have preferred a
service conducted by a black preacher.[45] The white preacher Mr.
Boyden may have presided, but when Judith used the word people, she meant slaves, indicating majority black attendance at the
service. While some slaves may have resented Mr. Boyden's presence, it was likely that many at the service accepted his preaching
as the mark of respect and honor Judith intended it to be.

In another letter to Alfred, also cited by Genovese, Judith
described the marriage of an 18-year-old slave named Pauline.
The Castle Hill kitchen and washhouse were decorated and lit
up for the reception of Pauline's numerous relatives and guests.
Expecting clumsy caricature of white wedding ritual, Judith was
impressed when "the imitation of a fashionable bridal was really
so perfect that it ceased to be ridiculous." Both males and females
had somehow found or made handsome clothes. The bride wore
a veil, and "to our surprise the ebony minister drew from his
pocket an Episcopal prayer book."[46]

Though benevolent slave ownership may have been an impossible contradiction, the Rives perceived themselves as benevolent
owners. Judith wrote her son Will, "we can only do our best with
the poor people by whom we are surrounded, leaving the rest
to Providence, which over-rules all."[47] Judith wrote her husband
from Oak Ridge in 1832 that "the old servants literally took me

in their arms and blessed me." An old slave, also named Judith, "said in a tone of triumph while talking about you, 'I raised Mas' William! God Bless him! I raised him!'"[48] Rives paid a Nelson County planter $1,400 to take two aged slaves named Dangerfield and Libby, to provide for them for the rest of their lives.[49] This payment for their welfare followed the large 1860 sale that may have included Dangerfield and Libby's children and grandchildren. When the Rives returned from their second sojourn in France in 1853, the Castle Hill slaves turned out to welcome them. Judith reported that "Old Mike took both his [Rives] hands in his own rough ones and fervently blessed Almighty God for seeing Master once more in this life."[50] Three slaves had accompanied the Rives to France, a coachman, a footman, and a maid. Rives told them that they were free as soon as they reached France, and was reassured when they returned to Castle Hill instead of remaining abroad.[51]

Francis R. Rives wrote his mother in 1856 that he had determined how to reduce the average cost of shoeing and clothing "our people" to $7.55 & 5/8 cents per head. "I have no doubt that the giving of an extra under-garment to the adults in summer would promote their cleanliness & health as you suggested in a former letter."[52] Economizing was apparently a greater consideration than cleanliness and health.

Rives had declared in the Senate in 1845 that he was a slaveholder more "from considerations of humanity than of interest." However, slavery was an economically beneficial arrangement for him, especially the $70,000 sale. Though he had criticized the institution as a younger man, and had favorably considered Randolph's 1831 emancipation scheme, Rives expressed harsher views on race and slavery as he aged. At the February 1861 Peace Convention, Rives sounded like Calhoun when he contended that the "very best position for the African race to occupy is one of unmitigated legal subjection."[53] He had apparently descended from the middle ground between Calhoun and Webster to a more harsh pro-slavery position. The tide of history was moving in the opposite direction, toward the termination of slavery. Rives served in the Congress of the Confederacy, whose Constitution (Article I, Section 9, and Article IV, Section 2) expressly endorsed the right to own slaves.[54] Slavery was an inescapable feature of the political, economic and social organization of Rives' central Virginia community. Even non-slaveholding white Virginians were still vested in the institution. Non-slave-owning farmers could lease slaves, and many aspired to the wealth and status of slave ownership. From a twenty-first century perspective, Rives' inability to remedy the problem of slavery, which he admitted was evil, and which contradicted the founders' ideals, was his greatest failure. Slavery was also a national failure, which would generate increasing conflict, dis-union and war.

✶ ✶ ✶

1 WCR, Jr., Biography, Rives MSS, LOC, box 103, 105.

2 Inventory of the Estate of Robert Rives, Nelson County Will Book G, 123-139.

3 Ibid, 401-412.

4 Albemarle County Will Book 18, 308.

5 Robert Rives to Rives, January 15, 1831, June 6, 1831, January 31, 1832; Rives MSS, LOC, box 22.

6 Bills of Sale issued to Peter Carr for the purchase of enslaved persons by Brown, Rives, & Co. of Milton, 1801-1810, Virginia Historical Society Mss2C2308b (James Brown of Richmond and Robert Rives' partnership lasted from 1790 to 1813, Cabells and Their Kin 240-242) *Cabells and Their Kin* does not mention Brown & Rives' involvement in the slave trade.

7 William M. Rives to Rives, September 22, 1831, Rives MSS, LOC, box 22.

8 Rives to T. W. Gilmer, October 29, 1831, Rives MSS, LOC quoted in Raymond C. Dingledine, Jr., "The Education of a Virginia Planter's Son,"

America The Middle Period Essays in Honor of Bernard Mayo, edited by John B. Boles, Charlottesville, University Press of Virginia, 1973, 228.

9 Rives to Robert Rives, May 19, 1832, Rives MSS, LOC, quoted in Dingledine, Ibid.

10 Clay expressed opposition to the institution of slavery although he was a slaveowner.

11 Mary Carmichael, "Louis Agassiz Exhibit Divides Harvard, Swiss Group," *Boston Globe*, June 27, 2012. Christopher Irmscher, *Louis Agassiz*, Houghton Mifflin Harcourt, 2013, reviewed in *The New Yorker*, March 11, 2013, page 75.

12 See Drew R. McCoy, *The Last of the Fathers*, New York, Cambridge University Press, 1989, 253-322 "Despair: The Peculiar Institution."

13 Rives to Earl Grey, August 24, 1850, Mary Elizabeth Thomas, editor, "William Cabell Rives and the British Abolitionists," *Virginia Magazine of History and Biography*, Vol. 89, No. 1, January, 1981, 64-66.

14 Gales & Seaton's Register of Debates, 24th Congress, 2nd session, 706.

15 Ibid, 722.

16 Madison biographer Drew McCoy calls this argument, made by other Virginians, "venerable Madisonian fiction." McCoy, Ibid, 354.

17 Washington freed his slaves in his will. See Henry Wiencek, *An Imperfect God, George Washington, His Slaves, and the Creation of America*, New York, Farrar Straus and Giroux, 2003. Rives mentioned in his speech anti-slavery passages from Jefferson's *Notes on the State of Virginia*, which is a problematic text. Although the book contains the passage about the consequences of slavery: "I tremble for my country when I reflect that God is just: that his justice cannot sleep for ever," *Notes* also contains extreme assertions of black racial inferiority, and Henry Wiencek calls the book "the Dismal Swamp that every Jefferson biographer must sooner or later attempt to cross." Henry Wiencek, *Master of the Mountain, Thomas Jefferson and His Slaves*, New York, Farrar, Straus and Giroux, 2012, 60, 43.

18 Register of Debates, Ibid, 722.

19 George Lockhart Rives, *The United States and Mexico*, Vol. I, New York, Charles Scribner's Sons, 1913, 414.

20 Register of Debates, Ibid, 720.

21 Ebenezer Boyden, "The Epidemic of the Nineteenth Century," University of Virginia Special Collections, E449.B79, 1860.

22 Rives to Robert C. Winthrop, March 5, 1857, Winthrop Papers, Massachusetts Historical Society, quoted in McCoy, Ibid, 355.

23 see William W. Freehling, *The Road to Disunion, Vol. I: Secessionists at Bay, 1776-1854*, viii.

24 Rives to Judith Page Rives, April 3, 1844, Rives MSS, LOC, box 26, quoted in McCoy, Ibid, 357.

25 William C. Rives "Draft of an Address for the Whig Convention of Virginia in 1847-1848," Rives MSS, LOC, box 120, quoted in McCoy, ibid, 358.

26 Judith Page Rives, Autobiography, 59-60.

27 Despite his dramatic gesture and his work to prevent Illinois from becoming a slave state, Coles was in favor of colonization, because he felt black people would never be fairly treated in the U.S. McCoy, Ibid. 315-317.

28 Judith Page Rives to William C. Rives, Jr. November 30, 1856, Rives MSS, LOC, box 34. The number sent to Liberia seems to be fewer than 10. The number of slaves on Castle Hill remained around 50, according to tax and census forms of the 1850s and 60s.

29 Judith Page Rives to William C. Rives, Jr., December 26, 1858, Rives MSS, LOC, box 35.

30 Account Book, Ibid, box 122, Seddon was married to a Cabell cousin of Rives & was later Confederate Secretary of War. Mason became famous in the "Trent Affair," when he and fellow Confederate diplomat John Slidell were taken from the British vessel Trent by US forces in 1861. Seddon owned plantations in Mississippi and Louisiana and presumably his share of the slaves purchased was sent there. See Gerard O'Brien, "James A. Seddon, Prototype of the Old South," University of Maryland Master's Thesis, 1960, 83, Seddon Papers, Special Collections Department, University of Virginia Library, Accession # MSS 14847.

31 Newton Bond Jones, "Charlottesville and Albemarle County 1819-1860." University of Virginia dissertation, 1950, 228.

32 Memorandum Book entry December 8, 1856, Rives MSS, LOC, box 122.

33 Wiencek, Ibid, 9, Wiencek cites David Brion Davis, *The Problem of Slavery in the Age of Revolution 1770-1823*, Ithaca, N.Y., Cornell University Press, 1975, pp. 174, 179.

34 Albemarle County Will Book 5, 207.

35 WCR, Jr., Ibid, 83-85.

36 Wiencek, ibid, 20. Wiencek cites a friend of Jefferson whose description appeared in the *Richmond Enquirer*.

37 Judith Page Rives to Jane Frances Page, June 23, 1852, Papers of the Walker and Page Families, University of Virginia Library, Special Collections Department, Accession #3098, Box 2.

38 See *Weevils in the Wheat: Interviews with Virginia Ex-Slaves*, edited by Charles L. Perdue, Jr., Thomas E. Barden, Robert K. Phillips, Charlottesville, 1976, University of Virginia Press. Most of the scores of accounts include incidents of brutality and humiliation.

39 Judith Page Rives to Jane Frances Page, June 23, 1852, Ibid.

40 Richard Channing Moore Page, *Genealogy of the Page Family in Virginia*, Second Edition, 1893, Reprinted, Harrisonburg, Virginia, C. J. Carrier Company, 1972, 216.

41 Judith Page Rives, *Home and the World*, New York, D. Appleton & Co. 1857, 27.

42 Ibid, 37.

43 Judith Page Rives to William C. Rives, Jr. December 18, 1856 Rives MSS, LOC, box 34.

44 Judith Page Rives to Alfred Landon Rives, December 5, 1856, A. L. Rives Papers, Duke University, quoted in Eugene D. Genovese, *Roll Jordan Roll, The World the Slaves Made*, New York, Vintage Books, a division of Random House, 1976, 196.

45 Ibid.

46 Judith Page Rives to Alfred Landon Rives, January 17, 1858, A. L. Rives Papers, Duke University, quoted in Genovese, Ibid, 480.

47 Judith Page Rives to William C. Rives, Jr., Feb. 1, 1858, Rives MSS, LOC, box 35.

48 Judith Page Rives to Rives, December 27, 1832, Ibid, box 22.

49 William C. Rives receipt from J. Bruce McClelland November 20, 1860 for $1,400, with engagement to support Dangerfield & Libby, Rives MSS, UVa., Accession #2313, box 2.

McClelland was apparently an agent in the Mason/Seddon transaction, which involved slaves from both Rives' Nelson and Albemarle farms as well as slaves belonging to William C. Rives, Jr. In a letter to McClelland, Mason suggested Dangerfield and Libby "should be kept in their own section of the country." Mason also noted his intention to "obtain the husbands of the married women who are scattered around to prevent separations in the families as far as possible." James M. Mason to J. B. McClelland, September 1, 1860, Rives MSS, LOC, box 91.

50 William C. Rives, Jr. biography, Ibid, 128.

51 Margaret Rives King, *Ancestors and Ancestral Homes*, Cincinnati, Robert Clarke & Co., 1890, 23-24.

52 Francis R. Rives to Judith Page Rives, April 26, 1856, Rives MSS, LOC, box 34.

53 Rives speech at the Peace Convention, as reported by Lucius E. Chittenden, *A Report of the Debates and Proceedings in the Secret Sessions of the Conference Convention*, New York, D. Appleton & Company, 1864, 139.

54 *The Confederacy*, edited by Albert Kirwan, New York, Meridian Books, 1965, 30-31.

CHAPTER SIXTEEN

Nestor in Politics

THE *NATIONAL INTELLIGENCER* in February 1846 published a letter from Rives expressing his fear that the Oregon
boundary dispute might lead to war with Great Britain. Rives
criticized aggressive statements by Secretary of State Buchanan,
and said war would greatly harm U.S. interests. Although "withdrawn entirely from political pursuits and without the slightest
desire again to engage in them, I have, nonetheless as a good
citizen, not been able to steel myself into indifference to what
so nearly concerns the interests and happiness of our common
country. . . ." Senator John J. Crittenden of Kentucky expressed
his agreement in a subsequent issue of the paper.[1] Despite his
claim, Rives never became withdrawn entirely from politics. He
no longer held political office, but he continued to participate
in national political dialogue. In newspapers as well as letters
to past and present leaders, he advocated government under
the Constitution, according to the principles of Madison and
Jefferson. Comparing him to the old wise ancient Greek King,
Historian Beckles Willson characterized him as "the Nestor
in politics of his native State."[2] Despite Polk's campaign slogan
"Fifty-four forty or fight," the Oregon dispute was peacefully settled. Both sides accepted the 49th parallel as the northwestern
U.S. and Canadian border.

In early 1847, a group of citizens from Bedford County, south
of Nelson and Albemarle, encouraged Rives to stand for election
as their Congressman. He declined.[3]

Rives served on the University of Virginia Board of Visitors. When Jefferson founded the University, he devised its governance by distinguished individuals who would meet to select professors and prescribe rules for discipline.[4] Rives was first appointed in 1828, but relinquished the position in 1829 when he left for France. He was re-appointed in 1834, and served until 1849. James Madison was Rector of the Board and James Monroe was a fellow member in 1828. At a July meeting that year the Board ordered that a bell should be rung every morning at dawn. Students were expected to rise immediately, dress themselves, and tidy their rooms for inspection by a Proctor. When the bell rang at 10:00 pm, students were required to extinguish all lighting, retire to bed, and maintain "perfect quiet."[5] The 10:00 curfew was rescinded the following October, when the Board outlawed backgammon and other games of chance.[6] The Board in 1837 prohibited keeping and raising hogs on University grounds. It prescribed a student uniform of dark grey coat and matching trousers. The Board also attempted to keep students away from retailers of "spirituous, vinous, or fermented liquors."[7]

All three of Rives' sons attended the University of Virginia. In 1843, his second son Will sent him an apologetic note, explaining that his debating society had served "wine and cakes of which with a few others I slightly partook." This was a violation of rules against "any festive entertainment given by any student within the precincts of the University." Will assured his father that only one student had become intoxicated (not himself); however, the Faculty reprimanded all members of the society. Will closed his note with a plea to conceal the painful news from "Mamma" and the neighbors.[8]

Will was not able to conceal later difficulty with University authority. Disorderly conduct had been a problem since the school's founding. Students rioted several nights in April 1845, breaking windows of faculty homes, shooting pistols, riding horses through Jeffersonian arcades, and breaking into the Rotunda. The faculty appealed to the sheriff and justices of the peace, who convened a county court and summoned a militia force of 200. Although he had not been one of the rioters, Will resented the troops. His uncle Alexander Rives, later to become Rector, and his father also felt the troops were unnecessary. Along with many of his fellow students, Will decided to resign.[9]

He transferred to Harvard, traveling to Cambridge with his parents in the fall of 1845.[10] The senior Rives was reportedly an "honored guest of Harvard alumni" in 1845, although he received no formal award.[11] Harvard considered Rives and William H. Seward among possible recipients for honorary LL.D. degrees in 1860, but neither made the final list.[12] Rives did receive LL.D. degrees from Hampden Sydney and Brown in 1845.[13] William C. Rives, Jr. received a Harvard Bachelor of Laws degree in 1847. He married, in 1849, Grace Winthrop Sears, who was the daughter of family friend David Sears, prominent Boston businessman and philanthropist.

Back in Charlottesville, Rives told his fellow Board members that the University needed a president to supervise and enforce discipline.[14] The University did not heed his suggestion until 1904, when it installed its first president.

Rives was named President of the Virginia Historical Society in 1847. The Society was founded in 1831. James Madison was its first honorary member, and John Marshall was its first President. Although not involved in its daily activities, Rives provided strong leadership, which revived the society after years of decline. In 1848, Rives convened the first annual meeting of the society in several years. He announced that the spirit of activity that had awakened the society was hoped to be an omen of "a better day about to dawn upon our ancient commonwealth."[15] His political and social ties were useful to the society.[16] Rives presented the society with a specially commissioned portrait of Benjamin Franklin, a copy by Parisian artist Louis Mathieu Didier Guillaume of an original by Jean Baptiste Greuze.[17]

Rives delivered a number of historical lectures which were subsequently published, including a "Discourse on the character and services of John Hampden . . ." and "Discourse on the Uses and Importance of History . . ." The first was delivered at Hampden Sydney College at the time he received his honorary doctorate of laws, and described one of its English namesakes. Hampden fought against abuses of power by Charles I. Rives argued he would have been the "George Washington of his country," a more wise and just ruler than Cromwell, had he not been killed in 1643.[18] The second lecture, delivered to University of Virginia alumni, was a comparison of the American and French Revolutions. Consistent with his conservatism, Rives argued that the American Revolution was more successful because its leaders followed lessons of the past whereas the French had tried to implement a new philosophy.[19]

Rives considered Virginia's future as well as its past. He sought advice from former Massachusetts Congressman Abbott Lawrence (1792-1855) on how to promote manufacturing in Virginia. Lawrence's 1846 letters to Rives were published in the *Richmond Whig* and separately printed for publication in Boston. Lawrence pointed out that Virginia should have been enjoying greater prosperity as she was blessed with excellent soil, plentiful waterpower and mineral wealth. Because other states were competing with Virginia's agriculture, manufacturing was essential for strengthening the state's economy. Lawrence advocated better education to elevate "less favored classes," even if this required raising taxes. Lawrence also advocated use of tariffs for developing industry and agriculture. The *Richmond Whig* saluted Lawrence as "truly national in his views and a true friend of the south." In published letters disputing Lawrence's advice and views,

Massachusetts merchant Samuel Dexter Bradford (1795-1865) feared southern manufacturing might compete with northern interests, and he opposed all tariffs.[20]

Closer to home, Judith led efforts to construct a stone English Gothic-style church to replace a wooden colonial structure. Though Rives served on the male-only committee nominally in charge, Judith was the one who recruited architect William Strickland, secured advice from General J. H. Cocke about stone masonry and laborers, and solicited funds from donors large and small. Judith proclaimed, "The house of God should be the best and most costly edifice in the parish."[21] Stone was first quarried in 1846, and walls rose steadily until the Rives left for France in 1849. Construction halted until the Rives returned in 1853. The church was consecrated May 9, 1855.

Rives took an active interest in the 1848 presidential campaign. Virginia Whig Congressman William Ballard Preston (1805-1862) wrote Rives in 1847 that Zachary Taylor was the best candidate. Preston considered Polk's conduct reckless, both on the Oregon dispute as well as the Mexican War. However, Polk chose not to run for re-election. Preston pronounced the slavery question most important, and said General Taylor was not embarrassed by it. Taylor could avoid alarming or exciting either section of the country. Preston pronounced Taylor the only southern candidate with hope of success.[22]

Rives agreed with Preston, and delivered a vigorous speech in Charlottesville in support of Taylor that was reprinted in the *Richmond Whig*. Rives was pleased to note that Taylor had not actively sought the Presidency. Rives declared Taylor was a Republican of the old school of Jefferson and Madison. The Democratic Party had nominated General Lewis Cass of Michigan. Rives opposed Cass because Cass advocated more territorial expansion. General Cass "has such an opinion of the American Anaconda powers of deglutition that he declared in the Senate we could swallow all Mexico without its hurting us." He also "plainly indicated that we must make a meal too, of all the British possessions in North America." Cass had declared in the Senate that, "War with England was inevitable." Rives advised his listeners to heed the example of Rome whose excessive foreign conquests sealed her fate. "My political career is ended, but I desire Virginia to take the side of liberty and popular rights. . . . The bitterness and delusions of party spirit are, I trust, passing away." Rives exhorted Virginia to be the foremost to salute the name of Taylor as the national deliverer.[23] Rives' prophecy that party bitterness was passing away proved to be wishful thinking. Also questionable was Rives' desire to bestow the Jefferson and Madison mantle upon Taylor and Fillmore.

Rives sent Taylor a copy of his speech with a letter congratulating him on his nomination. Rives insisted that the Whigs were the true representatives of Jefferson and Madison, and that Taylor would lead a "renewed ascendancy" of the old values. Taylor replied to Rives that they agreed on most subjects, including veto power (both felt it should be used seldom as possible). However, Taylor cautioned Rives against being "too sanguine in your expectations as to the benefit to be derived by the country from my elevation to the Presidency," because the President needed to be aided and sustained by the voice of the people and the various branches of government.[24]

Rives also wrote Taylor's Vice-Presidential running mate Millard Fillmore about his views on slavery. Fillmore replied that a letter, which he had written October 17, 1838, had been misinterpreted. Southerners were accusing Fillmore of claiming Congress had the Constitutional power to abolish the slave trade. Fillmore wrote Rives that he had never expressed such an opinion. He hoped that his five years in Congress would be sufficient evidence to the South that he was not hostile to their interests and that he would not do anything unjust or unconstitutional against them. Fillmore expressed distaste for writing anything for publication, and the letter was marked "Private."[25]

The 1848 campaign also included candidates from a third party, the Free Soil Party. Its platform proposed no interference with slavery in states where it existed, but maintained slavery should be forbidden in the territories. The Free Soilers endorsed the Wilmot Proviso, a law proposed by Pennsylvania Congressman David Wilmot in 1846 at the start of the Mexican War. The Proviso, passed by the House but not by the Senate, prohibited slavery in any territory acquired from Mexico. Free Soil delegates from 18 States met in Buffalo to nominate Martin Van Buren for President along with Charles Francis Adams for Vice President.

General Cass had suggested that actual residents of the territories might decide whether to allow slavery on their soil, which was designated "squatter sovereignty," and later renamed "popular sovereignty." However, Rives criticized Cass in a speech in Richmond for not promising to veto the Wilmot Proviso. Taylor was not a politician, and said little to encourage or enrage those on either side of the slavery debate. He was known for winning the Battle of Buena Vista February 23, 1847. Taylor won a close election. Van Buren did not win any states, but may have pulled enough votes from Cass to deliver the election to Taylor. Ten Free Soil candidates were elected to Congress.[26]

William Ballard Preston wrote Rives in December 1848 congratulating him on Taylor's victory. He said he and other Virginia Whigs, including fellow Congressman Thomas S. Flournoy, were hoping that Rives would be named Secretary of State.[27] This was Rives' third close call with the office. Van Buren said he would have offered the post to Rives in 1836, if Jackson's appointee had stepped down. Harrison told Rives he wanted to appoint him, but could not because of jealous Whigs. Taylor appointed Rives Minister to France, for which he possessed proven qualifications. Rives' name would reappear in future Secretary of State rumors.

The Rives prepared to return to Paris with four of their five grown children.

✳ ✳ ✳

1 *National Intelligencer*, Vol. XXXIV, Feb. 11, 1846, reprinted in letterbook, Rives MSS, LOC, Box 105.

2 Beckles Willson, *America's Ambassadors to France (1777-1927)*, London, John Murray, 1928, 254.

3 letterbook, Ibid.

4 Philip Alexander Bruce, *History of the University of Virginia 1819-1919*, Vol. I, New York, The MacMillan Company, 1920, 77.

5 Transcripts of the Minutes of the Board of Visitors, Box 1, 1817-1855, University of Virginia Manuscripts Reading Room, 199-201.

6 Ibid, 200-206.

7 Ibid, 391-395.

8 William C. Rives, Jr. to Rives, January 13, 1843, Rives MSS, UVa., Accession #2313, box 1.

9 Raymond C. Dingledine, Jr., "The Education of a Virginia Planter's Son," Chapter 12 in *America The Middle Period*, Essays in Honor of Bernard Mayo, Charlottesville, University Press of Virginia, 1973, 218.

10 Ibid, 220.

11 WCR, Jr., biography, Rives MSS, LOC, box 103, 105.

12 Harvard University Archives, Pusey Library, UAI 5.130, Corporation Papers, 2nd Series, Box 11, 1860, (Thanks to Robin Carlaw, researcher) Also *Quinquennial Catalogue of the Officers and Graduates of Harvard University 1636-1915* Cambridge, Harvard University Press, 1915, 831-832.

13 WCR, Jr., biography, Ibid, 108, verified by Gayle D. Lynch and Raymond Butti of Brown University Archives and Dr. William E. Thompson, Hampden Sydney Historian.

14 Transcripts of the Minutes of the Board of Visitors, Ibid, January 20, 1846, 492-493.

15 Melvin I Urofsky, "The Virginia Historical Society: The First 175 Years 1831-2006," *Virginia Magazine of History and Biography*, Vol. 114, No. 1, Richmond, Virginia Historical Society, 2006, 40-42.

16 Ibid, 45.

17 William Cabell Rives, "Letter in Regard to a Portrait of Franklin," *Virginia Magazine of History and Biography*, v. 40, 1932, 77-78. The portrait survived the Civil War and remains a part of the VHS collection. (Thanks to Heather Beattie, Museum Collections Manager, Virginia Historical Society).

18 William C. Rives, "Discourse on the character and services of John Hampden and the great struggle for popular and Constitutional liberty in his time," Delivered before the trustees, faculty, and students of Hampden Sydney College, Nov. 12, 1845, Richmond, printed by Shepherd and Colin, 1847.

19 William C. Rives, "Discourse on the Uses and Importance of History, Illustrated by a comparison of the American and French revolutions," delivered June 29, 1847, in appendix of "Proceedings of the Society of Alumni of the University of Virginia," June 1847, Richmond, Shepherd and Colin, 1847.

20 "Letters of S. D. Bradford to Hon. Abbott Lawrence in reply to those addressed by Mr. Lawrence to Hon. William C. Rives of Virginia," published in *Boston Post*, February 17, 18, 19, 1846, Boston, Beals and Greene, 1846 (Lawrence's letters as well as the Richmond Whig comments are included in this pamphlet).

21 Judith Page Rives, Pamphlet about construction of new church, Rives MSS, UVa. Accession # 2313 box 7.

22 William Ballard Preston to Rives, February 28, 1847, Letterbook, Rives MSS, LOC, box 20, 252-255, Preston was appointed Navy Secretary by Taylor. He later served in the Confederate Senate.

23 Rives speech, July 3, 1848, Albemarle Ratification Meeting, reprinted *Richmond Whig*, July 14, 1848, also in Letterbook, Rives MSS, LOC, box 105, 98.

24 Rives to Zachary Taylor, July 11, 1848, and Taylor to Rives, July 26, 1848, letterbook, Ibid, 94, 97.

25 Millard Fillmore to Rives, September 16, 1848, Ibid, 91.

26 Current, Williams, Friedel, Brownlee, *The Essentials of American History*, Third Edition, New York, Alfred a. Knopf, 1976, 156.

27 Preston, Fluornoy, Pendleton and other Whigs to Rives, December 1848, letterbook, Rives MSS, LOC box 105, 105.

CHAPTER SEVENTEEN

Paris Encore

THE RIVES SAILED August 22, 1849 on the RMS *America*, a Cunard mail and passenger steamship. Steam power shortened the crossing time to twelve days, which was a great relief to the chronically seasick Judith. The Rives' oldest son Francis remained in New York practicing law, having married Miss Matilda Barclay there in 1848. The other four children came along: Ella, Amélie, Alfred, Will, and his wife Grace. Judith wrote Grace that on the *America*, "the comfort of the ladies is assiduously sought by the stewardess, Mrs. Macbeth, who, notwithstanding her formidable name, is a very nice and efficient person."[1]

Secretary of State John M. Clayton had instructed Rives to go first to London and meet with British Foreign Secretary Lord Palmerston. The U.S. was interested in building a canal through Nicaragua. Apparently seeking to prevent this, Great Britain had been building forts and backing claims by the Mosquito Indians to the San Juan River in opposition to the government of Nicaragua. Rives sent a lengthy dispatch to Clayton September 25, claiming Palmerston gave him "a very cordial reception" and listened "with marked and earnest attention." Rives told Palmerston of U.S. desire to construct a canal, and that it viewed British activities in the San Juan with suspicion. Palmerston replied that Great Britain considered the Mosquito Indians as a separate nation from Nicaragua. However, Palmerston declared Britain did not wish to plant a new colony in Central America. He said it had plenty of colonies already. Great Britain did not wish to see U.S. monopoly of a canal between the Atlantic and

Pacific. Nevertheless, Palmerston assured Rives that if the U.S. would open a canal as a common highway for the use and benefit of all nations, it would receive "favorable consideration of Her Britannic Majesty's government." Rives reported that the lengthy interview was conducted "in that spirit of frankness which ought to characterize the intercourse of two such nations."[2]

This conversation between the two statesmen was a preliminary to the Clayton-Bulwer Treaty, which was signed April 19, 1850. The treaty established a joint Anglo-American protectorate over any ship canal through Central America. Both sides agreed not to seek exclusive control of a canal or the territory on either side of it.[3]

The Rives arrived in Paris in late October and took up residence at 30 Rue de la Ville Évêque. Rives faced an immediate diplomatic crisis. A U.S. Navy steamer *Iris* had rescued a French sailing vessel *Eugenie*, which had run aground off of Rojo, Mexico. The commander of the American vessel believed the French owed him compensation for his services, and briefly detained the *Eugenie* when his claim was denied. The French commander's howls of outrage reached Poussin, the French Minister in Washington, who wrote Secretary of State Clayton an arrogant letter of protest. Clayton wrote Poussin, inviting him to come explain his letter. Clayton also wrote about the situation to the French Foreign Minister Alexis de Tocqueville, author of *Democracy in America*, with whom he was personally acquainted.

Louis Napoleon, nephew of Napoleon I, had been elected President of the French Second Republic December 10, 1848. A February 1848 revolution had ousted King Louis Philippe. Louis Napoleon was shocked at the diplomatic irregularity of Clayton's writing directly to de Tocqueville. Wounded French dignity prevented him from receiving the new American Minister. Rives suggested that de Tocqueville meet him informally, to which the Foreign Minister agreed. The Frenchman explained his two grievances: Clayton's treatment of Poussin, and Clayton's writing to him personally rather than communicating through the U.S. Minister. Rives replied soothingly that Clayton had not summoned, but rather invited Poussin to come to Washington to explain matters. He assured de Tocqueville that Clayton had written directly to him because he feared Rives would be detained in London and that his predecessor Richard Rush would have already left Paris. De Tocqueville accepted the explanation and recalled Poussin. Louis Napoleon received Minister Rives November 8, and told him that such a diplomatic breach was more easily repaired in a Republic than under a monarchy. Clayton intended to publish his correspondence with de Tocqueville, but Rives convinced him that would cause further damage.[4]

Zachary Taylor died July 9, 1850. The new President Millard Fillmore named Daniel Webster Secretary of State. Rives wrote Webster about how the U.S. underpaid its Ministers in London and Paris. Expenditures were greater than remuneration, creating hardship for any American Minister who did not possess a large private fortune. Rives' salary in 1850 was $9,000. Rives calculated that annual food costs were $8,000; servants cost $3,000; carriage hire cost $1,200; house rental cost $3,000, and personal expenses cost $3,000. The British representative in Paris was much better compensated, and was furnished with a suitable residence. Unfortunately, Congress did not sympathize.[5] Rives had to borrow thousands of dollars to meet his Paris expenses.[6]

Alfred was enrolled in the prestigious *École des Ponts et Chaussées*, where he received advanced training as an engineer. He graduated in 1854 with the extra distinction of *brillamment*.[7] Fifteen-year-old Ella was devoted to her studies, but seventeen-year-old Amélie led a more active social life. She accompanied her parents to the opera, the ballet, a tour of Versailles, races at Longchamps, a costume ball given by Princess de Wagram, and dinner parties hosted by Baron James Rothschild.[8] When the Rives toured Switzerland, after seeing points of interest in Belgium, Germany, and Italy, Amélie met a "handsome young officer." This English Captain "had the most provokingly black hair and moustache, and really knew how to tie his cravat." He also waltzed "to perfection." Though the evidence is far from conclusive, Amélie's Captain, unnamed in her letters, may have been Edward Nolan, who died leading the Charge of the Light Brigade in the Crimean War.[9]

A former artillery general, Lahitte, replaced de Tocqueville as Foreign Minister. In a speech to the Chamber of Deputies, Lahitte criticized some American laws as "barbarous and savage." He expressed hope that France and England could persuade the United States that it was "out of the pale of the laws of nations." Lahitte was probably referring to the Fugitive Slave Act, part of the U.S. Compromise of 1850, which denied rights of blacks accused of being runaway slaves. When he read the speech, Rives called on the Minister at once. He told Lahitte his remarks were offensive and insulting. As a leading member of the French government, was he trying to provoke the United States? Rives countered Lahitte's accusations with specific cases of French legal misconduct. Lahitte promptly apologized. He claimed he had gotten carried away while addressing the assembly of his countrymen, and regretted any affront to America.[10]

Rives had noted rumors of Royalist and Imperialist plots since his arrival in 1849. President Louis Napoleon staged a *coup d'état* December 2, 1851. He later declared himself Emperor Napoleon III. Rives wrote in a dispatch to Webster, "The dénoument towards which events have been rapidly tending for some weeks past was brought upon Paris yesterday morning." Louis Napoleon dissolved the National Assembly and Council of State and proclaimed martial law. He had prominent legislators and journalists arrested, and he dissolved the courts. Paris was put under a state of siege. Rives reported that soldiers maintained the upper hand in street fighting, and cleared citizen-erected barricades.

Without waiting for direction from Webster, Rives did not attend the usual weekly receptions given by the President. He wrote that as the representative of a free Constitutional Republic, he should not appear to support Louis Napoleon's illegal actions. "In pursuing this course, I have taken counsel, not merely of the feelings and sentiments natural to the bosom of an American citizen under such circumstances, but also of those higher considerations of principle and duty which should control the conduct of a public agent."[11]

Louis Napoleon submitted his actions to a French vote of confidence, whose results were overwhelmingly in his favor. Once the nation had declared its support for Louis Napoleon, Rives decided to present himself at the next reception at the Elysée, and was cordially received. Letters from Secretary of State Webster, which severely criticized Louis Napoleon's actions, were published in the *New York Herald* as well as the French *Moniteur*. Rives deployed utmost diplomatic skill to assuage hurt feelings and control the damage. The French Minister in Washington complained to Webster that Rives' dispatches as well as his own were overly candid. Webster directed Rives to make a formal apology, which Rives declined to do as "derogatory to dignity."[12] Rives personally delivered a letter of congratulations from President Fillmore to Louis Napoleon. The French leader told Rives that their two countries were different. In the U.S., people did almost everything for themselves and did not call upon the government as much as the French, who relied on government for much more. Therefore, he said, the French needed a stronger central power.[13]

Before and after Louis Napoleon's coup, the status of Cuba was an issue for the French, who feared the increase of U.S. power if it acquired the island from Spain. Rives repeatedly assured Louis Napoleon that the U.S. would not annex Cuba.[14]

William Cabell Rives, 1853. Paul Gayrard, sculptor.

When the French declared in 1850 they had an agreement with Britain to protect Cuba with their joint naval forces, Rives wrote that efforts by persons to initiate conflict would be "frustrated by a policy of mutual frankness, cordiality and manliness on the part of both governments."[15] Rives suspected the British of trying to foment distrust between the French and Americans. The Sandwich Islands, (as Hawaii was then known), were another point of dispute between the three nations. The islands were independent, but the three powers grasped their strategic significance as a Pacific base.[16]

Daniel Webster died October 24, 1852, and was succeeded as Secretary of State by Edward Everett. In April 1853, Rives had a marble bust of himself sculpted by Paul Joseph Raymond Gayrard (1807-1855), who specialized in such likenesses of wealthy members of French society.[17] Rives tendered his resignation March 10, 1853 and wrote that the period of his mission "has been marked by many delicate and embarrassing questions which have been presented here in the relations between the

Government and that of the United States."[18] None of the incidents led to major rupture. Rives had served ably, though without a brilliant success like the reparations treaty he had secured during his previous service in France. The Rives sailed home on the SS *Arctic* and reached Castle Hill June 9, 1853.[19]

* * *

1 Judith to Grace Rives, July 21, 1849, Rives MSS, UVa., Accession #10596.

2 Rives to John Clayton, September 25, 1849, letterbook, Rives MSS, LOC, box 16.

3 WCR, Jr., Biography, Rives MSS, LOC, box 103, 123.

4 Beckles Willson, *America's Ambassadors to France 1777-1927*, London, John Murray, 1928 235-236.

5 Willson, Ibid, 237-238, Letterbook, Rives Papers, Library of Congress, box 103, 175-176.

6 Rives' Pocket Memorandum Book, Rives MSS, LOC, box 122. Rives borrowed $3,000 from his oldest son's father-in-law George Barclay and over $12,000 from his friend Lewis Rogers.

7 George Lockhart Rives, *Genealogical Notes*, New York, 1914, 12.

8 John Hammond Moore, "Judith Rives of Castle Hill," *Virginia Cavalcade*, Vol. XIII, No. 4, Spring 1964, 34.

9 John Hammond Moore, "Amelie Louise Rives and the Charge of the Light Brigade," *The Virginia Magazine of History and Biography*, Vol. 75, No. 1, January 1967, 89-96.

10 Willson, Ibid, 239.

11 Ibid, 242.

12 WCR, Jr. Biography, Ibid, 124.

13 Willson, Ibid, 243.

14 Polk had tried to purchase Cuba from Spain. General Narcisco Lopez of Venezuela led attempts to seize the island for the U.S. by groups of mostly American volunteers, and was executed after his third attempt in 1851. The Franklin Pierce administration actively tried to obtain Cuba in 1854.

Current, Williams, Freidel, Brownlee, *The Essentials of American History*, Third Edition, New York, Alfred A. Knopf, 1976, 165-166.

15 Willson, Ibid, 240.

16 Ibid, 240-241. The kingdom of Hawaii agreed to an annexation treaty with the U.S. in 1854, but a clause prohibiting slavery prevented approval by the Senate. Current, Williams, Friedel, Ibid, 165.

17 WCR, Jr., Biography, Ibid, 127.

18 Willson, Ibid, 244.

19 WCR, Jr., Ibid, 128, 157 (The *Arctic* sank September 27, 1854 after colliding with the SS *Vesta*) history1800s.about.com/od/steamships/a/wreckofarctic.htm.

CHAPTER EIGHTEEN

Emperor

WHILE ABROAD, Rives purchased a Cleveland Bay stallion he named Emperor, who preceded him across the Atlantic to Castle Hill. Seeking to improve the quality of horseflesh in Virginia and in the U.S., Rives had undertaken a three-year tour of stables and stud farms throughout France and England. He summarized his findings in a lengthy article published in *The Southern Planter* February 1853. After describing French breeds and types, he said England was more successful in breeding all equine varieties, from the thoroughbred racehorse to the heavy draught breeds like the Suffolk and Clydesdale. The English breed that he found most useful and attractive was the Cleveland Bay: "The Cleveland Bay is the horse best adapted to the whole range of our wants in Virginia, and suited in an especial manner to correct those errors of breeding by which our Virginia horses have become very much deteriorated." Rives said that Virginia farmers had relied too much on thoroughbred sires, which had resulted in horses that lacked the bone and substance for harness work. To remedy the problem, some had introduced heavy draft types who were too slow and coarse for a road carriage. Rives pronounced the Cleveland Bay the perfect happy medium, neither too light nor too heavy.[1]

The Cleveland Bay breed traces back to Yorkshire area peddlars' packhorses, known as "Chapman" mares, who were bred in the early 1700s to oriental stallions, including the Thoroughbred ancestors Darley Arabian and Godolphin Barb. Cleveland Bays are dark bay in color, with jet black manes and tails. Often possessing large ears, they are noted for their even disposition.[2]

Though of English ancestry, Emperor was foaled at the French government stables at Versailles in 1851. Horses were a vital part of the military, and the French had purchased Emperor's sire Cleveland[3] and his dam Georgette[4] as part of a massive equine improvement program. Rives admired both animals, and was determined to purchase their yearling colt in 1852. S. A. Gilbert, whom Rives employed as Emperor's stud groom recollected in 1876 that Rives had paid $10,000 to the French for Emperor.[5] Emperor was first shipped to New York, where Rives' two older sons saw him in June. Will noted in his diary: "Visited the Cleveland Bay colt which my father sent out to this country by the *Franklin*. The colt is now only a little over a year old and is very large. His legs were somewhat swollen—an effect which the ostler said is always produced by sending horses by sea."[6]

Francis regularly shipped horses and other livestock between Castle Hill and New York. They traveled by ship from New York to Richmond. Horses would then be ridden, driven or led sixty miles by road in two or three days.[7] Most likely Emperor reached Castle Hill in the summer of 1852.

Emperor won first prize as the best two-year-old colt or filly in the "Quick Draught and Saddle Horse" division at the Exhibition of the Virginia State Agricultural Society at Richmond, December 1853. The Chairman of the exhibition, Rives' old friend General John H. Cocke, declared: "The committee take leave to say in regard to Mr. Rives' two year old Cleveland Bay colt that the introduction of so perfect a specimen of one of the highly valued races of Great Britain may well be regarded as a public benefaction and entitles this distinguished member of our Society to its thanks."[8]

Emperor grew to be 16 ½ hands in height and weighed about 1,200 pounds, which was somewhat light by Cleveland Bay

Imported Cleveland Bay Stallion, Emperor. Engraving of a portrait by Guillaume.

standards. He was a deep bay color and all of his offspring were bay. He held his head high when trotting and could trot a mile in 2½ minutes when pulling a sulky. He beat Kossuth, Sea Breeze, and other noted speedsters on a Richmond track in 1858.[9] He won the prize for "Best Stallion for useful and elegant purposes combined" in Richmond in 1856, and his foals were also winners.[10] Emperor created such a sensation, that several other Virginians imported Cleveland Bays, including Col. R. H. Dulany of Welbourne, who founded the Upperville Horse Show.[11] Francis R. Rives made a tour of Yorkshire stud farms in 1855. He reported to his father that buyers from Spain, Prussia, and Russia had recently purchased Cleveland Bays from the area. Francis recommended breeding a Cleveland Bay stallion to a thoroughbred mare to produce a hunting horse. He said this would produce a more satisfactory offspring in the first generation than breeding a Cleveland Bay mare to a thoroughbred stallion.[12]

Emperor's stud fee and boarding rates for mares were:

> For the Season, $50, to be paid at the time of service, or when the Mare is taken away. Insurance, $70, of which $20 are to be paid down in any event for the services of the Horse, and the remaining $50 only when the Mare is ascertained to be in foal. Groom's Fee, $1. Good Pasturage 50 cents per week, and Grain, when desired, at the neighborhood prices.[13]

In 1856, to help generate demand for Emperor's services, Francis proposed that Emperor have his portrait painted. Francis first contacted Henri DeLattre, a well-regarded French sporting artist. DeLattre said he was busy with commissions until his expected return to France within the year. DeLattre also said he could not abide the Virginia summer heat, having previously suffered during a summer visit to Richmond. Francis then suggested an artist well known to the family, Louis Mathieu Didier Guillaume (1816-1892).[14]

As previously mentioned, Rives had commissioned Guillaume in Paris to copy an original portrait of Benjamin Franklin, which he donated to the Virginia Historical Society. Guillaume executed portraits of Rives' children, and he moved to the U.S. in 1853 when Rives returned from his mission abroad. Guillaume lived in New York 1853-1857, where Francis and Matilda Rives were his patrons.[15] Because Guillaume had little or no experience painting horses, Francis gave him a crash course on the subject. He brought him equestrian art to copy, including work by Harry Hall (1814-1882), who depicted formally posed English racehorses. After two months, Francis wrote his father that he thought Guillaume was ready for Emperor. He had specified to

Francis Robert Rives, pastel by Guillaume.

Guillaume how the horse should be posed so that all four legs were visible. Francis wrote that after Guillaume had sketched a preliminary outline, the horse "can look after the flies as much as he desires just as a child whose likeness is taking may run about the room." While Guillaume was in Virginia to paint Emperor, the Rives lined up half a dozen human customers for his $150 portraits, so that the artist's trip would be profitable and productive.[16]

Guillaume took his unfinished portrait of Emperor back to New York in the fall. Francis looked at the work with a critical eye and demanded several changes, which he said the artist willingly provided. He wrote his father that he told Guillaume that "the croup was so rounded that it looked as if it had been delineated with a pair of dividers. It is now much truer to nature, more horse-like and decidedly more aristocratic." The forelegs were repositioned on the canvas and the head was made smaller. The eye was initially too small and too dull. "Guillaume had wholly failed in the knowledge of the several causes of that effect of brilliancy, which are only to be found on a very close examination of the structure of the visual organ, the delicate bayish shading of the transparent cornea (which is the only part of the eye usually visible in good-tempered horses) revealing the limpid fluid beneath."[17]

Francis was very enthusiastic about the amended product. He compared Emperor's likeness with paintings by DeLattre, including one of a horse named Boston, and judged Guillaume's work superior. Francis arranged for an engraving of the portrait to be made by John William Orr of New York, and the engraving appeared in *Baltimore Farmer*, *The Southern Planter*, *Ohio Farmer*, other periodicals and a massive book, *Frank Forester's Horse and Horsemanship of the United States and British Provinces of North America*. Francis stated, "All think the woodcut is the best ever made in America, some say it can't be true to nature, the points are too remarkable. Others say it is an epic horse, a myth of the heroic age."[18]

Emperor was sent to Kentucky for the 1860 breeding season. On his way back to Castle Hill that fall, he tarried in Parkersburg (now West Virginia) to breed a host of mares in that vicinity.[19] At Castle Hill, he avoided gunfire and capture during the Civil War. Emperor spent some of the post war years in the Shenandoah Valley doing his part to replenish the horse population there.[20]

Guillaume moved to Richmond where he lived during the war. He painted portraits of Confederate leaders, some astride disproportionately slender equines. His most famous painting depicts the surrender at Appomattox and is part of the exhibition at the historic site.[21]

Rives was an innovative agriculturalist, who published the results of his experiments. He was a member of the Albemarle Agricultural Society, along with Jefferson, Madison, General

Cocke, T. M. and T. J. Randolph, James and Philip Barbour. His published address to the Society on the value of lime began, "Being somewhat of a pioneer in the lime husbandry in this portion of the State, I feel myself called on, gentlemen, to give you the results of my experience." His first use of lime was a disappointment because he applied it too late to his growing crop of wheat. Subsequently he achieved excellent results from earlier application of lime in combination with "putrescent manures from the farm-yard." Rives declared lime "the most permanent of all manures."[22] Rives also became enthusiastic about the use of Peruvian Guano [seabird excrement] as fertilizer, which became available in the 1840s.[23]

Rives attended the 1850 annual meeting of the Royal Agricultural Society of England and perceived that Cyrus McCormick's reaper would find a ready market there.

> I immediately wrote to our friend, C. J. Meriwether, as he will doubtless recollect, that if the 'Virginia Reaper' were sent out to the Great Exhibition of the next year, for which the arrangements were then commencing, it would make the fortune of its inventor. It has not only done this, but it has reaped a harvest of honor and renown for himself, his native State, and the reputation of American genius in general, which is a result far more to be prized.[24]

Rives suggested that Virginia develop scientific institutions for education and research to help produce additional useful inventions.

Castle Hill's orchards continued to produce Albemarle Pippin apples (introduced by Judith's grandfather) as well as grafted young trees.[25] Castle Hill and Rives' Nelson farms occasionally produced tobacco along with staple crops corn, wheat and oats.[26]

While Emperor was winning prizes at the 1853 Richmond Fair, Rives' bull named Red Rover won his class of Shorthorns and Herefords. His Oxfordshire Down sheep named Duke of Marlborough was named best buck in any breed.[27] Rives wrote about French merino sheep, which produced good wool, but whom he considered inferior for mutton production. Rives believed that the most useful breed was a cross between Cotswold and South Down breeds, which was called Oxfordshire Down. This new breed had a dark face, large carcass and heavy fleece.[28] Francis enclosed a clipping from the *New York Herald* in an 1856 letter to his father. The clipping about the Virginia State Fair is dated October 28, 1856:

> The display of sheep is as good as could be expected. The best specimens on the ground are those exhibited by Hon. Wm. C. Rives, whose success in raising this class of stock has rendered his name prominent among the farmers of Virginia. As an agriculturalist generally he is very successful; and from his zeal in that pursuit it would appear far more congenial than politics, with which, however, he occasionally identifies himself.[29]

Rives was the featured speaker at the New York State Agricultural Society in 1853. He praised the American farmer who owned and occupied the land he cultivated, as opposed to European tenant farmers who were not inclined to make improvements on land they did not own. Rives did not mention slavery.[30] Rives delivered another address at the conclusion of the Virginia Fair in 1858, where he declared:

> We sometimes hear it said that cotton is King. But the agriculture of America, as its political constitution, is Republican. It owns no dynasty of privilege or power.

If any one of those noble plants which constitute the chosen vegetable races of the new world, could fairly aspire to Royalty, it would be that prince of cereals, Indian corn, a proud native of the soil, lifting high its imperial form and tasseled banner above all its compeers and in the universality of its uses and its presence founding a claim to universal sway.[31]

Rives would later stress that the interests of Virginia and other middle states were different from those of the cotton producing states.

Though Rives had enjoyed political and diplomatic life in Washington and Paris, farming Castle Hill kept him occupied and fulfilled. His horse was saddled and bridled, waiting outside early every morning as soon as he rose. He liked to make a rapid survey of his farm before breakfast. After family prayers and breakfast, he devoted himself to correspondence and writing projects for several hours. He took another longer ride in the afternoon. Like his father, he often rode fast to save time. He and Judith enjoyed entertaining their neighbors or dining as their guests, but Rives generally retired at an early hour.[32]

* * *

1   William C. Rives to Frank G. Ruffin, December 24, 1852, published in *The Southern Planter*, February 1853, Vol. XIII, 51.

2   Sir Alfred E. Pease, "The Cleveland Bay and Yorkshire Coach Horse," reprinted from *Yorkshire Agricultural Journal*, 1937.

3   Cleveland was purchased by the French Agriculture Inspector General Lefebvre from J. Shaw of Yorkshire. Cleveland was by Master George out of a dam by Barnaby. "Emperor," *The Southern Planter*, Vol. XVII, April 1857, 232.

4 Lefebvre purchased Georgette from George Burton of Yorkshire. Georgette was by Alexander out of a dam by Golden Hero. Some of her other colts sold for high prices in England. Ibid.

5 "The Park Horse, Imported Emperor," *Wallace's Monthly*, Vol. II, June, 1876, 39. William C. Rives' will drawn up in 1866 mentions a debt owed to his son Francis "on our joint adventure on imported horses." Albemarle County Will Book 28, page 126.

6 William C. Rives, Jr. Diary, June 24, 1852, Rives MSS, LOC, box 103.

7 Francis R. Rives to Rives, July 7, 1856, Rives MSS, LOC, box 34.

8 *The Southern Planter*, Vol. XIV, January 1854.

9 "The Park Horse, Imported Emperor," *Wallace's Monthly*, Ibid.

10 *The Southern Planter*, Vol. XVI, December 1856, 267.

11 Alexander Mackay-Smith, "Cleveland Bays and Hunter Breeding in Virginia Before the Civil War," *The Horse*, published by the American Remount Association, Washington D.C., March-April 1937 3-6.

12 Francis R. Rives to Rives, January 15, 1855, reprinted in *The Southern Planter*, Vol. XV, March 1855, 65; April 1855, 98.

13 *The Southern Planter*, Vol. XVII, April 1857, page 5 of advertising sheet. Also printed Emperor brochure in author's possession.

14 Francis R. Rives to Rives, May 10, 1856, Rives MSS, LOC, box 34.

15 Annabel Shanklin Perlik, "Signed L.M.D. Guillaume," 1979 Master's Thesis, George Washington University, University of Virginia Special Collections #ND1329.G845P471979.

16 Francis R. Rives to Rives, July 10, 1856, Rives MSS, LOC, box 34.

17 Francis R. Rives to Rives, December 31, 1856, Ibid.

18 Francis R. Rives to Rives, February 4, 1857 and March 12, 1857 Ibid, box 35.

19 "The Park Horse, Imported Emperor," *Wallace's Monthly*, Ibid.

20 R. Tuck to Rives, September 15, 1866; John Walker to Rives February 11, 1867, Rives MSS, LOC, box 93.

21 Perlik, Ibid, 60.

22 *The Southern Planter*, Vol. II, no. 12, December 1842, 276.

23 John Hammond Moore, *Albemarle Jefferson's County 1727-1976*, University Press of Virginia, 1976, 167. Rives to Alfred Rives, September 1, 1866, Rives MSS, UVa., Accession #2312, box 2.

24 William C. Rives, "Virginia and Her Interests," *Plough, the Loom and the Anvil*, New York, published by Myron Finch. Jan. 1852, 428-429.

25 M. A. Littell to Rives, March 25, 1867, Rives MSS, LOC, box 93.

26 Miles L. Shipman to Rives, January 9, 1860, Rives MSS, LOC, box 91, 1850 census data on Rives in Newton Bond Jones, "Charlottesville and Albemarle County 1819-1860," 1950 University of Virginia Dissertation, Alderman Library Reference F232 Diss.0602.

27 Moore, Ibid.

28 William C. Rives, "Best Breed of Mutton Sheep," *The Southern Planter*, Vol. XIII, No. 10, October 1853, 301.

29 Clipping enclosed in letter from Francis R. Rives to Rives, December 2, 1856, Rives MSS, LOC, box 34.

30 "An Address Delivered at the Annual Exhibition of the New York State Agricultural Society at Saratoga Springs" September 23, 1853, by Hon. William C. Rives of Virginia, Albany, J. Munsell, 1853.

31 WCR, Jr., Biography, Rives MSS, LOC, box 103, 133.

32 Ibid, 117.

CHAPTER NINETEEN

No Prurient Desire for Public Office

RIVES VIEWED WITH DISMAY the rising sectional animosities of the 1850s. His daughter Amélie married Henry Sigourney[1] of Boston in 1854. Three of his five children married northerners and settled in the north. He and Judith enjoyed visiting their children and grandchildren in New York, Boston and Newport. The children and grandchildren made regular visits to their farms, which Rives and Judith had partitioned off of Castle Hill. Disunion threatened Rives' family routines as well as his cherished Union under the Constitution. Rives would spend the latter half of the decade absorbed in the life and papers of the Father of the Constitution.

Rives viewed the election of 1852 from abroad. He was a friend of the Whig Candidate General Winfield Scott. He called Democrat Franklin Pierce "a modest and respectable lawyer of New Hampshire," and predicted a Pierce victory despite Scott's more impressive service in the Mexican War.[2] The Virginian Scott lost the states of the Deep South because of his uncertainty over the Compromise of 1850 and the Fugitive Slave Act.[3] Free soil candidate John P. Hale won fewer votes than Van Buren had in the previous election.

Prominent citizens of Albemarle and Charlottesville, "irrespective of party," gathered for a welcome home dinner in Rives' honor Saturday, September 10, 1853. Attendees included T. J. Randolph, General Bernard Peyton (current owner of the Farmington estate where the Rives became engaged), Rives' youngest brother

Alexander, University of Virginia Faculty members, Rector and Board of Visitors. Some who were invited sent in their regrets along with praise for Rives, including his opponent in the 1840 Senate contest J. Y. Mason, Virginia's present Senator J. M. Mason, and former Illinois governor Edward Coles. Coles offered the following toast:

> William C. Rives—The pupil of Jefferson, and among the purest and greatest of our statesmen; he has ever conformed to the duties of a patriot, and never to those of a partisan.

Rives thanked everyone for the welcome and words of praise. He spoke of the need for Virginia to develop "a wise and diffusive system of public education," along with an effective railroad network. He said Virginia had been a sleeping giant, but the "railway whistle will rouse her from her dreamy repose. . . . the Schoolmaster and the locomotive are the twin missionaries of civilization and knowledge." Rives spoke of progress "in agriculture, in manufactures, in the mechanic arts, in commerce, in science, and I trust too in morals. The age is an age of movement everywhere. Those who do not move forward move backward." Rives said Virginia's prosperity was essential to the country because of geography. The state was in a unique position to be "the mediator of sectional controversies."[4]

Rives served on the Board of Directors of both the Virginia Central Railroad and the Orange and Alexandria Rail Road. The two roads formed a junction in nearby Gordonsville. Investing in railroad bonds and stock, he urged his children to do the same. He strongly supported the Virginia Central's construction of a link between Charlottesville and Lynchburg.[5]

Judge J. H. Sherrard of Winchester asked Rives to allow his

name to be considered for nomination by the American Party as a candidate for governor in 1855. Sherrard predicted that Whigs would unite with members of the American Party in support of Rives. The American, or Know Nothing Party began in the late 1840s as an anti-Catholic and anti-immigrant society. Its early meetings were secret, and members were instructed to reply, "I know nothing," if questioned by others. The party gained strength and broadened its appeal in the early 1850s, and nominated for President and Vice President former Whig President Millard Fillmore and Andrew Jackson's nephew A. J. Donelson in 1856. Rives and his northern Whig friends Robert C. Winthrop and Edward Everett preferred Fillmore in 1856 rather than the victorious Democrat James Buchanan or Republican John C. Fremont.[6] Fillmore wrote Rives during the campaign, expressing his frustration at the lack of support from Whigs. He complained that if he followed the rigid pro-slavery demands of Virginia Whigs, he would alienate his northern supporters. "I cannot be one thing to the North and another to the South."[7] The American Party failed to establish itself in the Deep South.[8]

Rives replied to Sherrard's request, "I have no prurient desire for public office." However, Rives agreed to allow his name to be considered, and if elected, he agreed to serve as governor. Rives stated that he would not campaign, letting his years of public service speak for themselves. The American Party met at Winchester March 14, 1855 and, instead of Rives, nominated the son of one of his Cabell first cousins, Thomas Stanhope Fluornoy[9]. Rives wrote his son that he was relieved that he was not chosen. "I am not tormented with any longings for public life and it would have looked rather odd for me, who have been trying to learn something all my life to be the candidate of the know nothings." Fluornoy, a Whig former Congressman, who later served with distinction as a Confederate colonel under Stonewall Jackson, lost the race to Democratic nominee Henry A. Wise. Wise ran a vigorous campaign of speeches and appearances that was unprecedented in Virginia politics.[10]

The Rives oversaw resumption and completion of construction of their neighborhood church. The building was consecrated as Grace Church May 9, 1855. No doubt pleased that the new church bore the same name as his youngest daughter, who had married William C. Rives, Jr., David Sears donated a bell cast in Boston weighing over 1,500 pounds.[11] The Rives raised church construction funds from the community, secured sizeable donations from wealthy friends, and also contributed thousands of their own dollars to the building, which cost a total of $20,000.[12] Rives often led the service of Morning Prayer when the preacher was absent. According to one parishioner, "He possessed a most musical voice... his clear, ringing tones and impressive manner rendered it [the service] most pleasing to his hearers."[13]

The Executive Committee of the Virginia Historical Society resolved on June 29, 1855, that, "The Life of James Madison should be written by one of Virginia's sons—by one qualified for the task." The committee designated Rives, the Society's President, as that person. Rives declined the request, but agreed to collect and organize materials on Madison for the use of some future biographer.[14]

In August 1856, Senator James Alfred Pearce of Maryland, Chairman of the Joint Congressional Committee on the Library of Congress, asked Rives to arrange and edit for publication Madison papers that Congress had purchased from Dolley Madison in 1848. Rives agreed on the condition that he could bring the papers to Castle Hill and do the work at home. On January 7, 1857, he left Washington with three trunks full of Madison papers from the State Department.[15] Although Congress had recently paid Professor Henry A. Washington $6,000 for similar work on an edition of Jefferson papers, Pearce offered Rives $3,000 plus additional costs for copying papers selected for publication.[16] Judith wrote Will that Rives agreed to do the job only because of his high regard for Madison. "Uncle Sam is too poor a paymaster to make the pecuniary compensation for the sacrifice of so much time much of an object."[17]

Rives began work as soon as he and the trunks reached Castle Hill. The papers were in "disordered condition and chaotic confusion," and some were barely legible.[18] Rives' friendship with Madison, his role in helping Dolley sell Madison's Constitutional Convention notes, and his grasp of history made him the ideal person for the job. As he began to sort through the mountain of paper, Rives realized important documents were missing. Rives had seen Madison's copy of a paper Madison (then a member of Congress) had written in February 1791 for George Washington in case Washington decided to veto the First National Bank Bill. Washington did not veto the bill; however, the paper showed Madison's opposition to the bank during that period. Madison's opinions evolved, because as president in 1816, he signed a bill chartering the Second National Bank. Rives asked Secretary of State William L. Marcy about the paper. When Marcy told him James K. Polk (1795-1849) had taken it, Rives sought help from James Buchanan, who had been Polk's Secretary of State. Buchanan was unable to find the missing document. Although a copy was later found among Polk's papers, and the original is now in the Boston Public Library, Rives' edition of Madison's Writings does not contain Madison's 1791 paper on the Bank.[19] Rives inquired about additional missing papers from Buchanan and others, including James C. McGuire of Washington, to whom Dolley's wayward son John Payne Todd had given important Madison papers without his mother's knowledge. McGuire allowed Rives to examine his Madison papers and to borrow some of them. He had copies made of some documents for Rives.[20]

Immersion in rich original source material made Rives reconsider the Virginia Historical Society's recommendation.[21] He began a biography of Madison as he continued to edit the Madison papers. Wanting to improve their mentor's image for posterity, Edward Coles wrote Rives to be sure to claim that Madison had intended to free his slaves.[22] In February 1859, Rives wrote Senator Pearce that he had nearly finished the task of editing the papers entrusted to him, and that he had also completed Volume I of a projected multi-volume history of the life of Madison. Rives suggested that the biography would boost sales of the collected writings, and that Congress should publish both *"pari passu"* [at the same time].[23] When Congress did not act, Rives had the biography published by Little, Brown and Company of Boston in 1859.

In his preface to Volume one of *The Life and Times of James Madison*, Rives suggested the work was more history than biography "though partaking of the character of both." The book covered the period from Madison's birth in 1751 to 1785, ending with Madison's Virginia "Memorial and Remonstrance against the Bill establishing a Legal Provision for Teachers of the Christian Religion." Rives saluted the Memorial, which was similar to Jefferson's Statute for Religious Freedom, as a vital expression of American religious and civil liberty. Rives' writing style is wordy and dense, and present day readers can choose works about Madison that are more accessible and pleasant to read. Rives' work was the first on its subject and received favorable notices. Historian Jared Sparks praised Rives for shedding new light on the history of the Revolution and following years, especially Madison's role. "The volume is in all respects a valuable addition to the historical resources of the country."[24]

Rives wrote Senator Pearce February 11, 1860 that he had the honor to be delivering the results of his editing work. Rives had prepared three volumes of approximately 1,000 handwritten pages each.[25] He suggested expanding the smaller fourth volume to match the first three in length with 23 additional Madison essays, including 18 that were published in *Freneau's National Gazette* of Philadelphia in 1791 and 1792.[26]

The Congressional Committee commissioned Washington attorney Philip R. Fendall, (who knew Rives and the Madisons) to make the suggested additions, create an index, and proofread. Fendall also added material from James McGuire's collection to Volume IV. Outbreak of the Civil War delayed completion of the project. Fortunately Castle Hill and the Madison manuscripts escaped Yankee torches and pillaging.[27] In August 1865, J. B. Lippincott and Company of Philadelphia printed 500 copies of each volume of *Letters and Other Writings of James Madison.* Despite their work, neither Rives' nor Fendall's name appears anywhere in the books. Rives had served in the Confederate Congress. Although Fendall had remained in D.C. during the war, he was a first cousin of Robert E. Lee. Vindictive northern congressmen apparently did not want Confederate tainted names soiling their publication.[28] Rives, once called Little Expunger, for supporting Benton's Expunging of Clay's Senate condemnation of Andrew Jackson, was now himself expunged. Congress would not provide copies of the volumes to either Rives or Fendall.[29] Though later editions of Madison's writings have been prepared and published, Rives' and Fendall's work in editing Madison's papers was a valuable, though unheralded, service to their country.[30]

The new chairman of the Congressional Library Committee, Senator Timothy Otis Howe of Wisconsin, wrote Rives demanding the return of the trunks of Madison papers. Although Rives had asked permission to retain the papers for use in his Madison biography, he sent the trunks promptly to Washington C.O.D.[31] Rives wrote his eldest son that he was relieved to get rid of the papers. Packing them up was a distraction from his work on Volume III of the biography. "I have Mr. Seward's receipt in due form for their return so I shall not be exposed to further annoyance respecting them."[32]

Though Rives thought he had returned all the papers, some would take over 70 years to find their way back to Congress. When Rives died, the bulk of his papers passed to his namesake, William C. Rives, Jr. (1825-1889) who bequeathed them to his son Dr. William C. Rives (1850-1938). Dr. Rives, who spent his last years in Washington, left the papers to his brother-in-law Bishop Philip Rhinelander. In 1940, Rhinelander's widow deposited the papers in the Library of Congress and in 1946 declared them a gift. These thousands of Rives papers contained nearly 900 haphazardly intermingled Madison items, which have been kept mostly as a unit that forms Series 2 of the Library of Congress Madison Papers.[33]

Little, Brown and Company published Volume II of Rives' Madison biography in 1866. Advertised at the front of Volume II was a second edition of Volume I, priced at $2.25 per volume. In the Preface, Rives stated that Volume II had been completed more than four years before, but was "prevented from publication by the inauspicious circumstances of the times."[34] Volume II covered the period from 1785 to 1789, dealing mostly with the Constitution. Rives idolized Madison at every opportunity. Patrick Henry spoke against ratification of the Constitution by the Virginia legislature, while Madison was its principal advocate. Comparing the two, Rives credited Henry with superior oratorical skills, but insisted Madison was more eloquent, brilliant and persuasive.[35] Later biographers and historians have stated more bluntly that Madison mumbled, and was a poor public speaker.[36] Rives wrote his sons that he was pleased with the reviews of the work in northern papers.[37] Robert C. Winthrop sent Rives a congratulatory letter from Boston: "I know of no American Biography more successfully done."[38]

Rives completed Volume III in February 1868. This installment covered the period up to the end of Washington's presidency in 1797. Rives included Madison's words of praise for Washington in the final pages. Little, Brown and Company were in no hurry to publish Volume III or the planned final Volume IV, having lost $600 on the second Volume.[39] The publishers only proceeded after William C. Rives, Jr., disobeying his father's instructions, assured the publishers he would cover their losses in the event of insufficient sales.[40] Judith served as clerk for the entire work, copying every page of her husband's manuscript into her own more legible hand for the printer.[41]

Volume III, containing an index to all three volumes, was published months after Rives' death in April, 1868. The volume's opening note stated, "no living writer is so qualified as he was, by intimate intercourse with Madison, and by special study to treat adequately the constitutional and early political history of this country."[42]

Rives' Madison work made him decline to be the featured speaker at Virginia's Jamestown 250 Jubilee in May 1857. The Jubilee committee then selected former President Tyler, who spoke for three hours, testing the endurance of his audience.[43] Had he accepted the opportunity, Rives might have proven even less concise.

Amid growing sectional bitterness and conflict, Rives made peace with one old foe. In March 1857, Rives and Judith attended a dinner at the Number 8 Washington Place, New York City home of George Barclay, father-in-law of Rives' eldest son. Guest of honor at the dinner was Martin Van Buren. After initial awkwardness, Rives and Van Buren had lengthy and pleasant conversation. Van Buren told Rives his four years as President were the most miserable of his life, and that he was happy to be out of politics now, spending time with his children and grandchildren.⁴⁴ This may have been one last instance of Van Buren's deceiving and outwitting Rives, as he had done decades before. Van Buren had twice sought re-election to that office he claimed had made him miserable. Whether or not he believed Van Buren, Rives was content to end the quarrel.

Rives hoped that national hostilities could also be settled amicably. In an address delivered before the Young Men's Christian Association of Richmond, Rives suggested that Christianity might play a decisive role in bringing peace to "the most doubtful and perilous stage of our national existence."⁴⁵

The Kansas Nebraska Act of 1854 had caused considerable peril and division. Proposed by Illinois Senator Stephen A. Douglas, the law provided for popular sovereignty to allow or deny slavery in the territories. The Act also repealed the Missouri Compromise, which had prohibited slavery north of latitude 36°, 30'. Southern Whigs and Democrats supported the Act. Northern Whigs opposed it, and Northern Democrats were divided. The Kansas Nebraska Act ended the national Whig party. Northern anti-Kansas Nebraska Democrats and Whigs joined to form the Republican Party in 1854. Armed conflict between pro and anti slavery forces spread through "Bleeding Kansas." ⁴⁶

Rives wrote a plea for peace and moderation to his northern friend Winthrop, which appeared in the *Daily National Intelligencer*. Blaming a familiar demon, Rives said the problem began with party agitation and factions. He said the violence in Kansas and on the Senate floor, where Brooks had brutalized Sumner with his cane, showed the nation was in revolution and the Union headed for rupture. Rives called for citizens to hold law and order meetings to promote the sentiment of loyalty to the Union over sectional differences. Rives argued that the Missouri Compromise deserved to be repealed, because it was unconstitutional. To support his argument, Rives attached a letter Madison had written to author and editor Robert Walsh, Jr. in 1819.⁴⁷

Madison's letter to Walsh explained that the majority of states at the Constitutional Convention had opposed the slave trade, but had compromised to allow it to continue until 1808 in order to secure the support of South Carolina and Georgia. The wording of Article V, which prohibited restriction of migration or importation of "persons" before 1808 pertained to slaves, though the framers did not want to use the word "slave." Madison said after 1808, importation of slaves was prohibited from abroad, but not between the states. Madison also wrote that the Constitution did not empower the government to emancipate slaves. Because a motion failed, which would have given the original 13 states higher status than new states, Madison wrote Walsh that powers and privileges enjoyed by existing states could not be forbidden to new states. Therefore if existing states had the right of slave ownership, that right could not be forbidden to a new state. Madison warned of sectional conflict: "Should a state of parties arise founded on geographical boundaries and other physical and permanent distinctions which happen to coincide with them, what is to control those great repulsive masses from awful shocks against each other?"[48]

Delaware Senator and former Secretary of State John M. Clayton (1796-1856) wrote Rives that he rejoiced while reading Rives' published letter to Winthrop and Madison's letter to Walsh, which he had not previously read. Clayton observed that he concurred with Rives on most of the great questions. At their advanced ages, he said, they were not motivated by political ambition, but aimed to do what was best for the country.[49] Rives would increase his efforts to save the country.

* * *

1   Pronounced with stress on the first syllable. Henry's French ancestors spelled the name Séjournée.

2   Rives to Alfred Rives, July 7, 1852, Rives MSS, UVa., Accession #2532, box 1.

3   Daniel W. Crofts, "The Southern Opposition and the Crisis of the Union," in Gary Gallagher and Rachel A. Shelden, editors, *A Political Nation: New Directions in Mid-Nineteenth-Century American Political History*, Charlottesville, University of Virginia Press, 2012, 87.

4   *Virginia Advocate*, J. L. Cochran, editor, O. S. Allen & Company, Proprietors, Vol. 28, no. 9, Charlottesville, Virginia, September 16, 1853, University of Virginia Special Collections.

5   Rives to William C. Rives, Jr., March 18, 1856, and December 30, 1856, Rives MSS, LOC, box 34, Notice of Orange and Alexandria Directors Meeting, September 6, 1860, Ibid, box 91.

6   Letterbook, Rives MSS, LOC, Box 105, 188.

7   Fillmore to Rives, July 23, 1856, Rives MSS, LOC, box 88, quoted in Michael F. Holt, *The Rise and Fall of the American Whig Party*, New York, Oxford, Oxford University Press, 1999, 974.

8   Crofts, Ibid.

9   Alexander Brown, *The Cabells and Their Kin*, Reprinted, 1994 by Randolph W. Cabell, Genealogy Publishing Service, Franklin, North Carolina, 393.

10 Letterbook, Ibid.

11 David Sears to Judith Page Rives, June 17, 1854, Rives MSS, UVa., Accession #2313, box 1, See Barclay Rives, *A History of Grace Church*, Cismont, Grace Episcopal Church, 2010 40-46.

12 William C. Rives pocket Memorandum Account Book, Rives MSS, LOC, box 122.

13 Edward C. Mead, *Historic Homes of the Southwest Mountains Virginia*, Philadelphia, J. B. Lippincott Company, 1898, 210.

14 Resolution of the Virginia Historical and Philosophical Society, June 29, 1855; Conway Robinson to Rives, July 27, 1855, Rives MSS, LOC,

box 86; Rives to Robinson, November 28, 1859, Ibid, Box 90, cited by Ralph L. Ketcham, "William Cabell Rives Editor of the Letters and Other Writings of James Madison," *The Virginia Magazine of History and Biography*, Vol. 68, No. 2, April 1960, 132, (Ketcham authored *James Madison: A Biography*, New York, 1971).

15 Ketcham, Ibid.

16 Rives to Alfred L. Rives, December 12, 1856, Rives to William C. Rives, Jr. December 30, 1856, Rives MSS, LOC, box 34.

17 Judith Page Rives to William C. Rives, Jr., December 13, 1856, Ibid.

18 Rives to Pearce, February 11, 1860, Rives MSS, LOC, box 91.

19 Ketcham, Ibid, 132-133. Ketcham cites a letter from Rives to Buchanan, January 17, 1857, Rives MSS, LOC, box 89. Rives mentions the missing paper in Volume III of his *Life and Times of James Madison*, footnote on page 171.

20 http://memory.loc.gov/ammem/collections/madison.papersmjmabout2. html#rives, see also Rives to Pearce, February 11, 1860, Rives MSS, LOC, box 91.

21 William C. Rives, *History of the Life and Times of James Madison*, Vol. I, Boston, Little, Brown, and Company, 1859, v.

22 Coles to Rives, February 3, 1857, Rives Papers, Library of Congress, box 89, cited in Drew R. McCoy, *The Last of the Fathers*, Cambridge, Cambridge University Press, 1989, 321 McCoy shows that Coles was inaccurately projecting views about slavery onto Madison.

23 Rives to Pearce, February 18, 1859, Rives MSS, LOC, box 90.

24 Jared Sparks to Rives, January 28, 1860, Rives MSS, LOC, box 91.

25 Handwriting of documents and remarks in her letters indicate that Judith and at least one other person assisted Rives in this monumental task. The four volumes are each about 650 printed pages.

26 Rives to Pearce, February 11, 1860, Rives MSS, LOC, box 91.

27 U.S. General Philip Sheridan led a March 1865 cavalry raid that inflicted much destruction in southern Albemarle and Nelson counties. See Richard L. Nicholas, *Sheridan's James River Campaign of 1865 Through Central Virginia*, Charlottesville, Historic Albemarle, 2012.

28 Ketcham, Ibid, 134-135. Ketcham quotes a November 27, 1865 letter from Fendall to Rives in the Yale University Library, reprinted in *Publications of the Colonial Society of Massachusetts*, X, 136.

29 Ketcham, Ibid, 135, cites letter from A. R. Spafford to Rives, October 12, 1865, Rives MSS, LOC, box 93.

30 Madison scholar Jack Rakove states Rives & Fendall's work "is especially valuable for Madison's extensive correspondence in retirement." Jack N. Rakove, *James Madison and the Creation of the American Republic*, Third Edition, New York, Pearson Longman, 2007, 246.

31 Ketcham, Ibid, 136. Cites letters: A. R. Spafford to Rives, October 12, 1865; Timothy O. Howe to Rives, January 18, 1866; Rives to Howe, January 22, 1866; William H. Seward to Rives, March 16, 1866; and W. Hunter to Rives, March 21, 1866, all in Rives MSS, LOC, box 93.

32 Rives to Francis R. Rives, April 25, 1866, Rives MSS, UVa., Accession #2532a.

33 http://memory.loc.gov Ibid. Mrs. Rhinelander bequeathed some papers to her nephew Laurens Rhinelander, a University of Virginia Law School Professor, who enlisted his daughter-in-law Ginger McCarthy to create typed transcripts, copies of which which he gave to the author, before donating the transcripts and originals to the University of Virginia Library, where they are kept as "Papers of the Rives, Sears & Rhinelander Families" Accession #10596.

34 William C. Rives, *The Life and Times of James Madison*, Volume II, Boston; Little, Brown and Company, 1866, v.

35 Ibid, 601-613

36 Monica Hesse, "For Many Presidential Inaugurations, the Second Time is Not the Charm," *The Washington Post*, Inauguration Supplement, January 15, 2013; www.richardrbeeman.com, "Principal Characters of the Constitutional Convention".

37 Rives to Francis R. Rives, April 25, 1866, University of Virginia Special Collections, Accession #2532a, Rives to William C. Rives, Jr. March 8, 1866, March 17, 1866, University of Virginia Special Collections, Accession #10596.

38 Robert C. Winthrop to Rives, August 13, 1866, letterbook, Rives MSS, LOC, box 20, 242.

39 W. C. Rives, Jr. to Rives, March 11, 1868, Rives MSS, LOC, box 38, cited in McCoy, Ibid, 366.

40 W. C. Rives, Jr. to Rives, March 18, March 25, 1868, Rives MSS, LOC, box 38, cited in McCoy, Ibid.

41 Judith Rives to William C. Rives, Jr., February 10, 1867, Rives MSS, UVa., Accession #10596.

42 William C. Rives, *The Life and Times of James Madison*, Volume III, Boston, Little, Brown and Company, 1868, iii These words may have been written by William C. Rives, Jr.

43 David James Kiracofe, "The Jamestown Jubilees: 'State Patriotism' and Virginia Identity in the Early Nineteenth Century," *The Virginia Magazine of History and Biography*, 2002, Volume 110, No. 1, Richmond, The Virginia Historical Society, 48-49.

44 Rives to William C. Rives, Jr. March 15, 1857, letterbook, Rives MSS, LOC, box 105, unnumbered page between 199 and 200.

45 William C. Rives, "Discourse Before the Young Men's Christian Association of Richmond, on the Ethics of Christianity," December 7, 1855, Richmond, John Nowlan, 28.

46 Current, Williams, Freidel, Brownlee, *The Essentials of American History*, Third Edition, New York, Alfred A. Knopf, 1980, 166-168.

47 William C. Rives to Robert C. Winthrop, June 10, 1856, followed by extracts of Mr. Madison's letter to Mr. Walsh, published in the *Daily National Intelligencer*, June 16, 1856.

48 Ibid, Madison's letter to Walsh, November 27, 1819, can also be found in *Letters and Other Writings of James Madison*, (Rives and Fendall editors), Volume III, Philadelphia, J. B. Lippincott and Company, 1865, 150. See also Drew McCoy, Ibid, 107-113 for interpretations of the letter.

49 John M. Clayton to Rives, June 27, 1856, letterbook, Rives MSS, LOC, box 20, 185.

CHAPTER TWENTY

Constitutional Union

JOHN BROWN'S RAID in Harper's Ferry, Virginia (now West Virginia), which took place October 16, 1859, agitated both northern and southern extremists. Northern abolitionists canonized Brown, who was hung December 2, as a man willing to die for his beliefs. Southern secessionists demonized him and warned that others like him would soon follow. Moderate Unionists like Rives faced greater difficulty making their appeals heard for a middle course.

Rives wrote a lengthy "Letter to a Friend On the Important Questions of the Day," dated January 27, 1860, which was published in the *Richmond Whig* February 4, and also published separately in pamphlet form. In the letter Rives stated that "the affair at Harper's Ferry" was not an isolated event. He was outraged by northern expressions of support for Brown, and reassured by northern denunciations of Brown. He cited specific recent spontaneous "pulsations for the maintenance of the Union," that occurred in Maine, Massachusetts, and Pennsylvania. Rives asserted that the people of the north did not believe in an "irrepressible conflict" between slave and free labor. Rives was referring to William H. Seward's 1858 Rochester speech "On the Irrepressible Conflict."[1]

The letter also denounced southern secessionists, and characteristically, Rives advised "dignity and coolness." He said Virginia should protect herself by building up her economy as well as her militia. He proposed that the question of slavery should be taken out of national politics, because it was "essentially a local

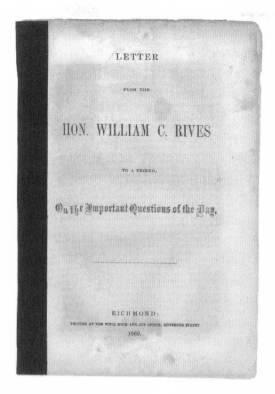

and domestic question," which should be governed by the judiciary. Rives believed that new states had to be able to choose for themselves whether to allow slavery. Rives mentioned South Carolina's invitation to Virginia to join in a convention of southern states to consider secession. Rives said Virginia declined the invitation, and that more than once she had "solemnly expressed her opinion to South Carolina against the adoption of this her favorite remedy."

Rives then referred to his May 27, 1844 Senate speech in reply to South Carolina Senator McDuffie on repeal of the 1842 tariff. McDuffie had suggested the nation might be split into three sections: a manufacturing confederacy of the northeast, a farming confederacy of the north and west, and a planting confederacy of the south. Rives refuted that view, arguing that Virginia had more in common with other middle states including Maryland and Delaware than the cotton states of the deep south. Rives pointed out that the Ohio River bound Virginia to Kentucky, Indiana, and Ohio (Virginia still included what is now West Virginia). Rives maintained that no scheme could compare with the present Union for maintaining rights and prosperity.

The letter continued with a quote from James Madison on Virginia's need to develop manufacturing to diversify its economy. Rives mentioned the compromises Madison and the other framers made regarding the slave trade to secure South Carolina and Georgia's support for the Constitution. The letter concluded, "let us not, upon the sudden appearance of a squall, or because one or two of the crew have mutinied, desert our good ship, the Constitution, abandon our comrades, and in a panic betake ourselves to the crazy raft of secession. . . ."[2]

U.S. Army General-in-Chief Winfield Scott numbered among the many who praised Rives' published letter. Scott wrote Rives that his letter would benefit both north and south "by assuaging passions, enlightening patriotism, and opening the vista of hope to all."[3] Another old Whig friend John Campbell of Abingdon (not to be confused with Judge John A. Campbell future C.S.A. Assistant Secretary of War) wrote Rives that he agreed with every sentence. "You have clinched the nail completely and given a mortal blow to all Southern Confederacies."[4]

Massachusetts industrialist Nathan Appleton (1779-1861) published a March 12 response to Rives entitled "Letter to the Honorable William C. Rives of Virginia on Slavery and the Union." Appleton praised Rives' letter, and laid the blame on both northerners and southerners for being in "hostile array" against each other over the issue of slavery. He called John Brown "a man of some character but of disordered intellect." Appleton claimed, "We of the North consider slavery a social evil." However, he pointed out that "many of the Free States pass the most stringent laws, in order to keep free negroes out of their borders, consid-ering them a public nuisance." Appleton argued that free states should not interfere with slavery in slave states. He predicted slavery would end when slaves ceased to be of value and not before. Addressing southern dis-unionists, Appleton asked why they should continue to agitate about extending slavery into the territories. He said the territories were unsuitable for slave labor. He advised southerners to be content to profitably enjoy slavery in their states where it was protected by the constitu-tion. He declared that a peaceful disunion was impossible. Civil war would result. The North and West would not relinquish the Mississippi as their highway or New Orleans as their great market. He concluded that the actual condition of North and South was favorable to mutually advantageous cooperation and trade. "The present estrangement is unnatural and unchristian."[5] Rives' plea for reasoned discussion resonated with old Whig friends like Appleton, Scott, and Winthrop. However, they were a minority of the population.

Kentucky Senator John Jordan Crittenden (1787-1863) is per-haps the best remembered southern Unionist because of his proposal that was the basis of efforts to save the Union in 1860-1861. The Crittenden Compromise would have restored the 36° 30' Missouri Compromise boundary, with slavery protected south of that latitude and prohibited north of it. Crittenden was a for-mer Whig, trying to follow the example of his late mentor, the Great Pacificator Henry Clay. For the 1860 presidential campaign, Crittenden was trying to unite former northern and southern Whigs to create a national party of moderation. The John Brown raid reduced his chances for success.[6]

Rives wrote Crittenden a letter of encouragement January 9, 1860. Rives said he was glad to hear that Crittenden's new party had adopted Henry Clay's words of 1850 as its plat-form: "The Union, the Constitution, and the execution of the laws." Crittenden had proposed that the new party be called the "National Union Party." Rives advised that "National" would be displeasing to southern ears, and that "Constitutional Union Party" would be a more suitable name.[7] Crittenden heeded Rives' suggestion. Rives wrote Constitutional Union Party organizer F. B. Deane, Jr. of Lynchburg in February stating his approval of the party committee's published writings as well as its proposed method of selecting candidates for the presidency and Vice-Presidency.[8] Crittenden appeared to be the logical candidate, but Rives' name was also "suggested widely" for the Constitutional Union Party nomination according to historian Patrick Sowle.[9]

Rives wrote Crittenden that he would be unable to attend the party convention in Baltimore in May. Rives said that because he had not attended a political meeting in a dozen years, he would be a "fish out of water." However, he promised Crittenden to do everything possible within his "sphere of action" to implement the party's aims. Rives said the Constitutional Union Party would unite "all the conservative elements in every part of the nation . . ." into "a great country party . . . frowning upon every form of sectionalism . . . showing a catholic and equal regard for the rights and interests of every portion. . . ." Rives closed the letter, referring to their days together in the Senate, that he recollected "with pride and pleasure our ancient fellowship in the public councils."[10]

At its convention, the Constitutional Union Party nominated former Whig Senator John Bell of Tennessee for President and former Whig Congressman Edward Everett of Massachusetts for Vice-President. A friend and correspondent of Rives, Everett had served as President of Harvard, Governor of Massachusetts, Secretary of State under Fillmore, and Minister to Great Britain. Francis R. Rives had assisted him as Secretary of the Legation in London. Everett is best known for his two-hour speech, which preceded Lincoln's more succinct Gettysburg Address.

The 1860 electoral field was crowded. Democrats had gathered in Charleston, South Carolina in April, but dissension caused them to have to reconvene in Baltimore in June. Members of eight Lower South states walked out of the Baltimore convention and assembled in Richmond. The Baltimore Democrats nominated Stephen A. Douglas for President, while the Richmond Democrats nominated the current Vice-President John Cabell Breckinridge. The Republican Party held its convention in Chicago in May. Republicans passed over the expected William H. Seward and instead nominated Abraham Lincoln.

The Constitutional Union Party was attempting to be a national party, which was otherwise lacking in the 1860 election. The Democrats had split into northern and southern factions. The Republican Party was a party of the northern section.

Rives expressed written support for the Constitutional Union ticket, but historian Sowle stated, that "Declining health and old age prevented Rives from campaigning vigorously."[11] He chose to travel to Newport with his family instead of accepting an invitation to speak at a Bell and Everett rally in Lynchburg.[12] Rives wrote Green Peyton, Secretary of the Charlottesville Constitutional Union Committee, a letter declining Peyton's invitation to preside and speak at a mass meeting at the end of September. In the letter, which was published in a Charlottesville newspaper, he said the great cause must be taken up by "younger and abler men" than himself. Rives called on Virginia "to repel . . . every unhallowed attempt at interference with the domestic institutions or the reserved rights of the States . . . and maintain the integrity of the Union against every attempt to weaken or subvert it, whether from the North or the South."[13]

During the early summer of 1860, political observers believed the four-way race might split the electoral vote so that no candidate would gain a majority. The House of Representatives would have to select the President as in 1824 and the Senate would have to select the Vice-President as in 1836. Bell and Everett supporters hoped such circumstances would favor their ticket. Although Bell and Everett were able to carry Virginia, Tennessee, and Kentucky, the pair came in last in the popular vote. Lincoln and the Republicans won only 40% of the popular vote, but secured an overwhelming electoral vote majority by winning every northern state. According to historian Daniel Crofts, "the informed echelon of Southern Unionists fully expected Lincoln's election a month in advance."[14] The election revealed that the solid bloc of northern states could select a president even if southerners united in opposition or cast no votes, which provoked southern anger and resentment.[15]

The *New York Herald* published a strange rumor days before the election that William C. Rives would be Lincoln's Secretary of State. The front-page article included comment from Senator Iverson of Georgia that "any Southern Man who would accept office from a Republican President ought to be condemned and ostracized."[16] This was the fourth time Rives' name was mentioned for the position; however, this rumor was ridiculous. The two would not meet until the following February. The rumor persisted long enough to inspire 15 citizens of Buckingham County to write Rives urging him to accept the offer to become Secretary of State "as a protection to Virginia, as a protection to the slave states."[17]

Rives concluded his sale of 114 slaves to James Mason and James Seddon November 12, 1860 for $70,000. He also sold his Nelson County Ranston property to Lemuel Turner, owner of an adjoining plantation Cherry Hill, for $30,632.00.[18] Rives and Judith sold other Nelson County properties in 1858 and 1862.[19] Rives was getting too old to travel to Nelson to inspect his plantations there. None of his children seemed inclined to take over the Nelson lands. The sales gave Rives a more plentiful cash flow than he had ever enjoyed, and he sought investment opportunities. The sales also appeared to be a hedge against an uncertain future. He converted some of the proceeds into gold.[20]

South Carolina seceded December 20, 1860, followed by six other states. Weeks earlier, on December 4, Virginia Congressman Alexander R. Boteler proposed the formation of a special House Committee consisting of a representative from every state, to assess the present crisis. This Committee came to be known as the Committee of Thirty-Three. The Senate created a similar Committee of Thirteen. Rives praised Boteler's idea for a "solemn family council" in a letter that summarized his views. The letter was published in the *National Intelligencer* and other papers as well as printed by itself as a broadside. Rives' letter stated that South Carolina was determined to go out of the Union, "and to drag as many of her sister States as she can after her."[21] However, Rives believed that Virginia could unite her neighbors Maryland, Kentucky, Tennessee, and North Carolina, along with Delaware, Missouri, Louisiana, Arkansas, and "possibly Mississippi," to demand that non-slaveholding states must obey the authority of the Constitution. "There must no longer be acts of States legislation in the guise of 'personal liberty laws' to nullify a solemn compact written in the Constitution, that there be no attempt covert or open by Congressional legislation to undermine their domestic institutions." Rives also proposed that if the Deep South and New England States should conspire to break up the Union, Virginia should be the leader of a band of middle states who would remain together and work to "win back to the fold those who might have temporarily strayed from it."[22] Circumstances forced Rives to contemplate an arrangement similar to the McDuffie division of the country, which he had previously condemned.

Virginia's Unionist Governor John Letcher commended Rives' letter in a message to the Virginia legislature.[23] Though Rives sounded a positive note at the end of the letter that Constitution and Union might be preserved and "placed on a more firm and lasting foundation than ever," he could see the nation breaking apart.

* * *

1 William H. Seward, "On the Irrepressible Conflict," delivered in Rochester, New York, October 25, 1858, www.nyhistory.com/central/conflict.htm.

2 "Letter from the Hon. William C. Rives on the Important Questions of the Day," Richmond, Printed at the Whig Book and Job Office, Governor Street, 1860, University of Virginia Special Collections, E438.R59 1860; also appeared in *The Richmond Whig*, February 4, 1860.

3 Winfield Scott to Rives, February 9, 1860, Rives MSS, LOC, box 91.

4 John Campbell to Rives, February 11, 1860, Rives MSS, LOC, John Campbell was appointed Treasurer of the U.S. in 1829 by Jackson and resigned the post in 1839 because of differences with Van Buren, www.huntsvillehistorycollection.org.

5 Nathan Appleton, "Letter to the Hon. William C. Rives of Virginia on Slavery and the Union," Boston, J. H. Eastburn's Press, 1860. Appleton owned textile mills in Waltham, Lowell and Lawrence, Massachusetts, and Manchester, New Hampshire. He served in the U.S. House of Representatives 1830-1832.

6 See Daniel W. Crofts, *Reluctant Confederates, Upper South Unionists in the Secession Crisis*, Chapel Hill, University of North Carolina Press, 1989, 17-18, 68-72.

7 Rives to Crittenden, January 9, 1860, (excerpt copy in Judith's handwriting) Rives MSS, LOC, box 91; original is in John Jordan Crittenden papers, Library of Congress.

8 Rives to F. B. Deane, Jr. February 22, 1860, Rives MSS, LOC, box 91 (The Deane family owned a metal foundry in Lynchburg).

9 Patrick Sowle, "The Trials of a Virginia Unionist, William Cabell Rives and the Secession Crisis 1860-1861," *Virginia Magazine of History and Biography*, Vol. 80, No. 1, January 1972, 3.

10 Rives to Crittenden, May 4, 1860, Rives MSS, LOC, box 91.

11 Sowle, Ibid, 5.

12 F. B. Deane to Rives, July 21, 1860, Rives MSS, LOC, box 91.

13 Rives to Green Peyton, September 17, 1850, newspaper clipping, Rives MSS, UVa., Accession # 2313, box 2, Folder 1860-1861 Misc. Correspondence Financial, Copy in Judith's handwriting, Rives Papers, Library of Congress, box 91.

14 Crofts, Ibid, 86. See Crofts' discussion of the campaign, 79-89.

15 Ibid, 87.

16 "News from the Nation's Capital," *New York Herald*, October 26, 1860.

17 Letter to Rives from citizens of Buckingham, November 15, 1860, Rives MSS, LOC, box 91.

18 Memorandum Book, Rives MSS, LOC, box 122.

19 Nelson Country Deed Book 15, pages 169, 317; Book 16, pages 128, 131, 275.

20 Sowle, Ibid, 6, cites letter of Judith Rives to A. L. Rives, December 2, 1860, A. L. Rives Papers, Duke University.

21 Rives to Boteler, December 11, 1860, with attached clipping, Rives MSS, UVa. Accession # 2313, box 2.

22 "Letter of Hon. Wm. C. Rives to Mr. Boteler," December 8, 1860, Virginia Historical Society, Broadsides 1860:14, #54.

23 Crofts, Ibid, 109, cites a letter from Letcher to James D. Davidson, James D. Davidson Papers, Wisconsin State Historical Society.

CHAPTER TWENTY-ONE

One of the Old Gentlemen

THOUGH HIS EFFORTS to prevent disunion were unsuccessful, Rives rendered devoted service to his country in the early months of 1861. He tried to save a Union being torn between two groups of extremists. Judith wrote Will in January that "Papa seems to dread the dogmatical rule of the secessionists as much as the pragmatical intermeddling of the abolitionists and would like to be at the queue of neither."[1]

Reacting to the crisis, the Virginia Legislature called for a State Convention in Richmond of members elected from every county, to consider the question of secession. On January 12, two days before the bill's final passage, a group of Albemarle County citizens called upon Rives to be a candidate. That same day, the Virginia Legislature also resolved to call for a Peace Conference of all the states to take place in Washington. Rives was one of the five members designated by the legislature to represent Virginia. Rives' brother Alexander urged him to undertake both missions, stressing the importance of having a Unionist represent Albemarle.[2] Rives accepted the Peace Conference appointment, but declined to run for the State Convention. He explained himself to the Albemarle group in a published declamatory letter.

The letter stated that trying to attend both meetings would present a scheduling conflict. Therefore, "another and more efficient person" should be chosen to represent Albemarle. Rives stressed the importance of "securing new and permanent guarantees for the rights of the slaveholding States in the Union, such as are embodied in Mr. Crittenden's resolutions." Rives hoped that the seceded states would not commit acts of aggression, and that the General Government would not attempt "coercion," which in his opinion would be "folly." Rives had backed Andrew Jackson's proposed use of force against South Carolina to collect revenues in 1833, but he opposed use of armed force or "coercion" to bring seceded states back into the Union in 1861. The two situations were not identical. Madison had written Rives in 1833 that as long as a State remained within the Union, it was bound to obey its Constitution and laws; however, he had expressed uncertainty about secession. Though Rives repeatedly said he did not believe in a state's right to secede, he recognized that leaders of the seceded states believed otherwise. Rives was mindful of the words of Jefferson's Declaration that government based upon consent of the governed lost its legitimacy if it became destructive of their rights. When Rives backed Jackson against the nullifiers in 1833, plenty of Virginians and other southerners agreed with him. Most Southern Unionists in 1860-61 opposed coercion.[3]

If the two sides could remain peaceful, Rives professed belief that they could be reconciled, and they could preserve "the noblest fabric of political wisdom the world has ever seen." Rives advocated that every diplomatic method should be tried to save the Union. However, he also declared, "Our rights must be maintained at all hazards," even if that meant "costly and bloody sacrifices."[4] Rives was still dedicated to preserving the Union, but not at the expense of forfeiting Constitutional "institutions" and rights.

Rives also explained in his letter that his reply was somewhat tardy because he had been absent from home for a week. Rives had visited Washington, hoping to promote the Unionist cause among old friends and new acquaintances. Rives met with General Winfield Scott, who agreed with him that a fight over Fort Sumter should be avoided.[5] John H. B. Latrobe of Baltimore, an engineer, lawyer and old friend of Rives, helped Rives arrange interviews with both Republicans and Democrats. He met with Virginia Senators James M. Mason and Robert M. T. Hunter (proponents of "states rights" who would become prominent members of the Confederate government) as well as New Hampshire abolitionist Senator John P. Hale and Senator Simon Cameron of Pennsylvania (who would be Lincoln's first Secretary of War). Rives had lengthy conversations with many lawmakers who agreed on the necessity for a national convention. Initially, Rives favored a formal constitutional convention, but he decided that an unofficial gathering of representatives could be more quickly accomplished, and was therefore preferable.[6] Rives was mostly pleased with his reception in Washington, and Senator Hale remarked that, if they "only had to deal with men such as Mr. Rives instead of bullies and blackguards, that the matter might have been amicably settled."[7]

Unfortunately, Rives' conversation with New York Senator William H. Seward was less pleasant. Seward was a former Whig, like Rives, who had served in the Taylor administration. He had been Lincoln's rival for the presidential nomination and would soon become Secretary of State. Seward made a speech in the Senate January 12 advocating concessions for the south, including a constitutional amendment protecting slavery where it existed. The amendment, known as the Corwin Amendment, named for Congressman Thomas Corwin, was approved by the House and Senate shortly before Lincoln took office, and would have been the Thirteenth Amendment had war not halted the process of ratification by the states. Seward persuaded Lincoln to use more conciliatory language in his March 4 Inaugural Address. He also urged Lincoln to evacuate Fort Sumter. Seward shared Rives' desire to prevent bloodshed.[8]

Rives and Seward conversed at a dinner party at the home of Henry S. Sanford, who had served as Secretary of the American Legation in Paris during Rives' second term as Minister. Rives asked Seward to explain what he meant by his speech on "The Irrepressible Conflict" between free and slave states. Seward replied that his words were meant to appease abolitionists in his home state of New York, and that he had not intended them to reach southern ears. Rives had nothing more to say to Seward, who was the first guest to leave.[9] Rives wrote his son Will, "I found every body in Washington, even among the Republican members of Congress, convinced of the necessity of liberal concessions to the slave-holding states, with the exception of Seward, who is a very small man, relying exclusively upon political maneuvering, & without the least pretension to true & manly statesmanship."[10]

Rives' dismissal of Seward as small and un-manly was counter-productive snobbery. He would have been wiser to overcome his personal distaste and seek cooperation with Seward, who possessed greater political power than Rives' other contacts. Throughout the country, considerations of manliness and honor were displacing reason.[11] Apparently not hindered by Rives' opinion, Seward kept up his peacemaking efforts. Unlike Lincoln, who never offered any concessions to fearful southerners, Seward tried to be a pacificator like Henry Clay.[12] Seward secretly communicated with Unionist leaders in Richmond about calling a convention to produce a settlement.[13]

In the same letter in which he criticized Seward, Rives told Will, "I feel great hopes that our approaching Convention at Washington will be animated with the right spirit. It is the last hope that is left us."[14] Historian Daniel Crofts credited Virginia Unionist Democrat James Barbour, Unionist Whig George Summers, and "perhaps others" for the plan of the Washington Peace Conference, to which Virginia invited her sister states to send delegates.[15] Rives sent a telegram from Washington to the Virginia Legislature suggesting appropriate wording for Virginia's invitation. The Legislature, according to Judith, "acted handsomely" in following his suggestions.[16]

Rives spent two weeks in Virginia, where he campaigned for his friend Valentine Southall's election to the State Convention. Rives was pleased that a large majority of Unionists were elected to the convention.[17] Popular majorities in the upper south states opposed secession during the winter of 1860-61.[18] Rives returned to Washington for the February 4 opening of the Peace Conference, held at the Willard Hotel. On that same day, representatives of the seven seceded states met in Montgomery Alabama to form a new government. None of those states sent delegates to Washington, nor did Arkansas, Michigan, Wisconsin, Minnesota, California, or Oregon. Some delegations arrived late, but at its full strength the Peace Conference included 132 delegates representing fourteen free states and seven slaveholding states.

The conference included former President John Tyler, six former cabinet members, nineteen former governors, eleven former senators and fifty former congressmen. A writer for the pro-compromise *St. Louis Daily Missouri Republican* declared that the group rivaled the framers of the Constitution in ability and reputation.[19] Their experience was accompanied by maturity in years. Most were older than fifty, and twelve were over seventy. Horace Greeley of the *New York Tribune* pronounced the gathering: an "Old Gentlemen's Convention [of] political fossils who would not have been again disinterred but for the shock. . . [of] the secessionist movement."[20]

Unionists from Virginia and other states wanted the Peace Conference to prevent war and restore the Union. Stephen A. Douglas wrote in a published letter that the hope for peace and Union depended on the actions of the Middle States, especially Virginia. "Save Virginia and we will save the Union," he declared.[21] Debates about whether to accept Virginia's invitation revealed fears of northern state radicals, that the Conference would deliver what they considered unacceptable concessions to slaveholders, such as the Crittenden plan. Some northern delegates saw

Peace Convention, from Frank Leslie's Illustrated Newspaper, *February, 16, 1861.*

the convention merely as means to delay secession of additional states, ensuring a quorum for counting electoral votes February 13. They also wanted to keep Maryland and Virginia in the Union until after Lincoln's inauguration on March 4.[22] Horace Greeley wrote that once Lincoln was inaugurated, he and fellow radicals would be "in a position to use daggers as well as speak them."[23]

Secessionists in Virginia and further south perceived the Peace Conference as a threat. Alexander wrote his brother that, "Its failure is ardently prayed for by the disunionists."[24] Those forming the new government in Montgomery, Alabama telegraphed their border state allies at the Conference "not to consent to compromise of any kind." A correspondent of the Charleston, S. C. *Mercury* wrote, "The only hope now is in the smashing up of the Peace Conference and getting Virginia out."[25]

Rives' fellow Virginia delegates were Judge George W. Summers of Kanawha Court House (now West Virginia), James A. Seddon of Goochland, Judge John W. Brockenbrough of Lexington, and former President Tyler. Rives expected Seddon and Tyler to advocate strong southern rights positions. Though Brockenbrough was from a majority Unionist area, he allied himself with Tyler and Seddon, and the three of them outvoted Rives and his fellow Unionist Summers.[26] Rives could not have been pleased to see Tyler elected as President of the Conference. Former Secretary of the Treasury James Guthrie of Kentucky suggested that a committee be formed, consisting of one delegate from every state, to create resolutions for preserving peace. Rives was again displeased when Seddon, Tyler and Brockenbrough united to install Seddon onto the Guthrie Committee. He privately told Guthrie and other friends on the committee that Seddon's views did not reflect Virginia popular opinion.[27]

On February 15, the Guthrie Committee submitted its recommendations, including: re-establishment of the 36° 30' Missouri Compromise Line, with slavery prohibited north of the line, and protected south of it, future territory to be acquired only by treaty ratified by four-fifths of the Senate, vigorous enforcement of the fugitive slave guarantee of the Constitution, and repression of illegal importation of slaves into the U.S.[28] All members of the Conference then proceeded to debate merits of the Committee Report and suggest amendments.

Believing he could accomplish more in private conversations, Rives delivered only two formal speeches to the conference, compared to Seddon's fifty-three. His first was a eulogy for Judge John C. Wright of Ohio, a Conference delegate who died after a final utterance, "May the Union be preserved!" Rives recounted how he first met Wright in 1824 when both served in the House along with Clay, Webster, and other "giants" of the day.[29]

Rives delivered his major speech to the Conference Tuesday, February 19, after a denunciation of "northern villainy" by Seddon, which provoked countercharges of southern corruption from radical Republican George Boutwell of Massachusetts.[30] Rives first addressed William C. Noyes of New York who had complained that the Conference was unconstitutional. Rives contended that the conference was as legitimate as the Constitutional

Convention, and more important because the country was more severely fractured than at any time in its history.

Although he asserted Virginia could live in the Union or stand on her own strength out of it, Rives declared that he did not believe in a Constitutional right of secession. "I proclaimed that thirty years ago in Congress." However, it was a fact that seven states had seceded. Virginia was attempting to mediate. Rives said he was surprised by the complaint of Mr. Boutwell of Massachusetts that Virginia was thrusting herself between the Republican party and its victory. "It is not so," said Rives.

Boutwell interrupted. "I said that Massachusetts thought her action had that appearance."

Rives said that he wished to make the victory worthwhile, to ensure that the victors would govern a whole nation, rather than a fraction of that nation, or a nation at war. Rives argued that armed coercion could not succeed in bringing states back into the Union. He believed the federal government might spend millions of dollars and shed oceans of blood, but it could not conquer seven states. Rives also recounted his experience of the 1830 Paris revolution, when he saw regiments throw down their arms rather than fire upon their fellow citizens. He predicted (inaccurately) that Americans would not kill their brothers.

Rives repeated the old accusation that Massachusetts, when it profited from the slave trade in colonial times, had forced slavery upon the south. Only now that she had ceased to profit from it did Massachusetts denounce the institution. Rives explained that to bring an end to slavery, the north must let it alone. "If you will say and let it be said in the Constitution that you will not interfere with slavery in the District, in the States, or in the Territories, and permit free transit of slaves from one state to another, then there will be peace."[31]

Rives' hour and a half speech reportedly impressed even the northern radicals. Delegate J. Z. Goodrich of Massachusetts

Ardent secessionist James A. Seddon served as
Confederate Secretary of War, 1862-1865.

wrote Governor John Andrew that everyone "had a good time generally."[32]

During a Peace Conference session on February 23, the "body servant" of James Seddon, "a man scarcely darker than himself," according to an eyewitness, entered the hall and handed his master a note that read "Lincoln is in this hotel." Waldo P. Johnson of Missouri, who was sitting next to Seddon, also read the note and exclaimed in a loud voice, "How the devil did he get through Baltimore?" Vermont Republican Lucius E. Chittenden, recorder of Peace Conference proceedings, implied that Johnson and other Conference delegates were aware of a plot to assassinate Lincoln in Baltimore. Word of Lincoln's arrival produced uproar. Some favored meeting with the President-elect; others did not. Lincoln agreed to receive members of the southern delegations that evening at 9 p.m. He told Chittenden that Rives and Judge Thomas Ruffin of North Carolina were influential southern statesmen he particularly wanted to meet.[33]

Chittenden's account of Rives' meeting with Lincoln differed from the previously mentioned narrative Rives wrote to his son. In Chittenden's version, Lincoln expressed surprise that Rives was not a taller man, then added, "every one is acquainted with the greatness of your intellect. It is, indeed pleasant to meet one who has so honorably represented his country in Congress and abroad." Rives thanked him for the compliment and said he felt himself a small man in Lincoln's presence. While Rives ended the story at that point in his letter, Chittenden wrote that Rives continued the exchange and told Lincoln, "Everything now depends upon you."

Lincoln replied, "I cannot agree to that. My course is as plain as a turnpike road. It is marked out by the Constitution." He suggested that obedience to the Constitution and the laws was the solution. James Seddon interjected that northerners freely disobeyed the laws, citing abolitionist editor William Lloyd Garrison and insurrectionist John Brown. Lincoln remarked that Garrison had been imprisoned and Brown had been hung. William E. Dodge of New York warned Lincoln he would be to blame if war destroyed the country and caused grass to grow in the streets of American cities. Lincoln claimed he was bound to obey, enforce and defend the Constitution, "let the grass grow where it may." However, he promised that his administration would protect the legitimate rights of the slaveholding states.

Afterwards, in Chittenden's account, Rives told his fellow southerners that Lincoln "has been both misjudged and misunderstood by the Southern people. They have looked upon him as an ignorant self-willed man, incapable of independent judgment, full of prejudices, willing to be used as a tool by more able men. This is all wrong." Though Rives said Lincoln lacked the statesmanship of Madison and the willpower of Jackson, he believed, "He will be the head of his administration, and he will do his own thinking. . . . I do not see that much fault can be found with the views he has expressed this evening." Ruffin agreed, though he did not like Lincoln's objection to making any concessions to the slaveholding states.[34]

In his letter to Will written the following day, Rives complained of the "narrowminded & impracticable" New England delegations, except for Rhode Island. He wrote "in confidence" to his son in Boston, that those of Massachusetts[35] and New York were the worst. Rives also feared Lincoln was not leading, but was being led by members of his party.[36] He concluded that Lincoln would not help the Conference.[37] Rives' opinion of Lincoln would continue to decline. In her autobiography written a few months later, Judith lamented that in earlier, nobler years of the republic, "A rail splitter might have been deemed a useful citizen, but he could never have aspired to the Presidency."[38]

On February 26, the Peace Conference voted on the first section of the Guthrie Committee Report, the protection of slavery in all territory south of the Missouri Compromise line. Each state would have one vote, determined by majority vote of its delegation. Republicans opposed it because it violated their party's "Chicago" platform (named for the city of their 1860 convention). The more extreme southerners opposed it because of an amendment limiting its reach to present territory only. Rives and Summers were outvoted, as Virginia sided with the majority that defeated the article by a vote of eleven to eight. The first section was the most important, and it seemed the Conference would end in complete failure. Then Thomas Turner, a member of the pro-compromise minority of the Illinois delegation made a motion for reconsideration. After much confusion, the Conference was adjourned until the next morning.

When the Conference reconvened and re-voted on the morning of the 27th, the article passed by a vote of nine to eight. Illinois changed its vote to aye and New York and Missouri abstained. The remaining articles from the Guthrie report also passed, and the Peace Conference adjourned. Its report was sent to Congress, where it subsequently failed to win approval.[39]

That evening, Rives and others called on Lincoln. Rives pleaded with Lincoln to withdraw troops from Fort Sumter, and Lincoln indicated he might do so, according to Governor Morehead's account. In the following weeks, Winfield Scott and Seward also urged Lincoln to evacuate Sumter. Sumter increasingly became the focus of attention and debates, assuming a symbolic importance far greater than its military value. A March 9 article in the *Richmond Dispatch* discussed "The Coming Assault on Fort Sumter," and the difficulties of bombardment and anticipated assault by "Palmetto regiments."[40] On April 4, Lincoln met with Virginia Unionist John B. Baldwin of Staunton. Lincoln had summoned George Summers, but requested that Summers send a like-minded friend if he was unable to appear. Summers did not want to be absent from the Virginia Convention, which was voting that day on a motion for secession, which failed 88-45.[41]

At the end of a long discussion with Baldwin about the crisis and Virginia's position, Lincoln indicated his supporters would be displeased if he abandoned Sumter, and that he might need to provision the troops there. Baldwin advised him not to. He added, "If there is a gun fired at Sumter — I do not care on which side it is fired — the thing is gone. . . . Virginia herself, strong as the Union majority in the Convention is now, will be out in forty-eight hours."

Lincoln said, "Oh, sir, that is impossible."

Baldwin replied, "Mr. President, I did not come here to argue with you; I am here as a witness. I know the sentiments of the people of Virginia and you do not."[42]

Rives hastened from Washington to Richmond after the Peace Conference to promote its result to the Virginia Convention and defend it from many critics. Though suffering from poor health, including a "blister on his chest,"[43] Rives delivered a two-hour speech on the Peace Conference before an overflow crowd in the African Church (First African Baptist), a large structure that also accommodated white-led assemblies.[44] Rives declared that though detractors labeled them "an abortion, a mockery, a delusion, and what not," the Peace Conference proposals were "the most comprehensive and satisfactory settlement of the unhappy controversies which divide the country, that has yet emanated from any quarter." Rives hoped the proposals would be approved by state legislatures even if they stalled in Congress. The issue, Rives observed, was the "delicate but fruitful topic of domestic servitude." Rives argued that the Peace Conference resolutions were based upon Crittenden's plan, but were superior in many respects. The required four-fifths congressional majority vote on territorial expansion enabled both south and north to restrain disproportional growth by the other section. The south would need northern approval to expand into Mexico, and the north would need southern approval to acquire territory from Canada. Rives praised New Jersey, Pennsylvania, Ohio, Illinois, Indiana and Rhode Island for standing with the south during the Conference. He criticized the seceded states for abandoning the opportunity to defend their interests by legislative means. He declared Virginia stood with her sister border slaveholding states, of which she was the leader: North Carolina, Tennessee, Arkansas, Missouri, Kentucky, Maryland and Delaware. He asked if Virginia should become the tail of a Southern Confederacy, or at the "head of the serried Macedonian phalanx of her sister border slave states?" If she chose to join the seceded states, "end-less feuds and strifes will follow," as in revolutionary France, Mexico, or South American countries. Rives concluded that such a reckless course provided "no warrant for believing that the laws of history . . . will be suddenly reversed in our favor."[45]

The speech received "prolonged and vociferous applause" according to the *National Intelligencer*[46] along with high praise from many Unionist friends. The *Richmond Dispatch* included a positive summary of the speech, though it did note that when Rives asked rhetorically if Virginia should join the seceded states, "Mingled cries of no and yes," echoed through the hall.[47] Worried that the speech had undermined their cause, secession-ists insisted that John Tyler deliver a rebuttal the following day.[48]

The secessionist *Daily Richmond Examiner* subsequently deliv-ered a personal, bitter, and severe criticism of Rives' speech and of his entire career. The editorial ridiculed his support of Jackson's Force Bill and the Expunging. It claimed his Reparations Treaty nearly caused a war with France. Rives' head allegedly became deranged when he "received a very hard fall in a wrestling match with a man named Johnson . . ." for the vice-presidency. This supposedly prompted him to bolt the Democratic Party and to commit the apostasy of supporting Clay for President. The writer stated it was appropriate that Rives returned to Paris for a second term as Minister, because the best lunatic asylums could be found there. The writer asked how Rives, who had declared in the Senate that slavery was evil, could believe himself "the pro-perest man to undertake its perpetuation." The writer asserted the Peace Conference proposal surrendered everything to the abolitionists. The article called Rives an "intellectual ichneu-mon," (a type of stingless wasp). It also mentioned prizes won by Rives' livestock, including a stallion "ambitiously named Emperor." Noting that Rives was writing a biography of Madison, the writer stated, "Thus one trimmer should embalm another."[49] (A "trimmer" is one who changes his opinions or policies to suit the occasion.)

This assault was likely the work of *Examiner* editor John Moncure Daniel, an ardent Virginia secessionist. Daniel would have known about Rives' livestock because he had previously written for *The Southern Planter*. The "ichneumon" insult was in the same vein as Daniel's characterization of Lincoln as "an ugly and ferocious old orang-outang from the wilds of Illinois."[50] Daniel had traveled to Washington during the Peace Conference and conferred with James Seddon. Both men would have known the main features of Rives' career.[51] Two nephews of Rives, Edward Alfred Pollard and his brother Henry Rives Pollard, joined Daniel as fellow editors of the *Examiner* later in the spring of 1861. The Pollards fled from Baltimore, fearing for their safety after Edward had published a vicious attack on Lincoln titled "Letters of a Southern Spy."[52] As loyal family members, the Pollards would not have assisted in, and hopefully would have objected to Daniel's attack on their uncle.

Rives had returned to Castle Hill to recover his health when the *Examiner* piece appeared. Fellow Unionists urged him to write out his African Church speech for publication.[53] He also wanted to return to his Madison work.[54] Among the many letters that had arrived in his absence was a note from a neighbor in Stony Point, to the west of the Southwest Mountains from Castle Hill, that warned of an impending slave insurrection. Five days after Lincoln's inauguration, slaves throughout Virginia were going to kill every white person "except the young and lovely virgins." The neighbor assured Rives, "This is no fiction."[55]

On April 6, Lincoln sent a message to the South Carolina Governor that he was sending ships to bring food to the garrison at Fort Sumter. Confederate forces began firing on Sumter April 12, and the commander of the fort surrendered April 14.[56]

From Castle Hill, Rives wrote on April 15 to Summers at the Virginia Convention that Virginia should not rush to secede, even though the shooting had started. He said Virginia and the border states should "maintain their meditational position."[57] In a more urgent tone, Rives wrote H. B. Latrobe in Washington on April 19 about the possibility of mediation by European nations. The prospect of war, Rives wrote, was "too afflicting to humanity, & I must add, too disgraceful to our civilization, not to call for every possible effort, even at this eleventh hour, to avert the catastrophe."[58] On April 15, Lincoln issued a proclamation calling for 75,000 militiamen to put down the insurrection. Rives wrote Summers that Lincoln's request for 2,460 militiamen, Virginia's portion of the total, was illegal, that Virginia should refuse to comply, and that the proclamation was insufficient reason for secession. He said Virginia should defend her rights within the Union "instead of resorting to the suicidal remedy of secession." Rives concluded gloomily, "If I had not had so many proofs of my utter inability to exert any influence on the course of events, I would go down to confer with you and our friends. But I could do no good."[59]

Judith also expressed hope that Virginia could somehow remain in the Union. She wrote Will of her affection for "the star spangled banner," how she had proudly seen it floating over foreign harbors, how it had protected "life and property in the blood stained streets of revolutionary France." She recalled that she and Will had been rolled up in a large U.S. flag and lowered from the deck of the *Constellation* into a barge, to be rowed ashore after they had first crossed the Atlantic in 1829.[60]

On April 17, Virginia Convention Delegate Robert Scott of Fauquier County proposed a referendum giving voters a choice between secession and a border state conference. The motion was defeated 77-64. Scott correctly predicted that immediate secession would divide the state.[61] The day before the vote, former Governor Henry Wise had organized extra-legal militia groups to seize the Harper's Ferry Arsenal and the Gosport Navy Yard in Norfolk. Similar pre-secession military strikes took place in other slaveholding states. Wise was a Convention delegate and after Scott's motion failed, he marched up to the podium brandishing a large horse pistol and waving his pocket watch, indicating there was no more time for delay. John Baldwin spoke in protest, but the Convention soon voted for secession 85-55. Caught up in the momentum, 85% of Virginia voters approved the Ordinance of Secession on May 23.[62]

Rives wrote Will on April 25 that a separation of sections into two nations now seemed inevitable. However, he hoped it would be "a peaceable one." Rives said he believed "a Christian people will never permit our present unhappy difficulties to go to the extremity of civil war."[63] Will's father-in-law David Sears wrote Rives from Boston that he hoped that the two countries could become "united allies if they cannot keep them as United States." Sears said that the boundary between North and South, "once drawn, will never be changed except by removal of slavery" from the South. He quoted Rives' letter, which he was answering, to assure Rives that their ties of friendship and family would "lose nothing of their perennial freshness and warmth from this unhappy national disruption."[64]

The Virginia Convention selected Rives to be one of Virginia's representatives at the Confederate Congress in Montgomery. Rives wrote John Janney, President of the Convention, how, while any hope remained, he had struggled to maintain the Union "on terms consistent with the rights and honor of the South." Now that the "Commonwealth of Virginia, the mother to whom I owe everything both of duty and affection," had chosen secession, Rives promised, "to devote all that I am and all that I have to the service of my native and honored commonwealth." Rives observed, "The authorities installed at Washington, crowding the brief space since their accession to power with acts of madness and infatuation of which there is no example in the records of official incompetence or delinquency, and invoking to their aid the blind and exterminating rage of party and sectional passions, leave us no alternative but to stand as one man in defense of our altars and our friends." [65]

For Rives and his compatriots, Lincoln's decision to invade changed a dispute about rights and honor to a struggle for survival. Threatened by an attacking enemy, southerners previously divided over secession and other issues, became united to protect their homeland. [66] Upper South Unionists faced only bad and worse choices: oppose their country or oppose their home state and neighbors. Though Rives had declared slavery an evil and had opposed secession, he had decided to stand with a secessionist government which guaranteed the rights of slaveholders. Rives had revered the Union and the Constitution, but he felt Lincoln had despoiled the Constitution. In making his choice, Rives reverted to fundamental love of home and of his land, where loved to ride at daybreak. He wrote his son, "Our justification . . . lies in the principles of the Declaration of American Independence . . ." of the right to reject a ". . . government, which no longer stands upon the only legitimate foundation, the consent of the governed, but seeks to rule by the sword." [67]

In his letter to Janney, Rives had declined the honor of being a representative, citing age and poor health. He wrote the letter May 1, the same day the Convention adjourned. Because there was no longer a convention to appoint a substitute, Rives decided to obey the summons. He wrote another former-Unionist friend Alexander H. H. Stuart of his mission to Montgomery, "I confess I . . . [see] but little prospect of my doing any good, but it is enough for me to know that my friends think otherwise." [68] Rives explained to Will, "Providence often casts upon us, in spite of ourselves, duties which it is impossible to avoid."[69] Rives had decided, "We must make good our independence, or submit to a government resting on force and the arbitrary will of a sectional majority."[70]

Rives set off for Montgomery, Alabama to take his place in the Confederate government.

* * *

1 Judith Page Rives to William C. Rives, Jr. January 14, 1861, Rives MSS, LOC, box 36.

2 Alexander Rives to Rives, January 17, 1861, Rives MSS, Ibid.

3 Daniel W. Crofts, *Reluctant Confederates: Upper South Unionists in the Secession Crisis*, Chapel Hill, University of North Carolina Press, 1989, 126.

4 "Correspondence": T. J. Wertenbaker . . . and 550 others to W. C. Rives, January 12, 1861, and "Mr. Rives' Reply," January 23, 1861, broadside, University of Virginia Special Collections, E438.R58 1861 Election for the Virginia Convention took place February 4, the opening day of the Peace Conference.

5 Patrick Sowle, "The Trials of a Virginia Unionist: William Cabell Rives and the Secession Crisis, 1860-1861," *The Virginia Magazine of History and Biography*, Vol. 80, No. 1, January 1972. Cites letters from Judith Rives to W. C. Rives, Jr. January 14, 27, 1861, Rives MSS, LOC, box 36 and J.H.B. Latrobe to Rives, January 16, 1861, Ibid, box 91. See Crofts, Ibid, 274, Scott advised Lincoln that defending Sumter would require an immense naval flotilla.

6 Sowle, Ibid, 9

7 Judith and Rives to William C. Rives, Jr. January 27, 1861, (written from Oak Ridge) Rives MSS, LOC, box 36.

8 See Crofts, Ibid, 236 for Seward's January 12 Senate Speech, for his suggestions on Lincoln's Inaugural address 254 (Seward threatened resignation), 271-274, 299 for his efforts toward withdrawal from Sumter.

9 Sowle, Ibid, 8-9, cites letter from Judith to A.L. Rives January 21, 1861, A. L. Rives Papers, Duke University.

10 Judith and Rives to William C. Rives, Jr., January 27, 1861, Rives MSS, LOC, box 36.

11 See Crofts, Ibid, 126-127 for discussion of the role of honor in opposition to coercion, even among Unionists.

12 See William J. Cooper, "Where Was Henry Clay? President-Elect Abraham Lincoln and the Crisis of the Union 1860-1861," in Gary Gallagher and Rachel A. Shelden, editors, *A Political Nation: New Directions in Mid-Nineteenth-Century American Political History*, Charlottesville, University of Virginia Press, 2012, 133, 138.

13 Sowle, Ibid, cites several works, including *Henry Adams, The Great Secession Winter of 1860-61 and Other Essays*, George Hockfield, ed., New York, 1958, 24.

14 Judith and Rives to William C. Rives, Jr., January 27, 1861, Rives MSS, LOC, box 36.

15 Crofts, Ibid, 138, cites article in *Washington Evening Star*, reprinted in Alexandria Gazette, January 25, 1861.

16 Judith and Rives, to William C. Rives, Jr. January 27, 1861, Rives MSS, LOC, box 36.

17 Sowle, Ibid, 10.

18 Crofts, Ibid, 130-131. Crofts explains how remnants of the Whig party (not found in the Deep South) provided a foundation for Unionists.

19 *St. Louis Daily Missouri Republican*, February 9, 1861, quoted in Robert G. Gunderson, "William C. Rives and the 'Old Gentlemen's Convention.'" Journal of Southern History, Vol. 22 (1956) 459-476, 467.

20 *New York Semi-Weekly Tribune*, February 1, 8, 1861, quoted in Gunderson, Ibid.

21 Public letter from Stephen A. Douglas, January 31, 1861, in Petersburg Express, February 2, 1861, *Richmond Whig*, February 4, 1861, cited in Crofts, Ibid, 139.

22 Robert G. Gunderson, *Old Gentlemen's Convention, The Washington Peace Conference of 1861*, Madison, University of Wisconsin Press, 1961, 33-34, 38-39. See entire Chapter 4 "Matters of Political Necessity," for debates in various states about sending delegates.

23 Horace Greeley to W. H. Herndon, December 26, 1860, in R. T. Lincoln Collection, Library of Congress, quoted in Gunderson, "William C. Rives and the Old Gentlemen's Convention," Ibid, 468.

24 Alexander Rives to Rives, February 17, 1861, Rives MSS, LOC, Box 36.

25 Charleston, (S.C.) Mercury, correspondence February 4, 1861, quoted in *New York Times*, February 14, 1861, correspondence from Montgomery, February 19, 1861, quoted in *New York Times*, February 20, 1861, cited in Gunderson, "William C. Rives. . . ." Ibid, 469.

26 Rives to William C. Rives, Jr., March 2, 1861, Rives MSS, LOC, box 36.

27 Rives to William C. Rives, Jr., February 11, 1861, Ibid. See Sowle, Ibid, 11-12.

28 Sowle, Ibid, 12. See Crofts, Ibid, 202-203 for a comparison of features of the Missouri Compromise, Crittenden Compromise, Committee of Thirty-Three and the Peace Conference Proposal.

29 Lucius E. Chittenden, *A Report of the Debates and Proceedings in the Secret Sessions of the Conference Convention for Proposing Amendments to the Constitution of the United States held at Washington D.C. in February A.D. 1861*, New York, D. Appleton & Company, 1864, 39.

30 Ibid, 133-141, Sowle, Ibid, 13.

31 Chittenden, Ibid. Also transcript of speech in letterbook, Rives MSS, LOC, box 105.

32 Goodrich to Andrew, February 19, 1861, John A. Andrew Papers, Massachusetts Historical Society, cited in Gunderson, "William C. Rives and. . . ." Ibid, 471.

33 Lucius E. Chittenden, *Recollections of President Lincoln and his Administration*, New York, Harper & Brothers, 1891, 66-69.

34 Ibid, 72-77.

35 Robert C. Winthrop to Rives, February 9, 1861 Rives MSS, LOC, box 91. Winthrop wished that his governor had appointed at least one Democrat and Unionist instead of seven Republicans to the Massachusetts delegation.

36 See William J. Cooper, "Where Was Henry Clay?..." Ibid. Cooper writes that Lincoln acted as head of the Republican Party rather than as President-elect of the entire nation.

37 Rives to William C. Rives, Jr. February 24, 1861, Rives MSS, LOC, box 36

38 Judith Page Rives, Autobiography, 60.

39 Sowle, Ibid, 16-17, Gunderson, "William C. Rives and. . . ." Ibid, 472-473

40 *Richmond Dispatch*, March 9, 1861.

41 William W. Freehling and Craig Simpson, editors, *Showdown in Virginia, The 1861 Convention and the Fate of the Union*, Charlottesville, University of Virginia Press, 2010, xiii.

42 John B. Baldwin, Interview between President Lincoln and Col John B. Baldwin, April 4th, 1861: Statements and Evidence Staunton, Virginia, : "Spectator" Job Office, 1866) 11-13, quoted in Crofts, Ibid, 305-306. Crofts notes that some people disputed Baldwin's account. Crofts' Chapter 11 289-307 "Reversal of the Hands-off Policy" explores the Sumter issue.

43 Judith Page Rives to William C. Rives, Jr., March 15, 1861, Rives MSS, LOC, box 36.

44 www.mdgorman.com "Civil War Richmond, Churches".

45 William C. Rives, "Speech of Hon. William C. Rives, on the Proceedings of the Peace Conference and the State of the Union, Delivered March 8, 1861, Richmond, printed at the Whig Book and Job Office, 1861, University of Virginia Special Collections, #A1861.R44.

46 *National Intelligencer*, March 12, 1861.

47 *Richmond Dispatch*, March 9, 1861, cited in Nelson D. Lankford, *Cry Havoc! The Crooked Road to Civil War 1861*, New York, Viking, 2007, 33.

48 Sowle, Ibid, 19, also Gunderson, "William C. Rives and. . . .", Ibid, 475-476.

49 *Daily Richmond Examiner*, March 23, 1861, cited in Lankford, Ibid.

50 Peter Bridges, "A Pen of Fire," *Virginia Quarterly Review*, Charlottesville, University of Virginia, Winter 2002, 41-53.

51 George W. Bagby, *John M. Daniel's Latch Key*, Lynchburg, J.P. Bell & Co., 1868, 7.

52 Charles F. Ritter, John L. Wakelyn, *Leaders of the American Civil War: A Biographical and Historiographical Dictionary*, Westport, Connecticut, Greenwood Publishing Group, 1998, 317.

53 Judith to William C. Rives, Jr., March 15, Rives MSS, LOC, box 36

54 Rives to Robert C. Winthrop, April 19, 1861, Winthrop Papers, Massachusetts Historical Society, cited in Drew R. McCoy, *The Last of the Fathers*, Cambridge, Cambridge University Press, 1989, 345.

55 J. F. Simms to Rives, February 20, 1861, Rives MSS, LOC, box 91.

56 James M. McPherson, *Battle Cry of Freedom*, New York, Ballantine Books, 1988, 273-274. See also Crofts, Ibid, "Epilogue" 353-360 for a discussion of Lincoln's options. Crofts states, ". . . it is dangerously ahistorical to see the outbreak of the Civil War as simply the first chapter of a morality tale and Lincoln as a secular saint or giant among pygmies." 359.

57 Rives to Summers, April 15, 1861, Rives MSS, LOC, box 92.

58 Rives to Latrobe, April 19, 1861, Ibid.

59 Rives to Summers, April 19, 1861, Ibid.

60 Judith to William C. Rives, Jr., April 14, 1861, Ibid, box 36.

61 Crofts, Ibid, 314.

62 Freehling and Simpson, Ibid, xiii-xvii, xxiv-xxvi, 193-195.

63 Rives to William C. Rives, Jr., April 22, 1861, Rives MSS, LOC, box 36.

64 David Sears to Rives, April 27, 1861, Ibid, box 91.

65 Rives to John Janney, May 1, 1861, Ibid, box 92.

66 see William W. Freehling, "Reviving State Rights," in Gary Gallagher and Rachel A. Shelden, *A Political Nation: New Directions in Mid-Nineteenth-Century American Political History*, Charlottesville, University of Virginia Press, 2012, 123. Freehling writes that Virginian John Hughes explained his conversion from Unionist to secessionist that Lincoln's demand for troops was an intolerable declaration of war upon Virginia's people. 123.

67 Rives to William C. Rives, Jr., May 6, 1861, Rives MSS, LOC, box 36, quoted in William W. Freehling, *The Road to Disunion*, Vol. II: *Secessionists Triumphant 1854-1861*, New York, Oxford, Oxford University Press, 2007, 527.

68 Rives to Stuart, May 7, 1861, Alexander H. H. Stuart Papers, Library of Congress Manuscripts Division, quoted in Gunderson, "William C. Rives and. . . ." Ibid, 476.

69 Rives to William C. Rives, Jr., May 6, 1861, Rives MSS, LOC, quoted in McCoy, Ibid, 360.

70 Ibid, quoted in Crofts, Ibid, 337. See also Rives to Alexander Rives (copy) June 7, 1865, Rives MSS, LOC, box 37, In this letter, composed under different circumstances, Rives wrote his brother that he had felt obliged to obey the call of his fellow citizens in order to work for an early termination of the war. Another possible incentive for Rives' acceptance of the post was that the convention selected him over James A. Seddon, although Seddon later joined the Provisional Congress. *Anatomy of the Confederate Congress*, Thomas B. Alexander and Richard E. Beringer, Nashville, Vanderbilt University Press, 1972, 39.

CHAPTER TWENTY-TWO

Rights and Liberties Assailed

AS RIVES TRAVELED SOUTH by train, assembled crowds at stations called for speeches from the famous orator. In Atlanta he told his audience:

> I feel highly complimented by this call from the citizens of Georgia to say a few words. I suppose you do not want to hear a speech from me, but that you do want to hear from Virginia. ['That's it.' And cheers from the crowd.] She is all right, I am most happy to inform you. She is heart and hand with Georgia in this struggle, and will faithfully do her part. You have been accustomed in political matters, in time past, to follow our lead; but now we will follow your lead in this great movement for the maintenance of the rights and independence of the South and her institutions. Our rights and liberties are assailed, and must be defended. Our cause is a just one, and brave hearts are rushing to uphold it. In the meantime, you may rely upon Old Virginia. Whether she is to lead or to follow, she will be along and give a good account of herself.

Rives continued that he had never been to Georgia, but he felt at home in a state with so many family ties to Virginia. Answering a question from the crowd, Rives said that Federal troops were not in Alexandria, and would fall into a trap if they tried to occupy that city. When the train jolted into motion, the crowd applauded and cheered as Rives concluded, "Thank you for this manifestation of your feelings towards Virginia. I now bid you adieu."[1]

In a letter accompanying this newspaper account, Rives observed to Judith that the mid-May Georgia temperature felt like July at Castle Hill. He reported that he had been received with "great kindness and consideration." He had dined at the home of Robert Toombs, who was the first Confederate Secretary of State. Rives was honored to be "assigned the privilege of conducting the Madame to the table. There is no great elegance or refinement, but their place is supplied by great cordiality and manliness."[2] Apparently Rives' highly critical, class-conscious eye perceived in Toombs a manliness that William H. Seward lacked, though Seward turned out to be a more successful Secretary of State. Toombs' brief term would end with his resignation in late July. Rives received the same honor when he dined at the home of President Jefferson Davis. He escorted "the Madame Presidentess" Varina Davis, whom he deemed: ". . . exceedingly clever, *spirituelle*, and *bien instruite* [witty and well-informed], but, according to the custom of the country, too free and easy to be of the highest order of elegance and refinement. She was very kind and flattering in her attentions to me. The President is a very intelligent man, civil, observant, and cordial . . . far above the average of the modern race of American Presidents."[3]

Rives took his seat in the Second Session of the Provisional Congress of the Confederate States in Montgomery on Monday, May 13, 1861. He was appointed to the Committee on Foreign Affairs. Three fellow Virginians, R. M. T. Hunter, John W. Brockenbrough, and Walter R. Staples had arrived and been seated before him. Some sessions were designated "Open" to spectators and other sessions were designated "Secret," and therefore closed to the public. Each open session began with a prayer led by a minister. Rives and his fellow legislators considered bills organizing the military, a postal service, operation of mints, and other functions of a new government.[4]

Legislators of the Confederacy have not enjoyed the acclaim of its military leaders, perhaps because the ablest men were in uniform. Historians rate the Confederate Congress as ineffective and greatly inferior to its rival U.S. Congress. The Confederate Congress drew criticism both for being too compliant as well as for obstructing the Davis administration. The body had no political party structure, which Rives may have welcomed, since he had trumpeted the evils of the two-party system since the 1830s. However, this lack of party organization and every-man-for-himself voting made passage of laws unpredictable and inefficient. [5]

After Rives' death in 1868, *The New Orleans Times* declared, "In the Confederate Congress he was the patriarch statesman whose venerable aspect and earnest zeal gave new vigor and encouragement to his younger associates."[6] The Second Session adjourned May 21 after resolving to re-convene in Richmond July 20.

Back at Castle Hill, Rives sent a note to Treasury Secretary Christopher G. Memminger with a contribution of $63.61 to the Confederate cause, gathered from members of Grace Church.[7] Rives invested thousands of dollars of his own money in Confederate bonds.[8]

The Third Session of the Provisional Congress in Richmond included additional members from Virginia well known to Rives, including Robert E. Scott, James Seddon, James M. Mason, and John Tyler. In an urgent message to Congress, President Davis noted that the United States was raising an army of half a million troops to invade the Confederacy. The following day, July 21, he announced to Congress that Confederate forces had won a glorious victory at Manassas.[9]

Rives wrote of the victory to his youngest son Alfred, who was a Captain in the Confederate Corps of Engineers. He reported that Alfred's Cousin Channing Page was in the fight as part of Captain Pendleton's artillery. Rives speculated that if Generals Beauregard and Johnston had 20,000 more men, they could have taken Washington. He feared that the enemy had to suffer additional defeats before they would think of peace. "Wicked men in power" in Washington would prolong the war only to prevent their political disgrace.[10]

When the firing began at Fort Sumter April 12, Alfred was a civil engineer in Washington, supervising construction of the Capitol Dome. His training at the French *École des Ponts et Chaussées* made him one of the most knowledgeable engineers in the U.S. Serving under U.S. Captain Montgomery Meigs, Alfred also designed the Cabin John Bridge, which in 1861 was the country's largest clear span masonry arch bridge.[11] At the end of March, Captain Meigs had sailed with an expedition to relieve the garrison of Florida's Fort Pickens,[12] and left Alfred in charge of the Capitol project, for which Alfred had invented a special derrick.[13]

Unlike his three siblings who had married northerners and settled in the north, Alfred married a fellow southerner, Sarah Catherine (Sadie) Macmurdo of Richmond in 1859. When Virginia seceded, he resigned his position in Washington, and was invited to join the Confederate cause as a Captain of Engineers.[14] He was later promoted to Colonel, and for much of the war was acting head of the Confederate Bureau of Engineering. Alfred helped design defenses at Drewry's Bluff, a high point overlooking the James River below Richmond. Those defenses prevented Union ships from steaming upriver and bombarding the city.[15]

Alfred and Sadie suffered the loss of a daughter who died shortly after being born in December, 1861.[16] They had three more daughters, who lived to advanced ages. Amélie, who was born in

Col. Alfred L. Rives   *Sadie Rives*

Richmond August 23, 1863, claimed General Lee as her godfather.[17] Her godmother was her Aunt Amélie Sigourney. Neither godparent was able to attend the christening.[18]

Rives' youngest daughter Ella never married, and remained at Castle Hill throughout the war. Rives and Judith did not see their other three children for the duration of the conflict. Correspondence between Castle Hill and the north traveled circuitous routes and dwindled in frequency.[19]

Eldest son Francis in New York sympathized with the southern cause, and rejoiced at news of Confederate victories. In letters to his brother Will, he criticized Lincoln administration policy, and described with disgust the "delirium for battle" sweeping the city in the spring of 1861. His wife Matilda gave birth to a son, Reginald William Rives, May 18, 1861. Francis wrote that he was glad his and Will's sons were not of military age. He speculated that because of their father's position in the Confederate Congress, he and Will might have been on a list of government suspects.[20]

As Rives headed for Montgomery in May, his namesake Will wrote him from Boston that the Confederacy should try to identify its cause as the same liberty of self-government the colonists sought in 1776. He advised his father to reject the proclamations of Confederate Vice-President Stephens that slavery was an essential feature of the new republic. "I trust the dogma of Mr. Stephens in reference to slavery will be discarded, and that the Rebellion will now be put forth on such grounds by the Southern Congress, as to conciliate the sympathy and win the respect of Europe."[21] Will criticized the "Imperial Despotism at Washington,"[22] while managing not to offend Bostonians holding opposing views, including his father-in-law David Sears. Sears praised Will's "gentlemanly discretion and personal self respect."[23] Judith wrote her son that she was horrified that "dear Willie" would hear his grandfather called "a rebel and traitor" at his school.[24]

Rives and his compatriots did view themselves as true heirs of the revolutionary founders. He had cited Jefferson's Declaration of Independence as an inspiration in his May 6 letter to Will.[25] An image of George Washington adorned the seal of the Confederacy.

Both Rives and Judith urged Will in April 1861 to frequently visit his nearby sister Amélie, who was soon due to give birth. Amélie and her Bostonian husband Henry Sigourney welcomed the birth of a daughter named Helen in May.[26] Helen died of Scarlet Fever in February 1864 without ever seeing her maternal grandparents.[27] Henry Sigourney was an ardent supporter of the northern Unionist cause, which Amélie feared would provoke resentment from Virginia relatives and neighbors. She decided against a visit to Castle Hill when the war ended. She would not expose her husband to insult, and she refused to leave him because he had "cherished and protected and comforted me through sickness and heart anguish and desolation."[28]

Many of Rives' nephews served in the Confederate Army, including three surgeons: Alexander's son and namesake Alexander Rives, Jr. MD, assistant surgeon with the 15th Alabama[29], and two sons of Dr. Landon C. Rives of Cincinnati: Landon Cabell Rives, Jr., MD, surgeon with the 1st Virginia Cavalry,[30] and Edward Rives, MD, surgeon with Pickett's Division.[31] Rives' brother George's son, Captain James Henry Rives, commanded a Nelson County Light Artillery Company.[32] Previously mentioned nephews, Edward Alfred Pollard and Henry Rives Pollard supported the Confederate cause in their *Daily Richmond Examiner* editorials, but were often critical of Davis. In 1866, Edward Alfred Pollard published *The Lost Cause*, "which gave currency to the use of that phrase, 'The Lost Cause,' as applied to the Confederate States of America."[33]

Rives felt his absent children's rights and liberties were assailed by his own government body. Rives wrote Judith from Richmond that he was trying to prevent his peers from committing "acts of disgraceful violence in their legislation."[34] The Confederate Congress passed a Sequestration Act in August 1861 to retaliate against U.S. government confiscation of slaves and southern property. The Sequestration Act specified that any property identified as belonging to an alien enemy should be seized by the government and sold. Proceeds supplied a fund to reimburse victims of Federal depredations. Rives voted for certain amendments to the bill, against others, and was absent during several days of debate and voting.[35]

He was appalled when Albemarle County officials initiated sequestration of property belonging to Francis, Will and Amélie. He wrote a letter of protest to Thomas Giles, Receiver of sequestration funds. Rives invoked numerous legal precedents in arguing that the law did not apply to his children. They could not be regarded as enemy aliens, because their loyalty to Virginia and the Confederacy was absolute. "In every stage of the controversy between the North and the south, they have boldly and manfully vindicated the rights of the South, and every throb and pulsation of their hearts are now with her in her noble struggle for independence." Rives said that an amendment had been proposed to the Sequestration Act to protect individuals like his children, who had demonstrated no hostility to the Confederacy and were prevented from returning to their lands by causes beyond their control. However the amendment was considered unnecessary, because the general understanding was that the bill would be applied only to avowed and flagrant enemies. Rives also explained that the lands in question were part of his wife's ancestral estate, "the slaves upon the whole estate have been interchangeably employed, and transferred from farm to farm, according to varying exigencies, subject to my discretion and control." Rives apologized to Giles for troubling him; however, his children's plight, Giles' official position, and the "mutual frankness and confidence I would wish to preserve in all our relations," had necessitated the communication.[36] The letter must have prompted the desired response. The land stayed in the family.

Judith worried that the Confederate government might mimic "the vulgar and brutal despotism at Washington." Sympathetic friends and neighbors at Grace Church wondered with her if there were "as many Yankees on this side of the Potomac as the other."[37]

Rives was soon worried about armed Yankees in blue uniforms. He wrote Alfred from Castle Hill, asking his son to make discreet inquiries in Richmond about the Confederate line of defense. Would it be the Rappahannock or the James? Would Albemarle County be defended or left to the enemy? Rives wished to avoid capture. "It will not do for me to be in the power of the enemy than which no greater humiliation could happen to me." He told his son that he had been sick and that Judith had been suffering from migraines. If enemy troops were coming, Rives hoped his son could provide "timely warning . . . to make the best arrangements I can with regard to my property as well as the safety of my family."[38]

Rives lost a beloved family member January 17, 1862 when his sister Margaret Jordan "Peggy" Rives died at Oak Ridge. John Tyler died the same day. After speeches in his honor, the Confederate Congress recessed January 21 for Tyler's funeral. The Provisional Congress adjourned February 17, 1862. The First Session of the First Confederate Congress would convene the following day. Rives was no longer a congressman and would return to Castle Hill. His name had not been on the ballot in the House election held the previous November. Rives' name was placed before the Virginia Legislature during its January election of Confederate Senators. Robert M. T. Hunter and William Ballard Preston bested Rives in that contest.[39] Although out of office, Rives maintained his interest and involvement in the Confederate cause.

* * *

1   Clipping from unidentified paper accompanying letter from Rives to Judith, May 15, 1861, Rives MSS, LOC, box 36.

2   Ibid.

3   Rives to Judith, May 18, 1861, Ibid.

4   *Journal of the Congress of the Confederate States of America 1861-1865,* Washington, Government Printing Office, 1904, Vol. I, 214.

5   See Wilfred Buck Yearns, *The Confederate Congress,* Athens, University of Georgia Press, 1960, viii, 42, and Thomas B. Alexander and Richard E. Beringer, *The Anatomy of the Confederate Congress,* Nashville, Vanderbilt University Press, 1972, 343-344, and James M. McPherson, *Ordeal by Fire, The Civil War and Reconstruction,* New York, Alfred A. Knopf, 1982, 363.

6 *The New Orleans Times*, William C. Rives obituary clipping, 1868, exact date uncertain, Rives MSS, UVa. Accession # 2313, box 3.

7 Rives to Memminger, June 24, 1861, Rives MSS, LOC, box 92.

8 Account and Memorandum Book, Ibid, box 122.

9 *Journal of the Congress . . .*, Ibid, 271-276, 303.

10 Rives to Alfred, July 26, 1861, Rives MSS, UVa., Accession #4498.

11 Meigs ordered Alfred Rives' name left off of the bridge's identifying plaque because of Alfred's Confederate service. *Washington Post*, April 21, 2010, B2. Meigs also turned Robert E. Lee's home Arlington into a Union cemetery.

12 Daniel W. Crofts, *Reluctant Confederates*, Chapel Hill, University of North Carolina Press, 1989, 298.

13 Judith to William C. Rives, Jr., March 15, 1861, Rives MSS, LOC, box 36, and Alfred Rives to Rives, April 13, 1861, Ibid.

14 Judith to William C. Rives, Jr. April 28, 1861, Ibid. In this letter Judith conveys reports that General Scott wept over the resignations of Lee and Johnston, whom he considered the finest officers of the army.

15 Robert E. Lee Krick, *Staff Officers in Gray*, Chapel Hill, University of North Carolina Press, 2003, 255. Also David S. Heidler, Jeanne T. Heidler, David J. Coles, editors, *Encyclopedia of the American Civil War: A Political, Social, and Military History*, New York, W. W. Norton and Company, 2000, 1658-1659, Also Rives to Alfred L. Rives, May 16, 1862, Rives MSS, UVa., Accession #4498.

16 Francis Rives to William C. Rives, Jr., December 26, 1861, Rives MSS, LOC, box 36 Francis noted that Sadie's "accouchement [delivery] had been difficult."

17 This Amélie Rives became a celebrated author of fiction, and available sources for this claim lead back to her, so that Lee's role may be overstated. He does not mention his godchild in a letter to Alfred, Nov. 1, 1865, Washington and Lee University, Robert E. Lee Collection, [home.wlu. edu].

18 Donna M. Lucey, *Archie and Amélie, Love and Madness in the Gilded Age*, New York, Harmony Books, 2006, 83. Lucey cites an autobiography in the Rives Papers, University of Virginia Library, accession #2532. Lucey discovered that the authoress Amélie's claim to have been presented to

the Russian Tsar was false; however, Lucey believes Lee was Amélie's godfather.

19 William C. Rives, Jr. to Rives, June 12, 1861, WCR, Jr. to Rives, July 8, 1861 Rives MSS, UVa., Accession # 2313, box 2. Item #559 in the April 13, 2000 catalogue for Siegel Auction Galleries was an envelope addressed to "Mrs. W. C. Rives" in Will's handwriting, hand stamped "Ship" that had been carried in May 1863 by the blockade runner *Cornubia* from Nassau to Wilmington, N. C.

20 Francis R. Rives to William C. Rives, Jr., March 13, April 18, 23, 1861, Rives MSS, LOC, box 36, Also Francis R. Rives to William C. Rives, Jr. January 10, 12, 1862, Rives MSS, UVa., Accession #10596.

21 William C. Rives, Jr. to Rives, May 10, 1861, Rives MSS, LOC box 36.

22 William C. Rives, Jr. to Judith Page Rives, June 13, 1861, Rives MSS, UVa., Accession # 2313, box 2.

23 David Sears to Rives, April 27, 1861, Rives MSS, LOC, box 92.

24 Judith Page Rives, to William C. Rives, Jr., July 1, 1861, Ibid, box 36.

25 Rives to William C. Rives, May 6, 1861, Ibid.

26 Grace Rives to Judith Rives, May 30, 1861, Rives MSS, UVa., Accession #2313, box 7.

27 William C. Rives, Jr. to Rives, June 12, 1861 and to Judith Page Rives February 8, 1864, Ibid, box 2.

28 Amélie Rives Sigourney to Sadie Rives, April 30, 1865, Ibid.

29 James Rives Childs, *Reliques of the Rives*, Lynchburg, J. P. Bell Company, 1929, 601.

30 Ibid, 571.

31 Ibid.

32 Ibid. 598.

33 Ibid, 595.

34 Rives to Judith, August 11, 1861, Rives MSS, LOC, box 36, quoted in Drew R. McCoy, *The Last of the Fathers*, New York, Cambridge University Press, 1989, 362.

35 Yearns, Ibid, 191, 196, *Journal of the Confederate Congress*, Vol. I, 417-419, 426-427, 450.

36 Rives to Thomas T. Giles, (copy), September 23, 1861, Rives MSS, LOC, box 92. James Seddon proposed an amendment to the Sequestration Act February 11, 1862 that the next of kin of aliens, if faithful citizens of the Confederacy, could have land decreed to them. Journal of the Congress, Ibid, 807.

37 Judith to Rives, October 14, 16, 1861, Rives MSS, LOC, box 36 quoted in McCoy, Ibid.

38 Rives to Alfred L. Rives, March 17, 1862, Rives MSS, UVa., Accession # 4498.

39 Ezra J. Warner and Wilfred Buck Yearns, *Biographical Register of the Confederate Congress*, Baton Rouge, Louisiana State university Press, 1975, 207.

CHAPTER TWENTY-THREE

Scenes of Great Excitement

ROBERT M. T. HUNTER resigned his position as Secretary of State to take his seat in the Confederate Senate. The cabinet vacancy prompted rumors that Rives might be appointed Secretary of State (the fifth time in his career he was mentioned for the office). "The *Petersburg Express* and *Lynchburg Virginian* both concur in commending Mr. Rives as a person eminently fit for the station. We entirely agree with our respected contemporaries in their estimate of Mr. Rives. We regard him as the foremost statesman on this continent. . . ."[1] Instead of Rives, President Davis chose Judah P. Benjamin, who had also served as Attorney General and Secretary of War. Historians regard Benjamin as the most (some say the only) capable and effective member of the Confederate cabinet.[2]

Rives was interested to learn that Count Robert Mercier, French Minister to the U. S., had visited Richmond in April 1862. Mercier's declared purpose was to inspect stores of French-owned tobacco. Rives wrote Alfred that he would have enjoyed discussing with Mercier "the true policy of his government towards the American quarrel."[3] Mercier conferred with Judah Benjamin, who offered the French 100,000 bales of cotton and free trade in exchange for breaking the blockade. Mercier reported to his superiors that the Confederacy was unconquerable. However, the French declined Benjamin's offer.[4]

When McClellan's Union army threatened Richmond in the spring of 1862, Alfred sent his wife Sadie to the safety of Castle

Hill. He wrote on June 2, that General Robert E. Lee had assumed command in place of the wounded General Joseph E. Johnston, "a change which it is thought by many persons in high positions and capable of judging will be to our advantage." Alfred reported having ridden to inspect the Confederate defenses "by direction of the President."[5] On June 11, Alfred wrote, "Richmond is in danger of falling for the enemy are only 5 miles from town."[6]

In late June, General Lee drove McClellan away from Richmond in a series of battles known as the Seven Days. Lee had summoned Stonewall Jackson and his army from the Shenandoah Valley for support. Sadie Rives wrote to Alfred how Jackson's men marched through the neighborhood June 20 and 21, causing "quite a scene of excitement." Ladies of the parish transported wagonloads of provisions to Grace Church in order to feed the soldiers as they marched by. "Poor creatures, it seemed like a mere drop in the bucket however, there were so many of them." General Richard S. Ewell and several of his officers had tea at Castle Hill. Sadie sang "Casta Diva" for them, an aria from Bellini's opera *Norma*. In the aria, the title character pleads to the Moon, the Queen of Heaven, for peace between the Romans and the Druids, of whom she is High Priestess. The officers stayed so late that the ladies of the house, Judith, Ella and Sadie, prepared beds for them. However, they departed at 11:30, declaring they had to sleep in the field and make an early start in the morning. Reports of Confederate victories prompted her to insist days later that Richmond must be safe and she should rejoin her husband there.[7]

General Lee wrote Rives after the Seven Days, thanking him for his kind note of May 28, and also thanking "Almighty God, who has heard your prayers. . . . To him alone we owe our success." Lee reported how the enemy had retreated to the cover of his "war steamers" on the James. Prisoners had claimed that

McClellan intended to "advance upon Richmond by the South side of the James River, which Lee said would "require all our strength to be prepared to meet him." Lee dictated the letter to his aide, former U.S. Congressman A. R. Boteler, noting, "I am away from the conveniences of writing." Lee also specified that the communication was intended only "for your own eye." As a fellow gentleman, Lee knew he could depend upon Rives' honor and discretion.[8]

Lee sent a note to Judith the following winter, thanking her and Ella for a camp blanket they had made for him, which he deemed "more precious in my eyes than if wrought on the looms of Persia. Accept my grateful thanks and most sincere wishes for the happiness and prosperity of that home from which it came."[9] Ella and Judith had spent three weeks weaving the blanket, which contained eight pounds of fine wool.[10] Judith was a member of the "Ladies Relief Society of Albemarle County," which provided clothing for soldiers. The ladies asked county residents to donate clothing, leather and wool. They also purchased garments of deceased patients from the hospital at the University of Virginia.[11]

General Lee thanked Rives for his congratulations after the battle of Chancellorsville, as well as his condolences over the loss of Jackson. Lee commended his soldiers: "If properly led they will go anywhere and never falter at the work before them. Since it has pleased Almighty God to take from us the good and great Jackson, may he inspire our Commanders with his unselfish, devoted and intrepid spirit, and infuse his indomitable energy through our ranks. Then indeed we shall be invincible and our country safe."[12]

Rives had visited with Jackson a few days before the August 9, 1862 Battle of Cedar Mountain. Colonel Boteler, who served Jackson as well as Lee,[13] conveyed Jackson's thanks to Rives for his visit as well as for the "beautiful and acceptable present" from "Mrs. and Miss Rives" (perhaps another blanket). "He wishes me also to say that he hopes at some future day when his presence will not be so necessary in the field, to accept your hospitable invitation."[14]

Rives asked Alfred for help in finding an overseer in 1862. Judith had foreseen that the "universal draft will probably take away the most important of our overseers."[15] Rives complained, "I am losing $50 a day from neglect and mismanagement of many things by negroes."[16] The situation had improved by 1864 when Judith observed, "our servants have never been so reasonable and so well behaved as during the war."[17] Later she said "our people have stuck with us with as much tenacity as the barnacles to an old ship."[18]

Selling the Nelson County lands and slaves before the war allowed Rives to pay all debts and provided him surplus cash for the first time in four decades. He had difficulty finding sensible ways to invest it. Rives dutifully purchased nearly $50,000 of Confederate, Richmond City, and State of North Carolina Bonds. He periodically traveled to Richmond to discuss investments with William H. MacFarland, President of the Farmer's Bank of Virginia. Rives observed that in contrast to hard times endured by most households, MacFarland managed to dine in luxurious style.[19] Rives contributed $20,000 while MacFarland and other investors contributed "much larger funds" toward the purchase of cotton grown west of the Mississippi. Texas cotton was an attractive commodity because it could be easily transported to Mexico, the only neutral country not cut off by the blockade. Speculation in Texas cotton soared.[20] Rives' and MacFarland's money was sent to an agent, Col. Stevens of Monroe, Louisiana, who died before making the purchase. Rives then entrusted the funds to the care of his nephew George Cabell Rives in Galveston.[21]

Inflation plagued the Confederate economy. Neither the Confederate government nor the states ever imposed sufficient taxes to finance the war.[22] The value of Confederate currency depreciated till it was nearly worthless. While in Congress, Rives received letters from constituents complaining about the rising cost of food.[23] Rives complained to Alfred, "My debtors in Nelson, with the cunning instinct of low minds, have informed me that they were now ready to pay me what they owe me, about twenty three thousand dollars, the depreciation of money having reached a very low point. I have concluded to receive it, as I might otherwise run the risk of losing it altogether." Rives then asked his son, "What are the opinions of the probable effects of the enemy, and tax bills on the safety and value of Confederate Bonds?" In the same letter, Rives noted that Judith was recovering from a mild case of "varioloid" (smallpox) and that he and the Castle Hill servants had been re-vaccinated.[24]

In 1864, Rives and William Morris of Richmond invested $30,000 to purchase 3,000 barrels of Number One Rosin, which were stored in Cumberland County North Carolina. Rosin was used in the manufacture of varnish and other products. The rosin was guaranteed, "to be delivered in such quantities as may be required and in like condition as received. Risks of fire and ravages of enemy excepted."[25] This was not a reliable investment. After the war ended, Rives lamented that all of his financial assets had vanished in "a general wreck."[26]

Rives' 1863 Tax Bill noted 1,762.13 acres of land worth $20 per acre, 41 slaves worth $24,600, 22 horses and mules worth $3,300, 21 cattle, 85 sheep, 70 hogs, a piano, and other possessions amounting to nearly $68,000. For this property as well as a declared $20,000 investment in bonds, Rives paid $1600.97 in taxes. Rives also paid the taxes on the properties belonging to his children residing in the North.[27]

The battle of Gettysburg (July 1-3, 1863) has become known as the unmistakable turning point of the Civil War. The so-called "high water mark of the Confederacy" occurred when Pickett's men crested Cemetery Ridge, before being repulsed during their charge on the battle's third day. At the time, Rives and many fellow citizens of the Confederacy did not perceive the battle this way, nor did they perceive themselves on an inevitable decline toward defeat. Rives wrote a cautiously optimistic assessment of the situation to member of the Virginia House of Delegates Francis B. Deane of Lynchburg in late August 1863. Rives congratulated Deane for retaining his "accustomed erectness and buoyancy of spirit" though some fellow citizens were discouraged. Rives speculated that the many successes at the beginning of the war may have spoiled them and "unstrung our minds for the discipline of these occasional reverses, which none can hope to escape amid the inexorable vicissitudes of war."

Rives did not consider Sharpsburg or Gettysburg as defeats. The Army of Northern Virginia, he stated, "under its illustrious leader, made two bold and successful incursions into the enemy's territory, levied contributions upon it, gave battle to his concentrated legions on his own soil, crippling and inflicting heavy losses upon him, and then returned at leisure to resume its attitude of calm defiance and proud invincibility at home."

He admitted that the war in the west had not gone as well. However, despite the loss of Vicksburg, Confederate sharpshooters and moveable batteries could still harass enemy shipping on the Mississippi. Rives reminded Deane of the dark days of the American Revolution, when Washington had to retreat from Long Island and New York, and when Cornwallis overran the south. With habitual thoroughness, Rives invoked other historical precedents, including the invasion of Greece by the Persian hordes of Darius and Xerxes that were finally defeated at Salamis. He also cited Rome's defense against Hannibal of Carthage, who won a string of decisive victories before being ultimately destroyed. More recently, the Dutch fought off the Spanish and gained their independence in the 16th century.

Rives believed:

> What any of these people accomplished, we are capable of accomplishing. We have the same love of liberty: we have the same devotion to our native land; we have the same martial ardor; we have the same, and even greater, motives to exert every faculty for our deliverance. With most of them, the great stake involved was national independence and political rights. With us, in addition to all this, everything precious to the human affections, everything sacred to the human heart is at issue. From the ruthless spirit in which this war has been waged by our adversaries, from the specimens we have had of their infamous proconsular governments in parts of our territory occupied by him; from the appeals they are now making to the vindictive and brutal passions of an uncivilized race as their allies in this unholy crusade against us, it is impossible for the imagination to picture a fate more horrible than ours would be, if we were once subjected to their power.

Rives claimed that the citizens of the Confederacy were much more supportive of the war than citizens of the North. Alluding to the recent New York anti-draft riots, Rives predicted that the military and moral strength of the North would decrease "while ours will certainly increase." The "demands of the crisis, appealing to the instinctive courage of men, and enforced by the pleading loveliness of woman will keep our active army full. . . ." He concluded, "No local or occasional disaster can check the onward progress of a great cause, blessed with approving smiles of heaven and sustained by stout hearts with unceasing vigilance and unfaltering faith."[28]

The letter, which was published in several newspapers, drew praise from the *Richmond Enquirer*. The *Enquirer's* editor favorably compared Rives' letter to a more pessimistic piece written by former Confederate Secretary of State Robert Toombs. While Rives was "buoyant with hope and confidence . . . and redolent with patriotic enthusiasm," the *Enquirer* declared that Toombs' letter conveyed "no encouraging word to his countrymen, but is calculated to destroy confidence in the Administration . . . and shows that he has permitted personal pique and individual resentment to eclipse the public good, and the final success of our cause." The *Enquirer* noted that Toombs was an early advocate of secession while Rives worked to preserve the Union until Virginia seceded. The writer considered it ironic that Rives now appeared to be more supportive of and more useful to the Confederate cause.[29]

An Albemarle County political mass meeting, "large, unanimous, and enthusiastic," returned Rives to Congress.[30] His restoration was part of a backlash against aggressive secessionists, whom some voters were now blaming for causing the trouble. The Albemarle County tax collector Lit Macon told Judith, ". . . if people would have listened to Mr. Rives, they wouldn't have been in such a fix."[31] In 1861, Democrats and Secessionists in the Confederate Congress held a two to one majority over Whigs and Unionists. The 1863 elections reduced that majority to five to four.[32] The Second Congress convened May 2, 1864.

General Lee's Army of Northern Virginia spent the winter of 1863-64 encamped south of the Rapidan River, while the Union Army of the Potomac lurked on the Rapidan's northern bank. Lee's winter headquarters were near the town of Orange. Some troops spent the winter on lands of James Madison's Montpelier. At Castle Hill, Judith noted "a numerous lot of beaux in the neighborhood." The Confederate government had instituted a ten percent tax-in-kind on agricultural produce. Judith noted that those Confederate beaux consumed Castle Hill's tax contribution of $3,000 worth of meat in a single day.[33]

Returning to Virginia in April from an unsuccessful Tennessee campaign under General Longstreet, General Micah Jenkins' Infantry Brigade and McIntosh's Artillery Battalion of Hill's Corps spent several weeks on Castle Hill property.[34] Commissary Officer Captain S. T. Stuart gave Rives compensation certificates for 1,500 pounds of oats worth $555, $481.50 worth of wheat, and $384.80 worth of potatoes consumed by the army. The men chopped down acres of trees for shelter and firewood.[35]

Rives complained about damage inflicted upon Castle Hill's farmland to Secretary of War Seddon. Rives had offered his pastures for the artillery horses, but the Quartermaster had insisted on placing them in the better grass of his hay fields. The famished horses consumed every blade, destroying the entire hay crop "in embryo." Rives asserted this action damaged the Confederacy because the one tenth of his previous hay crop had facilitated the "renovation of our cavalry and artillery horses, after their severe and exhausting service in Pennsylvania." Now he would have nothing and the Confederacy would receive one-tenth of nothing. He suggested better safeguards and compensation to protect the vital agriculture of the country.[36]

A letter from General Charles P. Field indicates that Grace Church may have also sustained damages from the visitors in gray.

In Camp, May 1st '64
My Dear Mrs. Rives,

I thank you for your polite note, and pamphlet just   .
received.

My division will march from this neighborhood early tomorrow, thus relieving you of the necessity of having Guards. Meanwhile I will see that your beautiful Church is not further molested.

I very much regret that my duties will probably debar me the pleasure of paying my respects to the ladies of Castle Hill before my departure; but your book will be a pleasant reminder of them during the weary hours of Camp.

With Sentiments of high respect & esteem

I am truly yours,
Chas. P. Field"[37]

The men and horses revived by the bounty of Castle Hill soil joined their comrades for General Lee's last grand review, which took place in the neighborhood April 29. Thousands in formation cheered and saluted Lee on Traveller. Artillery General Edward Porter Alexander termed the event "a military sacrament, in which we pledged anew our lives."[38]

Many would soon lose their lives. As these men prepared for relentless fight against the forces of U. S. Grant, beginning at the Wilderness, Rives returned to Richmond for the Second Confederate Congress.

★ ★ ★

1 Clipping from unidentified newspaper in Rives MSS, UVa., Accession #11375.

2 Eli N. Evans, Judah P. Benjamin, *The Jewish Confederate*, New York, The Free Press, 1988, 154-158, also James M. McPherson, *Ordeal by Fire, The Civil War and Reconstruction*, New York, Alfred A. Knopf, 1982, 363-364.

3 Rives to Alfred Rives, April 20, 1862, Rives MSS, UVa., Accession #4498.

4 Wilfred Buck Yearns, *The Confederate Congress*, Athens, University of Georgia Press, 1960, 167-168.

5 Alfred Rives to Sadie Rives, June 2, 1862, Rives MSS, LOC, box 36.

6 Alfred Rives to Sadie Rives, June 11, 1862, Rives MSS, UVa., Accession #2313, box 2.

7 Sadie Rives to Alfred Rives, June 23, 25, 1862, Ibid. Unfortunately these letters are fragmentary. A collector of Confederate stamps snipped his plunder off of envelopes containing folded letters, leaving gaping holes on each page.

8 Robert E. Lee to Rives, July 4, 1862, Rives MSS, LOC, box 92.

9 Robert E. Lee to Judith, February 22, 1863, Ibid.

10 Judith Rives to Sadie Rives, February 15, 1863, Rives MSS, UVa., Accession# 2313, box 2.

11 Ervin L. Jordan, Jr., *Charlottesville and the University of Virginia in the Civil War*, Lynchburg, H. E. Howard, Inc. 1988, 35.

12 Robert E. Lee to Rives, May 21, 1863, Rives MSS, UVa., Accession #2532, Box 1 (typed copy of the letter with a note from Amélie Rives Troubetzkoy that "the original had to be sold in a hard time").

13 Yearns, Ibid, 18.

14 A. R. Boteler to Rives, August 4, 1862, Rives MSS, LOC, box 92.

15 Judith Rives to Sadie Rives, March 12, 1862, Rives MSS, UVa., Accession #2313, box 2.

16 Rives to Alfred Rives, August 5, 1862, Rives MSS, UVa., Accession #4498.

17 Judith Rives to Alfred Rives, April 6, 18, 1864 Rives MSS, LOC, box 36, quoted in Drew R. McCoy, *The Last of the Fathers*, Cambridge University Press, Cambridge, 1989, 363.

18 Francis Rives to William C. Rives, Jr., (quoting letter from his mother), May 19, 1865, Ibid, Box 37, quoted in McCoy, Ibid.

19 Rives to Judith Rives, October 26, 1862, Rives MSS, UVa., Accession #2313, Box 2.

20 See Wilfred Buck Yearns, *The Confederate Congress*, Athens, University of Georgia Press, 1960, 136.

21 Account and Memorandum Book, Rives MSS, LOC, box 122.

22 Albert D. Kirwan, *The Confederacy*, New York, Meridian Books, 1959, 117.

23 J. J. Hopkins to Rives, June 10, 1864, Rives MSS, UVa., Accession #2313, box 2.

24 Rives to Alfred Rives, March 29, 1863, Ibid. See also Rives to James Seddon, September 17, 1864, Rives MSS, LOC, box 92 Rives tells Seddon he is unhappy about receiving installment payments for the 1860 slave transaction in depreciated Confederate currency.

25 Receipts February 3, 15, May 13, 14, 1864, Rives MSS, UVa., Accession # 2313, box 2.

26 Rives to Alexander Rives, June 7, 1865, Rives MSS, LOC, box 37 A posthumous inventory of Rives' investments shows less than $10,000 in stocks and bonds. Rives MSS, UVa., Accession #2313, Box 7, Miscellaneous Folder "Note on Finances" WCR, Jr.'s handwriting.

27 Rives' 1863 Taxes, Ibid.

28 Rives to Francis B. Deane, clipping (date and paper unknown) in Rives MSS, UVa., Accession # 2495, box 1, Also, letterbook, Rives MSS, LOC, Box 105, 242. The letter was reportedly dated August 24, 1863, and appeared in the *Richmond Whig* September 1, 1863 and the *New York Herald* September 12, 1863.

29 "Rives, Toombs and Foote," *Richmond Enquirer*, undated clipping attached to previously cited clipping, Rives MSS, UVa., Ibid. About H. S. Foote of Tennessee, the article commends his advice to Jefferson Davis to dismiss personal favorites and replace them with more competent generals. The writer also suggests Foote should be in the cabinet.

30 Judith Rives to Alfred Rives, April 21, 1863, Rives MSS, UVa., Accession #2313, box 2.

31 Judith Rives to Rives, November 25, 1864, Rives MSS, LOC, box 36, quoted in McCoy, Ibid, 363.

32 Yearns, Ibid, 58.

33 Judith Rives to Sadie Rives, January 26, 1864, Rives MSS, LOC, box 36.

34 Douglas Southall Freeman, *Lee's Lieutenants A Study in Command*, Vol. III *Gettysburg to Appomattox*, New York, Charles Scribner's Sons, 1944, Chapter XVII "Winter Tests Temper" 315-341.

35 National Archives, Record Group #109, Publication #M346A, Confederate Papers Relating to Citizens or Business Firms 1861-1865, Roll No. 868, documents relating to William C. Rives.

36 Rives "To the Secretary of War," (copy) April 26, 1864, Rives MSS, LOC, box 92.

37 Charles P. Field to Judith Rives, Rives MSS, UVa., Accession #2313, box 2.

38 Gary W. Gallagher, editor, *Fighting for the Confederacy The Personal Recollections of General Edward Porter Alexander*, Chapel Hill, The University of North Carolina Press, 1989, 345-346. The review took place within a few miles of Castle Hill. Lee had ordered Longstreet to camp near Mechanicsville, Louisa County, south of Gordonsville. (There was also a Mechanicsville in Hanover County). See also Freeman, Ibid, 342.

CHAPTER TWENTY-FOUR

A Matter of Much Importance and Delicacy

HISTORIANS REFER to the series of battles from May to Mid-June 1864, fought between the forces of Lee and Grant, as the "Overland Campaign." Both armies sustained heavy casualties. The Confederates prevented the Union forces from capturing Richmond, but they were not able to drive them back. After Grant crossed the James and threatened Petersburg on June 15, the contest then became an extended siege in which Union numerical and material superiority eventually proved decisive.

In late May, Rives still believed that the Confederate military situation was favorable. He wrote Judith that Lee had maintained "his ground against that bull-dog Grant...." and that "Great confidence is felt in Lee's continued success." Rives also admitted being fatigued from delivering a two-hour speech.[1] He proposed that Congress should take advantage of the military success and issue a Manifesto, declaring the Confederacy's desire for peace and righteous independence. Lincoln's prospects for re-election in November seemed far from certain in May. Rives likely hoped his Manifesto would help persuade war-weary northerners to vote Lincoln out of office and abandon the conquest. The Manifesto was intended also to strengthen support for the Confederate cause within its borders as well as to "be laid before foreign governments."

Rives submitted his resolution for a Manifesto on May 28.[2] A joint committee of both the House and Senate considered the measure, but the final product exhibited Rives' distinctive prose. Rives invoked the words and style of Jefferson and the philosophy of Madison in asserting the rights of the Confederacy. The Manifesto was approved by the House and Senate, and signed by President Davis on June 14. The Manifesto was Rives' most notable contribution to the Confederate Congress, and appeared in northern as well as southern newspapers.[3]

The Manifesto of the Confederate Congress claimed its purpose was:

> to enlighten the public opinion of the world with regard to the true character of the struggle in which they [the Confederate States] are engaged, and the dispositions, principles and purposes by which they are actuated. . . . They have ever deeply deplored the necessity which constrained them to take up arms in defense of their rights and of the free institutions delivered from their ancestors; and there is nothing they more ardently desire than peace, whensoever their enemy, by ceasing from the unhallowed war waged upon them, shall permit them to enjoy in peace the sheltering protection of those hereditary rights. . . . The series of successes with which it has pleased Almighty God . . . to bless our arms . . . enables us to profess this desire of peace in the interests of civilization and humanity without danger of having our motives misinterpreted, or of the declaration being ascribed to any unmanly sentiment or any distrust of our ability fully to maintain our cause.

The document maintained that the Confederacy was unconquerable. Its members would continue to fight before accepting the "Egyptian bondage that awaits them in the event of their subjugation." It labeled "our adversaries" as the aggressors who had invaded along with "black and foreign mercenaries." Those adversaries could end the war any time they chose. "Will they be willing, by a longer perseverance in a wanton and hopeless contest, to make this continent, which they so long boasted to be the chosen abode of liberty and self government, of peace and a higher civilization, the theatre of the most causeless and prodigal effusion of blood which the world has ever seen, of a virtual relapse into the barbarism of the ruder ages, and of the destruction of constitutional freedom by the lawlessness of usurped power?"

The Manifesto then invoked Jefferson, declaring that, "Government, to be lawful, must be founded on the consent of the governed. . . . We were forced to dissolve our federal connection . . . and in doing so we exercise a right . . . of a free people . . . to recur to original principles and to institute new guards for their security." The argument then assumed a Madisonian tone in explaining why armed coercion of seceded states was unjust, and had to be resisted: "The separate independence of the States, as sovereign and co equal members of the Federal Union, had never been surrendered, and the pretension of applying to independent communities, so constituted and organized, the ordinary rules of coercion, and reducing rebellious subjects to obedience, was a solecism in terms, as well as an outrage on the principles of public law." This assertion was debatable. Rives did not cite specific words of support from his former mentor. Madison had mentioned secession "without the consent of the co states" in his March 12, 1833 letter to Rives, but had not rendered a definitive opinion on the subject, only praying that actual events would not require the "painful task" of deciding the question.[4]

In apparent denial of the Sharpsburg and Gettysburg campaigns, the Manifesto claimed that Confederate conduct had been "strictly defensive. . . . We have not interfered . . . with the internal peace and prosperity of the States arrayed in hostility against us. . . . All we ask is . . . to be left in the undisturbed enjoyment of those inalienable rights of 'life liberty and the pursuit of happiness,' which our common ancestors declared to be the equal heritage of all the parties to the social compact."

If the enemy would "forbear aggression," the writer suggested negotiations conducted "in a spirit of peace, equity, and manly frankness" could solve any remaining disputes. "Strong in the persuasion of the justice of our cause, in the gallant devotion of our citizen soldiers, and of the whole body of our people, and above all in the gracious protection of Heaven, we are not afraid to avow a sincere desire for peace on terms consistent with our honor and the permanent security of our rights. . . . With these declarations of our dispositions, our principles, and our purposes, we commit our cause to the enlightened judgment of the world, to the reflection of our adversaries themselves, and to the calm and righteous arbitrament of Heaven."[5]

Though Rives had applied his utmost passion and eloquence to the document, his rhetoric had little effect, compared to battle-field results. The Manifesto might have gained more acclaim if the Confederacy had secured its independence. The Manifesto offered no new proposals or points of negotiation. Rives' plea for peace on terms consistent with honor and rights had failed to prevent the conflict in 1861, and the same plea would not halt the bloodshed in 1864. Lincoln was never willing to recognize Confederate independence, rendering a negotiated peace impossible.

Rives remained optimistic about the Confederate cause through the summer. On June 2, Alfred wrote his wife Sadie, whom he had sent to the safety of Castle Hill, "The Army has been increased in size and is confident of victory. . . . Father and myself think Europe on the verge of recognizing us on the first favorable opportunity."[6] Ten days later Alfred reported that, "General Lee still keeps General Grant completely at bay. General Hampton is reported to have defeated and driven back Sheridan with his raiders who seemed disposed to pay you a visit."

Cavalry forces of Hampton and Sheridan clashed at the Battle of Trevillians, Louisa County on June 11 and 12. Ten miles away, residents of Castle Hill could hear the sound of artillery. Hampton and the Confederates did prevent Sheridan from venturing further west towards Charlottesville. Railroad damage inflicted by the Yankees necessitated Rives' travel by canal to Columbia and the rest of the way by buggy to Castle Hill, when Congress adjourned June 14.[7] Alfred had hoped to accompany his father home, but he was busy with "great engineering operations," including building a bridge over the James two miles below Drewry's Bluff.[8] In August, Alfred conveyed predictions that Lincoln would lose the election to a peace Democrat, and that a satisfactory peace would soon follow. In the same letter, Alfred described the situation in Georgia as "more and more favorable," and that Atlanta was "as safe as Richmond and Petersburg, which as you know are considered very very safe."[9] Union forces under General Sherman entered Atlanta less than a month later on September 2. Sherman's victory helped secure Lincoln's re-election.

As late as October, Rives wrote Dr. Robert W. Haxall that, like Mr. Micawber, he hoped "something will turn up to our advantage" regarding military and political events.[10] Rives stayed at Dr. Haxall's Richmond home during sessions of Congress. Micawber was an eternally optimistic character in Dicken's *David Copperfield*. Rives' optimism seemed to be fading after he returned to Richmond when Congress reconvened November 7. He wrote Judith, "While an empty and boisterous speech is going on, I take the opportunity of holding a little sweet converse with my wife, my better and dearer half." Rives had just enjoyed a breakfast "at Mr. McFarland's, in company with Mr. Benjamin,"[11] which featured a Castle Hill ham as "the principal attraction and ornament." Rives doubted reports that McClellan had beaten Lincoln in the U.S. Presidential contest. "I think there is but little doubt that Lincoln is again elected. . . . His election will soonest bring on what seems to be the only solution of our troubles, a further disintegration of the Union."[12]

Rives again served on the Foreign Affairs and Flag and Seal Committees.[13] President Davis declared in a message to Congress, when it reconvened, that if the U.S. government desired peace, the Confederate government was willing to discuss the matter. Rives had opposed several administration measures in the Provisional Congress, but was mostly supportive of Davis during the Second Congress.[14] Although Vice-President Stephens and others, including Rives' Pollard nephews at *The Richmond Examiner*, formed a growing chorus of Davis critics, Davis received less interference from his Congress in the conduct of the war than did Lincoln.[15]

Davis conferred with Rives on a number of occasions. Although Davis was criticized for his lack of personal warmth, he and Rives maintained a cordial relationship. Davis invited Rives to dine at the Executive Mansion.[16] Rives thanked Davis for a conversation "when you did me the honor to communicate to me your views of our pending military operations with a frankness and unreserve which were duly appreciated."[17] Davis summoned Rives to Richmond March 19, 1864:

> My dear Sir,
>
> I wish to consult you on a matter of much importance and delicacy. Will your convenience permit you at this time to visit Richmond?
>
> With great respect I am very truly yours
>
> Jefferson Davis[18]

Davis was having conferences with many people at that time about the Army of Tennessee, according to Lynda Crist, head of the Jefferson Davis Papers Project at Rice University. Crist suggested that subject might have been the matter of much importance and delicacy.[19] Perhaps Davis wanted to discuss a delicate family matter: Rives' nephews Henry Rives Pollard and Edward Alfred Pollard, who were harassing Davis with their editorials in the *Examiner*. The Pollards criticized Confederate Generals Bragg, Hood and Longstreet, and reportedly received insider information about the government from Rives and his brother Alexander, who served in the Virginia legislature. The Pollards attracted gunfire from angry subjects of their articles after the war. An irate victim of his slander assassinated Henry in 1868.[20]

Mrs. Davis expressed a high opinion of Rives, and said that she would like to visit Castle Hill. Judith wrote her daughter-in-law Sadie that, "The old place has been a presidential resort ever since the days of Jefferson and Madison, and perhaps it might bring some good luck to Mr. Davis to pay a visit to us." Judith vainly hoped that the military situation would be sufficiently peaceful to allow a visit.[21]

The military situation compelled Davis to ask Congress to authorize suspension of the writ of habeus corpus. Under the writ of habeus corpus, a prisoner cannot be held indefinitely without being charged, and must be brought to court to determine punishment. Lincoln suspended habeus corpus in the North for most of the war. The Confederate Congress granted Davis the power in 1862 and reauthorized the suspension February 15, 1864. This measure enabled Confederate military authorities to promptly punish acts of desertion and treason. Vice-President Stephens and others vehemently opposed the measure. Rives spoke in support of the suspension, which provoked an interminable letter of outrage from John Harmer Gilmer.

Gilmer was an attorney and brother of Rives' late friend and foe Thomas Walker Gilmer.[22] His letter exceeded Rives' own epistles in lengthy circumlocution. Gilmer accused Rives of inflicting "a severe blow on the main pillar of all constitutional government," in his support of suspension of the writ of habeus corpus. After discussing numerous legal principles and historical precedents, Gilmer explained the case involving his clients, native Marylanders who had enlisted in a Maryland Confederate company in 1861. After three years of service, they felt entitled to an honorable discharge from further duty. Their discharge had been denied under a conscription act, which required all able-bodied resident men between the ages of 17 and 50 to serve, with certain exceptions. Gilmer argued that the Marylanders should be exempted from conscription, because they were not technically residents of the Confederate States, but citizens of the foreign state of Maryland. After much strenuous effort, Gilmer was able to secure their release from prison and their discharge from the army. Gilmer asserted this was an affirmation of liberty that would inspire Confederate soldiers and citizens. He declared that Secretary of War Seddon, in trying to enforce conscription, had "stained her [Virginia's] escutcheon." Gilmer urged Rives to affirm state sovereignty in future deliberations of Congress. "Remember sir, you deliberate for posterity."[23] A major problem for the Confederacy was that the war required centralized power, which was anathema to states rights proponents. Rives and fellow Whigs better understood the need for strong central government than Democrats.[24]

Rives supported the Davis administration's fiscal program,[25] and delivered a speech in favor of the pending Currency Bill. He spoke of the necessity of "some specific practical tangible security given for the redemption of the notes." He recommended setting aside tithes received by the government of cotton, corn and wheat. He declared that the remnant of the cotton crop on hand, if sold in England, could pay five times the amount of the Confederacy's funded debt.[26] As Rives must have known, the blockade and capture of southern ports made shipment of cotton to England impossible. His prescription for stabilizing the currency might have been more useful if the Confederacy's condition not been so precarious.

Rives' health was also precarious. Suffering from pleurisy, he requested a temporary leave of absence from Congress, which was granted January 28. His absence became permanent when he submitted his resignation in a March 1 letter addressed to voters of the Virginia Seventh Congressional District. He could no longer serve due to "the shattered condition of my health. . . . For the last six weeks I have been confined to my bed by a severe and complicated illness." He thanked the voters for their support during his "long career of public service." The letter, which was entered into the official journal, concluded with the promise of solidarity from the Book of Ruth, 1:16 "Whither thou goest I will go. . . ."[27] Awareness of the Confederacy's desperate condition, and the futility of legislating for a shrinking territory, also likely contributed to Rives' decision to resign.

Despite his illness, Rives was involved in some final efforts to salvage some concessions for the Confederate cause beyond unconditional surrender. According to the published diary of Robert Garlick Hill Kean, *Inside the Confederate Government*, Rives on January 10, 1865 proposed "a special embassage to the European powers to show our real condition and solicit intervention, coupling it with a proposition for prospective emancipation."[28] European powers had not intervened when the Confederacy's prospects were brighter. Rives' idea was impractical also because shipping diplomats to Europe was no more possible than shipping cotton.

One last time, Rives' name was mentioned for the office of Secretary of State. The Virginia delegation in Congress urged President Davis to make changes within his cabinet. Some suggested replacing Secretary of State Judah P. Benjamin with Rives, because they distrusted Benjamin to negotiate terms of peace with the U.S.[29] The only change Davis accepted was replacing James A. Seddon with John Cabell Breckinridge as Secretary of War.

Davis confided to Rives at the end of January that he was fully aware of the terrible condition of the country, and that he was willing to take any necessary action. Rives was "impressed with his honesty of purpose and anxiety to do what is best." Davis told Rives he was willing to send commissioners to meet with Lincoln, and that even the issue of Confederate independence was negotiable.[30] Although Rives was considered for the mission, Vice-President Stephens, Senator R. M. T. Hunter, and Assistant Secretary of War John A. Campbell (Former U.S. Supreme Court Judge) were chosen for the February 3 conference with Lincoln and Seward at Hampton Roads. Lincoln demanded unconditional surrender of all Confederate armies and emancipation. He offered no concessions, and the three commissioners returned to Richmond having gained nothing. Campbell urged Davis to authorize another peace mission, but Davis declined.[31]

Davis declared he would be willing to talk with Union representatives if the Senate formally advised him to do so. The Senate refused to take this action. Apparently, no one wanted the responsibility or the blame of surrendering to the Yankees. Although officially no longer connected with the Confederate government after March 1, Rives continued to seek an active role in its ultimate fate. The faction that distrusted Davis and Benjamin unofficially selected Rives, Hunter, Campbell, Senator William A. Graham of North Carolina, and Senator James L. Orr of South Carolina to devise a sensible course of action.[32]

On Saturday March 4, General Lee left his Petersburg Headquarters for two days of talks with government leaders in Richmond. Lee presented the desperate situation of his army to President Davis, Secretary of War Breckinridge, and others, including Rives.

Rives also examined an analysis of the entire Confederacy's military condition that had been prepared by Campbell. The report noted that manpower and supplies were exhausted, desertion was increasing, the currency was near collapse, and enemy forces continued to tighten their grip. Campbell's report concluded:

> The South may succumb, but it is not necessary that she should be destroyed. I do not regard reconstruction as involving destruction unless our people should forget the incidents of their heroic struggle and become debased and degraded. It is the duty of their statesmen and patriots to guard them in the future with even more care and tenderness than they have done in the past. There is anarchy in the opinions of men here, and few are willing to give counsel. Still fewer are willing to incur the responsibility of taking or advising action.[33]

Rives resolved to take action. He prepared a Peace Resolution for the Senate, for which he hoped Graham, Orr, and Hunter could secure passage:[34]

> The Senate of the Confederate States, cherishing with undiminished attachment the cause of national independence, but convinced by a careful and conscientious study of their situation, compared with the overwhelming numbers & unlimited resources of their adversary, increased by accessions from every part of Europe & favored by the partial & unjust policy of foreign powers, that a longer prosecution of the war, with any reasonable prospect of success on their part, has become impracticable; and yielding, as the proudest & most valiant national powers have done in like

circumstances, to the stern law of necessity & the apparent decrees of Heaven, do in order to prevent a further effusion of blood, to husband the lives & interests of so many of their fellow citizens committed to their guardianship, and to avert the horrors of a savage & relentless subjugation by a triumphant armed force of every race and complexion, advise the President to propose to the enemy, through the General in Chief, an armistice preliminary to the re-establishment of peace & union, and for the special purpose of settling whether the seceded states, on their return, will be secured in their rights & privileges as states under the Constitution of the United States.[35]

Members of the Senate considered Rives' resolution, but failed to vote on the measure. President Davis was determined not to surrender, and might have resisted the proposal even if it had passed.[36] On the back of his copy of the resolution, Rives wrote that Lee was still considering how the Confederate cause might be continued:

This paper was prepared & put into the hands of Judge Campbell, Assistant Secretary of War, on the 6th of March, 1865, after receiving from him a communication of his letter to the Secretary of War in which he developed the exhausted condition of our military resources & the apparent hopelessness of farther prosecution of the war on our part. On the day previous I had a very long and full conversation with General Lee, in which, while he said that as a soldier it was his duty to fight it out to the last extremity as long as the contest continued, yet as a patriot & citizen, he thought true policy required us to close the war on the best terms we could, & to husband our resources for a future & more propitious occasion, when we might profit of favorable conjunctures to extend our connections in the Middle & Western States, & to obtain foreign co-operation in the event, which seemed imminent, of a war between the United States & France or England or both. The Resolution here drawn, I considered as virtually embodying his views, as well as my own.[37]

Rives' peace efforts were well intentioned but ineffectual. Though U.S. relations with Great Britain and France were strained by the Civil War and by French occupation of Mexico, the tensions ebbed peacefully. By the time Lee surrendered at Appomattox on April 12, he no longer hoped for future "favorable conjunctures," and he urged his men to accept the war's decisive result.

Following Lee's surrender, occupying Union forces moved through Virginia. A Pennsylvania regiment camped within a mile of the Castle Hill house. Rives, who had returned to Castle Hill before Lee's evacuation of Richmond, rode his horse to the camp and invited the officers to his home for tea. The Colonel reciprocated the friendly gesture by ordering guards to protect the house.[38] The occupying force issued a safeguard, declaring that the Castle Hill house and buildings should not be harmed, and that the penalty for any soldier forcing a safeguard was death.[39] Rives signed an Amnesty Oath, agreeing to support and defend the constitution, as well as to accept and abide by the Emancipation Proclamation.[40]

Rives wrote Alfred of his great relief to hear that he had safely returned to Richmond as a paroled prisoner. God had been "gracious and merciful" in bringing us through this dreadful war with our family circle unbroken." Rives asked his son to try to procure shaving soap and a toothbrush for him. He also asked him to

see Mr. Lancaster and "ascertain . . . whether my papers with him, some certificates of Insurance & Bank & R. Road stock, escaped the dreadful conflagration."[41] Rives closed the letter: "Bring your saddle & bridle with you as I have a nice horse for you."[42]

* * *

1 Rives to Judith Rives, May 21, 1864, letterbook, Rives MSS, LOC, box 20, 199.

2 *Journal of the Congress of the Confederate States of America 1861-1865*, Vol. VII, Government Printing Office, 1904, 112.

3 WCR, Jr., Biography, Rives MSS, LOC, box 103, 155.

4 James Madison to Rives, March 12, 1833, *Letters and Other Writings of James Madison*, (edited by Rives and Fendall), Philadelphia, J. B. Lippincott and Company, 1865, 289-292. The letter, concerning the 1833 Nullification crisis, is cited in chapter 8: Lieutenant Randolph Outrage.

5 "Manifesto of the Confederate Congress," Rives MSS, LOC, box 120, Available online, transcription from *The Daily Dispatch*: June 15, 1864, http://www.perseus.tufts.edu/hopper/text?doc=Perseus%3Atext%3 A2006.05.1093%Aarticle%3Dpos%3D14. This transcription notes the Manifesto "is understood to be from the pen of the Hon Wm. C River [sic] of Virginia.

6 Alfred Rives to Sadie Rives, June 2, 1864, Rives MSS, UVa., Accession #2313, box 2.

7 Alfred Rives to Sadie Rives, June 12, 1864, Ibid.

8 Alfred Rives to Sadie Rives, June 15, 1864, Ibid.

9 Alfred Rives to Sadie Rives, August 5, 1864, Ibid.

10 Rives to Dr. Robert W. Haxall, October 18, 1864, Swem Library Digital Projects, Swem Library, William and Mary, http://scdb.swem.wm.edu/index.php?p=collections/findingaid&id=7190&q=william+cabell+rives&rootcontentid=4383id4383.

11 Apparently Mr. Benjamin did not observe kosher dietary restrictions.

12 Rives to Judith, November 11, 1864, Rives MSS, LOC, box 36.

13 *Journal of the Congress of the Confederate States of America 1861-1865*, Vol. VII, Washington, Government Printing Office, 1905, 35, 36.

14 Wilfred Buck Yearns, *The Confederate Congress*, Athens, University of Georgia Press, 1960, "Biographical Notes" 243. Also Ezra J. Warner and W. Buck Yearns, Baton Rouge, *Biographical Register of the Confederate Congress*, Baton Rouge, Louisiana State University Press, 1975, 206-208.

15 Yearns, Ibid, 140.

16 Invitation, August 16, 1861, Rives MSS, LOC, Box 92.

17 Rives to Davis, June 28, 1862, *The Papers of Jefferson Davis*, Vol. VIII, Baton Rouge, Louisiana State University Press, 1995, 273.

18 Jefferson Davis to Rives, March 19, 1864, Rives MSS, UVa., Accession #2313, box 2. Also Rives to Judith Rives, October 26, 1862, Rives MSS, UVa. Rives spoke with Mr. and Mrs. Davis after church, "the latter . . . very gracious and kind. I must therefore, call to pay my respects at the great house."

19 Lynda Crist email to the author, February 2, 2013.

20 Charles F. Ritter, and John L. Wakelyn, editors, *Leaders of the American Civil War: A Biographical and Historiographical Dictionary*, Westport Connecticut, Greenwood Publishing Group, 1998, 317-318.

21 Judith Rives to Sadie Rives, January 16, 1863, Rives MSS, LOC, box 36.

22 R. C. M. Page, *Genealogy of the Page Family in Virginia*, Harrisonburg, C. J. Carrier company, 1972, 222.

23 "Letter Addressed to Hon. Wm. C. Rives by John H. Gilmer on the Existing Status of the Revolution," Richmond, 1864, also available online at http:docsouth.unc.edu/imls/gilmerlet/gilmer.html.

24 Thomas B. Alexander and Richard E. Beringer, *The Anatomy of the Confederate Congress*, Nashville, Vanderbilt University Press, 1972, 334.

25 Ezra J. Warner and Wilfred Buck Yearns, Ibid, 207.

26 Rives Speech in the House of Representatives on the Currency Bill, December 19, 1864, reprinted in the *Richmond Whig*, December 31, 1864, WCR, Jr. Biography, Rives MSS, LOC, box 105.

27 *Journal of the Confederate Congress*, Vol. VII, 510, 674.

28 Edward Younger, editor, *Inside the Confederate Government, The Diary of Robert Garlick Hill Kean*, New York, Oxford University Press, 1957, 186.

29 Ibid, 191 (January 23, 1865).

30 Ibid, 192-193.

31 Yearns, Ibid, 182.

32 John Hammond Moore, "The Rives Peace Resolution—March, 1865," *West Virginia History*, Charleston (WV) Vol. 26 (1964-65), 155.

33 Ibid, 156, Moore quotes *The War of the Rebellion, A Compilation of the Official Records of the Union and Confederate Armies*, Series I, Volume LI, Part II, 1064-1067, Washington, Government Printing Office, 1899.

34 Moore, Ibid, 156.

35 Rives MSS, UVa., Accession # 2313, box 2.

36 Moore, Ibid, 160.

37 Rives MSS, UVa., Accession # 2313 box 2.

38 Letterbook, Rives MSS, LOC. box 105, 252.

39 Safeguard, Rives MSS, UVa. Accession #2313, box 2.

40 Amnesty Oath, Ibid.

41 Rives purchased a number of bonds from John A. Lancaster and Son during the war. Richmond financial institutions and their contents were

consumed when the city burned April 3. A few of Rives' bonds survived, perhaps because he had kept them at Castle Hill. However Confederate bonds were now worthless.

42 Rives to Alfred Rives, May 15, 1865, Rives MSS, UVa. Ibid.

CHAPTER TWENTY-FIVE

A Multitude

FRANCIS AND WILL JOURNEYED south to Castle Hill for a joyful reunion. The family members who had spent the war years in the north were in better financial condition than their Confederate father and brother. Rives was confident that Alfred's qualifications as an engineer would guarantee employment and enable him to assist in "reconstruction, in its best sense." Rives found his own "starting afresh" more difficult at age 72.[1]

Alfred told Judith an anecdote that mirrored her political sentiment, which she passed along to Will. Jefferson Davis was captured and imprisoned in May, after Lincoln's April 14 assassination. Alfred's story concerned a six-year-old boy named John, who was playing on a Richmond street. A Federal officer walked by him and said, "Good morning Johnny."

"How did you know my name was Johnny?"

"I didn't know, but we call all you rebs Johnny. Say Johnny reb, we've got your president in a hot place, haven't we?"

"Yes sir," replied John, touching the end of his nose with his thumb and telegraphing with his fingers, "but we've got yours in a hotter!" and "off he scampered, . . . leaving the officer *bouche béante.*" [open-mouthed][2]

Lincoln's successor Andrew Johnson issued an Amnesty Proclamation May 29, which pardoned many former Confederates. However, the plan required special certificates signed by the President for certain groups, including Confederates who had held civil or diplomatic posts and those who held more than $20,000 in taxable property.[3] Rives' brother Alexander wrote Rives that he would like to help him resolve his amnesty issues. Though two of his sons served in the Confederate army, Alexander did not hold office in the Confederate government. Alexander became a Virginia Supreme Court of Appeals Judge in 1866 and a U.S. District Court Judge in 1870.⁴ Rives wrote Alexander, claiming that his congressional seat was not technically a civil office. Furthermore, because Castle Hill was his wife's hereditary estate to which he was a tenant by courtesy, and because he had lost most of his investments, he declared his net worth was less than $20,000. Rives also stressed his anti-secessionist efforts of 1860-61, and how reluctantly he had accepted a position in the Confederate Congress, only doing so with the hope of promoting peace. He did not mention his published pro-Confederate exhortations of 1863-1864. Rives suggested the peace efforts of Judge Campbell deserved consideration by those determining Campbell's fate.⁵ Alexander forwarded the letter to President Johnson.⁶

Johnson signed a parole July 25, which permitted Rives to travel to Carnwath in Dutchess County, New York to visit Francis and his family. Located near Wappinger's Falls, Carnwath was the country estate of Francis' father-in-law George Barclay. Rives had hoped to join Judith and Ella, who were visiting Amélie Sigourney in Newport, but his sons advised him that malevolent anti-Confederate sentiment there might make his visit unpleasant. Francis also told his father to avoid "places of public and idle resort" in traveling to and from New York, which Rives said was not a hardship.⁷ Judith and Ella came to Carnwath from Newport, and accompanied Rives back to Castle Hill in September.

Rives and Judith had to reorganize Castle Hill's labor force. Emancipation prompted many slaves to leave Castle Hill. Rives referred to them as "seceding blackies," and said he wished, as he recalled General Scott had said of the seceding states in 1860, that they would depart in peace and never come back.⁸ Rives helped some of the freedmen join their relatives in Liberia.⁹ Freed people from other farms moved onto Castle Hill property, causing trouble for the Rives as well as for Castle Hill's two-dozen remaining freed black residents. Rives complained to federal authorities in Gordonsville, who removed the offenders. Rives and Judith hired white men to cultivate the farm, while employing six black servants for household work.¹⁰ In January, Judith boasted that the "seven fine young confederates" working the farm had filled the smokehouse with meat, filled the ice house with ice, and were repairing dilapidated fences and buildings.¹¹ Months later Judith observed, "No doubt we must have a certain amount of trouble with servants of any kind, but having tried both, I decidedly prefer white people."¹²

Emancipation would not soften the scorn for black people Rives had expressed in his 1863 *Richmond Whig* letter and the 1865 Peace Resolution. Judith was disgusted that her husband and Alfred were disfranchised, while former slaves could vote and run for office.¹³ When a former Oak Ridge slave named Hervey addressed a Nelson County political meeting, Judith wrote her son, "Papa says he was a notorious rogue, though a very smart fellow, when he was acquainted with him."¹⁴

Rives could also extend his condescension to white neighbors. Captain George C. Dickinson of Rougemont wrote Rives to complain that Rives' horses had invaded his fields, trampled his wheat, and knocked down his "fodder shocks." Dickinson advised, "please keep them out or I shall use my gun."

Rives replied:

Castle Hill 15 Dec. 1865
Dear sir,

I received a note from you this evening, expressed in a language & tone to which I am not accustomed. After telling me that 'your patience is exhausted,' you call upon me 'to keep my horses & colts' out of a field, the enclosure of which, my overseer tells me, was burnt by the negligence of your people, and that if I do not do so, 'you will use your gun,' whether upon me or the animals, you do not say. If you do not already know, I beg leave to inform you that I am not in a situation, as to health or age, to 'keep' animals from trespassing upon your fields; that I have, as you may perhaps know, a manager who is charged with such matters; & that in future you will address yourself to him, when you have complaints to make of the kind contained in your note.

Respectfully,
WC Rives
George C. Dickinson Esq."[15]

Like most of his neighbors, Rives was short of cash immediately after the war. Only the providential arrival of a check repaying an old debt enabled Rives to pay his 1866 taxes to Lit Macon, the Sheriff of Albemarle.[16] James Seddon paid the remainder of his debt to Rives for the 1860 slave purchase in railroad and city bonds.[17] Even though Seddon and Rives had differed on secession, and the purchased slaves were now emancipated, Seddon was related by marriage, and felt bound by gentlemanly honor to erase the debt. Rives' tax receipt showed that, in January 1866, Castle Hill had 22 horses, 46 cattle, 31 sheep and 32 hogs.[18] This livestock had escaped requisition and theft by Confederate as well as Union Army forces. Rives had sold six horses and two mules to the Confederate Army in 1862.[19]

Apparently anti-Confederate sentiment had abated sufficiently to permit Rives to accompany Judith to Newport as well as to Carnwath in the summer of 1866. While in Newport, Rives read

William Cabell Rives   *Judith Page Rives*

reviews of his recently published second volume of the Madison biography.[20]

Rives answered a favorable review by the *Richmond Whig*, that had also lamented the "downfall of the Constitution." While admitting the difficulties they faced, Rives remained optimistic. "Bad men, who are now in power, are certainly perverting it [the Constitution] in the grossest manner and to the worst possible purposes. This has happened before in our history, and yet the Constitution was restored, and even re-invigorated in its true principles." Rives noted that during the Adams presidency, "Mr. Jefferson said, 'the Constitution was at its last gasp,' and yet by perseverance in asserting and holding up its legitimate doctrines in a firm and Constitutional manner, it was fully restored to life, and gave sixty years of uninterrupted freedom and prosperity to the country under the auspices of the party which restored it." Rives also mentioned parallels in English History, when liberty and rule of law were threatened before being rescued. Rives strongly disagreed with the reviewer's opinion that the Articles of Confederation had been more satisfactory than the Constitution.

Rives observed:

> There is another reflection which we of the South must not lose sight of. If the Constitution has, in truth, been finally overthrown by the consequences of the war, did not we of the South, renouncing constitutional meth-ods of redress, which there is every reason to believe would, with a little patience, have secured all our rights, make the appeal to force, which has terminated in the catastrophe complained of?[21]

The "bad men in power," in Rives opinion, were the Radical Republicans, who implemented more punitive Reconstruction measures than President Johnson advocated. Rives had written Senator Reverdy Johnson of Maryland (who had argued the case against Dred Scott in 1857) to express his approval of President Johnson's approach. Using his superlative, Rives said Johnson realized "the true Madisonian" balance between state and federal power.[22] Andrew Johnson narrowly escaped being impeached from office.

Rives' last role in public service was his work as a trustee of the Peabody Education Fund. George Peabody, a Massachusetts native and founder of the George Peabody and Company London banking firm, provided approximately two million dol-lars to be distributed among southern educational institutions to help the region recover. Peabody, with the help of former House Speaker Robert C. Winthrop and others, selected distinguished northerners and southerners as trustees, including: General U. S. Grant, Admiral David Farragut, Hamilton Fish of New York (future Secretary of State), William Aiken of South Carolina (former governor and congressman), and Rives. Winthrop and

Peabody attached Rives' name to their project even before they heard he had accepted the appointment.[23] Peabody sent letters to those he had chosen February 7, and the first meeting, at which Rives was not present, was held in Washington February 8.[24] As soon as the *Richmond Whig* announced on February 9, 1867, that Rives was a trustee of the fund, he began receiving requests for money from numerous academies and colleges. Judith noted, "the applications are legion, and if a tenth part are indulged in their wishes, it will be like watering Papa's hundred acre wheat field with a watering pot."[25]

Though his health had been frail, Rives journeyed to New York for the second Peabody Trustees meeting March 19-22, 1867 at the Fifth Avenue Hotel. Rives stayed with Francis and family at 8 Washington Place, arriving during a snowstorm. Francis and his wife Matilda let Rives occupy their first floor bedroom, to save him the effort of climbing stairs.[26] Rives attended the meeting as well as a banquet in honor of General Grant March 22, at which Francis and Matilda were also guests. Rives helped the fund's general agent identify Virginia's educational needs.[27] Rives fell dangerously ill in New York. He observed, "The truth is my zeal for the interests of Mr. Peabody's very munificent donation was, as the circumstances of weather, exertion &c turned out, greater than my strength."[28] Fearing the worst, Francis summoned his mother to New York. Rives did not recover sufficient strength to return to Castle Hill until late May. Judith served as both nurse and secretary to her husband. She met with Mr. Peabody, who recounted how she and Rives had offered him a seat in their carriage when they had met in Niagara 38 years earlier. She wrote her son, "Happily I had heard this just before from Papa, whose memory for such things is so much better; so I was not surprised."[29]

Francis accompanied his parents to Washington to help his father change to the Orange and Alexandria train. He wrote

Peabody Education Fund Trustees. From left, Admiral David Farragut,
George Peabody, Hamilton Fish, Ulysses S. Grant, William Aiken,
Robert Charles Withrop, Charles Petit McIlvaine,
William Cabell Rives, Samuel Wetmore.

Alfred about the planned journey: "He was better yesterday than
at any time since his illness, but today the reaction from undue
mental labor has produced some demoralization."[30] Rives was
delighted to return to Castle Hill where, "Nature has put on her
sweetest and most attractive garb."[ɪ] He regained strength by taking walks about the lawn and gardens. He was able to visit the
Virginia springs in July, and saw General Lee and other former
Confederates at White Sulphur Springs.[32]

Rives continued to work on his Madison biography, complet-
ing Volume III in February 1868. He spent much of his time lying
on a sofa in the dining room. He grew a long gray beard. His
face became pale and emaciated.[33] Judith wrote Will in March

that "Papa" had overexerted himself in an hour-long speech to the family about George Washington.[34]

Rives died at Castle Hill Saturday, April 25, 1868. Judith wrote a dramatic description of his passing for Amélie and Will:

> I cannot let this mournful day pass, my precious child, without writing you some of the particulars of the last hours of our darling, which may help to comfort your sad and tender heart. After all his delicate health, he was very ill only two days. Last Thursday he was better than usual, dressed himself with particular care & neatness, and with help, drove out for an hour enjoying the sweet air. In the evening he said he felt so much better, that he begged us to go out & walk, but Ella lingered in the house, and in a short time pushed out to tell us he was ill & in great pain. I sent Henry with the horses to fetch the doctor, & in twenty minutes he was here, and by various remedies afforded him some relief. He had a restless night, and in the morning I telegraphed for Francis, fearing the worst. Henry brought his telegram saying he would be with us Saturday, leaving in the first train. Dear Alfred came Friday, which was a blessed comfort, as he could lift him about like a baby, and though suffering little pain, he wanted continual change from the bed to the sofa & back. I told him Francis was coming next day.
>
> Another restless night. In the morning he was more tranquil, spoke of all his dear absent children, of 'dear Will & dear Amélie,' and often asked if it was not time to send the carriage for Francis, adding 'dear Will and Amélie are too far off to come.' At one o'clock Francis arrived. He was so agitated he had to wait a little before embracing his dear father. 'I am so glad to see you my

dear Son,' he said, asked after his family. He called Alfred & said, 'My Son, you must bring me a pen and ink. I want to sign a check for the man who renewed the carriage. He is ill in bed & very poor.' Alfred said, 'Father don't trouble yourself. I have brought money with me on purpose to pay him.' 'I must sign a check my son,' he said. To put the matter at rest, Alfred brought the paper & a pen, and he wrote something illegible but which he meant for his name. Every few minutes he would look at me & say 'don't leave me my blessed wife.' 'Not for one moment,' I always said. Dr. Nelson had been sent for as consulting physician and came in. He spoke to him kindly, and asked about his family and friends. And now the hour all but himself dreaded drew on apace. The previous day he asked me to kneel by him & join him in prayer. I obeyed as far as my broken voice would allow. The next morning (Saturday) I repeated some of the sweet promises of eternal life to him. 'I wish I could repeat the blessed words' he said, 'but I am too weak.' About two hours before the last he raised his arms, looked steadfastly upward, and made a gesture as if beckoning with his hand. 'What do you see my darling?' I said. 'A multitude, more than I can number,' he replied, he then repeated this gesture, raising both his arms. 'You see the angels of God,' I said, 'coming to take you to heaven. You know you are going there to be with God and our blessed Saviour for ever!' 'I trust so,' he said. 'My darling,' I said, bless your dear children, before you go,' 'I do, I do,' he said 'every one of them.'

These were his last words. He then closed his eyes as if going to sleep, the breath came faintly and more faintly and became as gentle as that of a sleeping infant.

His hand was still clasped in mine, and I laid my other hand softly on those loved and lovely eyes, so we all sat in deep & solemn silence, not a struggle, not a sigh. He fell asleep in Jesus. Half an hour more the gentle breathing ceased, and all was over! God supported me to fulfill my answer to that plaintive request, 'don't leave me!' and also to say, 'I thank thee my God that this thy saint hath departed in thy faith & fear & love!' Please send this to our dearly beloved Son. I can write no more.[35]

* * *

1 Rives to Alfred Rives, December 22, 1865, Rives MSS, UVa. Accession #4498.

2 Judith Rives to William C. Rives, Jr. January 15, 1866, Rives MSS, UVa. Accession #10596.

3 "A Scarce Presidential Parole for an Important Southerner," Explanatory online text accompanying Johnson's signed parole of Rives dated July 25, 1865, which was offered for sale for $3,000 in 2012 at www.barnesautographs.com.

4 James Rives Childs, *Reliques of the Rives*, Lynchburg, J. P. Bell Co., 1929, 599-600.

5 Rives to Alexander Rives, June 7, 1865, (rough copy) Rives MSS, LOC, box 37.

6 Thomas B. Alexander, Richard E. Beringer, *The Anatomy of the Confederate Congress*, Nashville, Vanderbilt University Press, 1972, 39.

7 Rives to Alfred Rives, August 3, 1865, Rives MSS, UVa. Accession #4498, and Rives to William C. Rives, Jr. August 7, 1865, Rives MSS, LOC, box 37.

8 Rives to Alfred Rives, September 2, 1865, Rives MSS, Ibid.

9 Judith Rives to Sadie Rives, February 28, 1866, Alfred Landon Rives Papers, Duke University, cited in Drew R. McCoy, *The Last of the Fathers*, Cambridge, Cambridge University Press, 1989, 364.

10 Judith Rives to William C. Rives, Jr. September 28, 1865, Rives MSS, UVa. Accession # 10596 Also available online http://sewanee.edu/reconstruction/html/docs/judith28th.html.

11 Judith Rives to William C. Rives, Jr., January 15, 1866, Rives MSS, UVa., Accession #10596.

12 Judith Rives to Alfred Rives, April 16, 1866, Alfred Landon Rives Papers, Duke University, quoted in McCoy, Ibid. George Barclay sent a letter from New York congratulating Rives on his change to white farm labor, which "will enable you to secure a larger net income from your farms . . . than you could derive from that of the Black, who is, generally, a lazy thriftless animal." George Barclay to Rives, December 20, 1865, Rives MSS, LOC, box 93.

13 Judith Rives to William C. Rives, Jr. March 19, 1867, Rives MSS, UVa. Accession #10596.

14 Judith Rives to William C. Rives, Jr. June 15, 1867, Ibid.

15 George C. Dickinson to Rives, Rives to Dickinson, December 15, 1865, Rives MSS, LOC, box 93.

16 Judith Rives to William C. Rives, Jr., January 15, 1866, Rives MSS, UVa. Accession #10596.

17 Memorandum Book, Rives MSS, LOC, box 122.

18 1866 tax receipt, Rives MSS, UVa. Accession #2313, Box 2.

19 William C. Rives, Receipt#12, National Archives, Record Group #109, War Department Collection of Confederate Records, Publication #M346A, Confederate Papers Relating to Citizens or Business Firms 1861-1865, Roll #868.

20 Judith Rives to William C. Rives, Jr., July 20, August 4, August 17, 1866, Rives MSS, UVa. Accession #10596.

21 Rives to McDonald, Editor of the *Whig*, (copy in Judith's handwriting), February 9, 1867, Rives MSS, LOC, box 93.

22 Rives to Reverdy Johnson, December 7, 1865, Ibid.

23 Robert C. Winthrop to Rives, February 18, 1867, Ibid.

24 Letterbook, Rives MSS, LOC, box 105, 255.

25 Judith Rives to William C. Rives, Jr. March 19, 1867, Rives MSS, UVa. Accession #10596.

26 Ibid.

27 Letterbook, Rives MSS, LOC, box 105, 255.

28 Rives to William C. Rives, Jr. April 7, 1867, Rives MSS, UVa. Accession # 10596.

29 Judith Rives to William C. Rives, Jr. May 1, 1867, Ibid.

30 Francis Rives to Alfred Rives, May 17, 1867, Rives MSS, UVa. Accession # 2313, box 2.

31 Rives to William C. Rives, Jr. June 5, 1867, Rives MSS, UVa. Accession #10596.

32 William C. Rives III to Judith Rives, August 3, 1867, Ibid.

33 Letterbook, Rives MSS, LOC, Box 105, 256.

34 Judith Rives to William C. Rives, Jr., March 8, 1868, Rives MSS, LOC, box 38, quoted in McCoy, Ibid, 367.

35 Judith Rives to Amélie Sigourney, April 27, 1868, Rives MSS, UVa. Accession #2313, box 3.

CHAPTER TWENTY-SIX

Maintenance of Constitutional Liberty

ON MONDAY, APRIL 27, Rives was buried east of the Castle Hill house, half a mile from the Walker family graveyard, which lies at the foot of Walnut Mountain. Alfred designed a wrought iron enclosure that was later erected around the grave.[1] Rives' brothers George and Alexander, his children Francis, Alfred and Ella, Dr. James L. Cabell of the University, neighboring land-owners, and many of his former slaves gathered for the graveside service read by the Reverend Ebenezer Boyden.[2]

Robert E. Lee expressed his condolences to the widow with gentlemanly eloquence:

> Lexington Va: 29 April 1868
> My dear Mrs. Rives
>
> The sad news of the death of your husband has just reached me; & though I know that Virginia in all her length & breadth is this day mourning the loss of her great Statesman, there is not one of her Sons who more deeply laments his death, or more truly sympa-thizes with you, in the great Sorrow which has befallen you & your house, than myself. His long & illustrious career has been marked by usefulness to the country & devotion to his native State; & his pure patriotism & earnest efforts for the maintenance of Constitutional liberty will be an example to posterity. But I need not recite his virtues to you, who have observed them so

constantly & appreciate them so highly. Any object was to sympathize in your grief, & to assure you of my sincere participation in your affliction.

May God in his mercy support you in this sad hour is the prayer of yours most truly

RE Lee
Mrs. Wm C. Rives[3]

Robert C. Winthrop, who was President of the Massachusetts Historical Society at the time of Rives' death, praised Rives at a subsequent meeting. He said, "Virginia certainly had sent no more accomplished statesman to the councils of the nation." He remembered Rives' opposition to secession. Of Rives' accomplishments, Winthrop chose to mention his role in bringing Louis Philippe to the French throne in 1830.[4]

Newspaper obituaries praised Rives. The *Richmond Whig* stated, "His reputation was in no part due to the ultraism of the partisan, or to the seductive arts of inflammatory power of the orator; his popularity was acquired without flatteries to the multitude, or any attempt to become a people's man." Though the preceding was accurate, the obituary then extravagantly claimed: "Altogether, there is not much risk in saying that Mr. Rives was, with the exception of his great teacher, Mr. Jefferson, the most accomplished man the State of Virginia has produced; and we are not prepared to name any living person in the whole country who has higher claims in this respect."[5]

Rives displayed talent as a legislator, diplomat, scholar, and agriculturalist, but ranking him second only to Jefferson was overly generous. Rives was well known during his political career, but his labors produced modest results, compared to his great predecessors and even to his contemporaries. Rives belonged to a generation of Virginia political leaders who have suffered from comparisons to founders such as Washington, Jefferson, Madison, Patrick Henry and George Mason. Any other group of leaders would fail in that comparison, because no state ever again produced such a distinguished cast of great men.

Among Rives' notable achievements, the reparations treaty with France was his most productive diplomacy. In the Senate, his helping to secure passage of the Webster Ashburton Treaty, his support of President Tyler even as Tyler was expelled from the Whig Party, his work in the purchase of Madison's papers, and his unflinching support of Jackson against the bank and against nullification, all demonstrated courage and ability. He cultivated Madison's reputation in his Senate speeches as well as with his scholarly work.

Rives' reverence for Madison and Jefferson was sometimes a liability. He continued to invoke the words and policies of Madison and Jefferson when innovative thinking and action might have served him better. His reverence for history and his conservative nature prompted his constant hearkening back to a supposed golden age of the republic. Madison himself was not frozen in time. His thinking evolved on several issues according to Madison scholar and Stanford Professor Jack Rakove. For instance in the 1780s, Madison distrusted public deliberation. In the 1790s, he indicated a growing belief that people could be guardians of their liberties.[6] Madison was initially disappointed in the Constitution, because he had to sacrifice many of his proposals to achieve compromise.[7] Madison's remark in his March 12, 1833 letter to Rives, about how the Virginia Resolutions and the Constitution might have been better written, showed that the "Father of the Constitution" viewed his creation as less than perfect.[8]

Rives' solution to sectional controversy was to cling to the argument that Union was most important and that grievances about slavery or trade issues must be put aside for the Union's sake. He argued that slavery could not be forbidden, since Madison's Constitution had guaranteed it. Rives' avowed middle course between abolitionists and secessionists would never have resolved what was, in fact, an irrepressible conflict. Slavery was a nearly fatal flaw in the framers' legacy. Even with historical hindsight, devising a solution to the issue, which would have pleased all parties in 1860-1861, seems impossible.

Examination of Rives' life affords the view of a witness and participant in nearly 75 years of major events in the nation's history. With the inclination of a historian and archivist, he saved nearly all of his own papers for posterity, most of which survive as the 50,400-item Library of Congress Rives Papers. Many historians have utilized the collection, but its potential is hardly exhausted.

Rives' attempts to position himself between extremes of party and section, including Democrats and Whigs, and Calhoun and abolitionists, may explain his omission from the history books. Vehement leaders of opposing factions tend to be more memorable than moderates. Henry Clay earned a reputation for brilliance in crafting compromises and mediating disputes. Rives lacked Clay's genius at conciliation.

Rives failed in his bid for the vice-presidency, and he failed to become Secretary of State, despite his diplomatic credentials.[9] The Conservative Revolt he helped lead against the Democratic Party, and his opposition to party discipline proved to be vain struggle against relentless forces of change. His avowed insistence upon placing principle above party, and his transition from Democrat to Whig, gained him enemies in both parties, which limited his influence and effectiveness. Rives warned of the possibility of Civil War from 1833 until 1861, but was unable to prevent secession and conflict. Rives' obituary in the *Lynchburg Virginian* noted that Rives had declared during the war, "I thank my Heavenly Father that none of the blood shed in this dreadful war is on my skirts, I did all I could to prevent it. If it were otherwise, I could not rest on my pillow at night."[10]

When Virginia seceded, Rives could have maintained his opposition to secession and, with Judith, sought refuge with their children in the North. That would have meant abandoning Castle Hill. Their love for the ancestral home and their connection to the land rendered such a course unthinkable. Reversing himself with the zeal of a convert, as he had when he turned against Van Buren, Rives supported the Confederate cause as vigorously as his health allowed. After the war, he became reconciled to the result. Many former Confederates would have disputed the passage in his letter to the *Richmond Whig*, in which he said that the South had brought her troubles upon herself by abandoning the Constitution and resorting to armed conflict.

The Constitution has continued to serve his country, justifying Rives' faith in the document and its creators. He would certainly have valued maintenance of the Constitution far above lasting fame for himself.

William C. Rives, Jr. crafted the words inscribed upon a marble plaque memorializing his father on a wall inside Grace Church. Every Sunday, people file by it on their way to receive communion:

IN MEMORY OF ONE OF THE FOUNDERS OF THIS CHURCH

WILLIAM CABELL RIVES, LL.D.

STATESMAN, DIPLOMATIST, HISTORIAN

BORN 4TH MAY 1793

DIED 25TH APRIL 1868

UNITING A CLEAR AND CAPACIOUS INTELLECT

A COURAGEOUS AND GENEROUS TEMPER,

WITH SOUND LEARNING

AND COMMANDING ELOQUENCE

HE WON A DISTINGUISHED PLACE

AMONG THE FOREMOST MEN

WHOM VIRGINIA HAS CONSECRATED

TO THE SERVICE OF THE COUNTRY

WHILE HE ADDED LUSTRE TO HIS TALENTS

BY THE PURITY AND DIGNITY

OF HIS PUBLIC CAREER

AND ADORNED HIS PRIVATE LIFE

WITH ALL THE VIRTUES

WHICH CAN GRACE THE CHARACTER

OF HUSBAND, FATHER, FRIEND

AND

CHRISTIAN.

"Blessed are the dead which
die in the LORD."

* * *

1   Alfred Rives "drawing of enclosure around Father's grave," Rives MSS, LOC, box 120.

2   WCR, Jr., Biography, Rives MSS, LOC, box 103, 258.

3   Robert E. Lee to Judith Rives, April 29, 1868, Lee Papers, Washington and Lee University, available online: http://home.wlu.edu/stanleyv/29apr68.htm

4   Robert C. Winthrop, "Remarks on the Death of Hon. W. C. Rives and Hon. Edward Coles," *Proceedings of the Massachusetts Historical Society*, Series 1, Vol. 10 (1867-1869) 397-402.

5   *Richmond Whig* William Cabell Rives obituary notice, quoted in Alexander Brown, *The Cabells and Their Kin*, Franklin, N C., Genealogy Publishing Service, 1994 reprint edited by Randolph W. Cabell, 447-448.

6   Jack Rakove May 5, 2013 lecture on Madison at Montpelier.

7 Jack N. Rakove, *James Madison and the Creation of the American Republic*, New York, Pearson Longman, 2007, 78.

8 Madison to Rives, March 12, 1833, *Letters and Other Writings of James Madison*, [edited by Rives and Fendall], Philadelphis, J. B. Lippincott & Co., Vol. IV, 292.

9 One of his grandsons, George Lockhart Rives, served as Assistant Secretary of State under Grover Cleveland. A great great grandson Lloyd Michael Rives was a career diplomat, serving in the difficult post of Cambodia during the 1960s.

10 *Lynchburg Virginian*, Tuesday morning, April 28, 1868, "Death of Hon. William C. Rives" clipping in Rives MSS, UVa. Accession #2313, box 3.

Acknowledgements

Many wise and generous, old and new friends helped create this book. Despite his innumerable other commitments, University of Virginia Professor Gary Gallagher read my first draft and suggested improvements. Because he did not read the amended version, all blame for remaining imperfections rests upon the author, including inadvertent omissions from this list. Robert K. Krick, another great Civil War historian, passed along multiple research files and much needed advice. Gallagher, Krick and William W. Freehling, a third giant in the field, all encouraged me to write about my nearly forgotten ancestor.

I met these three experts through the Charlottesville Civil War Round Table. I have learned much from CWRT's distinguished speakers and well informed members, including past presidents Bob Tatum and Dick Nicholas (*Sheridan's James River Campaign of 1865*), both of whom provided advice and encouragement. The group's articulate scribe Sandy Von Thelen, invited me to join CWRT and has been educating me about the Civil War since we were in grade school.

My cousins in the Cabell Foundation have been an inspiration, including Archer Minardi, who organized a group tour of Cabell graveyards, Randy Cabell, Ran Cabell and Bob Self, who supplied photographs and historical background. My cousins Frank Moore in Boston and Bob Rives in Texas have been trusted authorities on Rives family matters. Cousin Jane Potts and her late mother Bette, shared Rives photos, documents and stories during pleasant visits to Richmond.

Endnotes of this book reveal my enormous debt to the late Raymond C. Dingledine, Jr.'s PhD dissertation on WCR's political career, and to Drew McCoy's chapter, "The Strange Career of

William Cabell Rives" in his study of Madison's later years, *The Last of the Fathers*.

Writer friends have been ever ready to respond to my plaintive emails, solve my dilemmas, and cheer me up, including Daniel Morrow (*Murder in Lexington*) who convinced me to start writing, Thomas Holliday (*Falling Up*), and Donna Lucey (*Archie and Amélie*). Donna's husband Henry Wiencek (*Master of the Mountain, Imperfect God, The Hairstons*) inspires with his diligent and courageous scholarship. K. Edward Lay (*The Architecture of Jefferson Country*) helped me navigate county tax records.

At the University of Virginia, Heather Riser, Margaret Hrabe, and the entire staff of the Albert and Shirley Small Special Collections Library made my extensive research there productive and pleasant. Warner Granade, Director of Circulation at the Alderman Library, plucked missing volumes out of thin air for me. Rachael Salisbury, Assistant Registrar of Collections of The Fralin Museum of Art, kindly made available four Rives family portraits, and William Auten, Digital Resources Coordinator, went to considerable trouble to provide a perfect image of FR Rives.

Margaret M. (Peg) O'Bryant, Librarian of the Albemarle Historical Society, provided frequent direction and assistance.

Staff members of the Rare Book and Special Collection Division of the Library of Congress (Madison Building) were always helpful and efficient. La Vonda Broadnax in the Digital Reference Room (Jefferson Building) guided me through online labyrinths. David and Page Winstead of Chevy Chase provided comfortable DC area lodging.

Hampden-Sydney historian and former chaplain William E. Thompson (*First in War, The Hampden-Sydney Boys*) verified that WCR received an LLB from Hampden-Sydney. Brown University archivists Gayle D. Lynch and Raymond Butti did likewise for their institution. Jessica Axel of Harvard Alumni

Online Help forwarded my questions about Harvard honors to Pusey Library Researcher Robin Carlaw, who discovered that Harvard had considered WCR and Seward for honorary doctorates in 1860. Perhaps Rives and Seward could have worked more productively together in 1861 if they had mingled in the Yard in 1860. Harvard Magazine Senior Editor Jean Martin answered my "mackerel in the moonlight" query. Heather Beattie, Museum Collections Manager of the Virginia Historical Society, verified that WCR's portrait gift survives.

Georgetown Law Professor Jim Oldham and Stanford History Professor Jack Rakove explained contents of Jefferson's law library. Lynda Crist, head of the Jefferson Davis Papers Project at Rice University, shared Rives/Davis files and was willing to venture an opinion about the matter of importance and delicacy. I am grateful to the staff at Montpelier, especially Tiffany Cole, Assistant Curator for Research and Documentation, for assistance and for hosting a highly informative 2012 Jefferson/Madison symposium.

Seeking publishing advice, I called John Conover, who printed my first book at his Papercraft Printing and Design in 1993. John directed me to my friend Fran Smith, a graphic designer who had directed me in a play in 1983. Fran introduced me to book designer Josef Beery, who has been a pleasure to work with.

My late mother Mary Jo Rives collected some of the archival material I utilized, including copies of letters, which the late Laurens Rhinelander donated to UVa. I wish my mother and my late father Alexander Rives were here to read this book. As a child, I shared a room with my brother William Cabell Rives, who lives up to his distinguished name, and has cheered me on, along with our older brother Sandy, my neighbor and hunting companion. The three of us miss our late oldest brother George. My wife Aggie, and my daughters Caroline and Mayo have given me constant love and support, which made the writing possible and worthwhile. My beloved family members have all qualified for the dedication of the 1929 family genealogy *Reliques of the Rives*, which is to all who "have shed lustre upon the name of Rives."

Bibliography

MANUSCRIPT COLLECTIONS

Confederate papers relating to citizens or business firms 1861-1865. William C. Rives papers, Microform Publication #M346A, Roll #868, Record Group #109, War Department Collection of Confederate Records, National Archives Building, Archives I, Washington D.C.

Minutes of the University of Virginia Board of Visitors. Albert and Shirley Small Special Collections Library, University of Virginia.

Papers of James McDowell, Accession #Mss1755, Albert and Shirley Small Special Collections Library, University of Virginia.

Papers of the Rives, Sears and Rhinelander Families, Accession #10596; Rives Family Papers, Accession #s 2313, 2532, 11375, 38-348, 6435, 7797, 1273, 4331, Albert and Shirley Small Special Collections Library, University of Virginia.

Papers of William C. Rives, Rare Book and Special Collection Division, Library of Congress. (Madison Building)

Rives-Barclay Family Papers, 1698-1941(bulk 1790-1880). Accession 37776. Personal Papers Collection, The Library of Virginia, Richmond, Va. 23219.

Seddon Papers, Accession # Mss14847, Albert and Shirley Small Special Collections Library, University of Virginia.

Virginia Historical Society Manuscript Collection. Mss2C2308b, Bills of sale 1801-1810 issued to Peter Carr for purchase of enslaved persons by Brown, Rives and Company of Milton.

GOVERNMENT RECORDS

Albemarle County Will Books, Albemarle County Clerk's Office

Congressional Globe. published by Blair and Rives (23rd-29th Congress)

Gales and Seaton's *Register of Debates* (19th-25th Congress)

Journal of the Congress of the Confederate States of America 1861-1865. Volumes 1-7, Washington, Government Printing Office, 1904

Nelson County Will Books, Nelson County Clerk's Office

NEWSPAPERS

National Daily Intelligencer

New York Herald

Richmond Dispatch

Richmond Enquirer

Richmond Examiner

Richmond Whig

Virginia Advocate

ARTICLES AND PAMPHLETS

Appleton, Nathan. "Letter to the Hon. William C. Rives: On Slavery and the Union," Boston, J. H. Eastburn's Press, 1860.

Boyden, Ebenezer. "The Epidemic of the Nineteenth Century." Richmond, C. H. Wynne, 1860.

Bradford, S. D. "Letters of S. D. Bradford to Abbott Lawrence in reply to those addressed by Mr. Lawrence to Hon. William C. Rives of Virginia." Boston, Beals and Greene, 1846.

Bridges, Peter. "A Pen of Fire," *Virginia Quarterly Review*. Charlottesville, University of Virginia, Winter 2002.

Carmichael, Mary. "Louis Agassiz Exhibit Divides Harvard, Swiss Group," *Boston Globe*. June 27, 2012.

Clarke, Raymond B., Jr. editor, "Observations on Washington Society: Mrs. W. C. Rives --- Miss Maria L. Gordon Letters, 1842," *Papers of the Albemarle Historical Society*. Charlottesville, Albemarle Historical Society, 1951, Vol. XI, 53-61

Clay, Henry. "Senate Speech February 19, 1838," Washington, Gales and Seaton, 1838.

Dingledine, Raymond C., Jr. "The Education of a Virginia Planter's Son," *America the Middle Period Essays in Honor of Bernard Mayo.* edited by John B. Boles, Charlottesville, University of Virginia Press, 1973.

Downing, Charles (attributed). "Reception of General Lafayette in Albemarle," *The Magazine of Albemarle County History.* Vol. 24 (1965-1966), Charlottesville, Albemarle County Historical Society.

Gilmer, John Harmer. "Letter Addressed to Hon. William C. Rives on the Existing Status of the Revolution," Richmond, 1864.

Gunderson, Robert G. "William C. Rives and the Old Gentlemen's Convention," *Journal of Southern History,* Vol. 22 (1956) Baton Rouge, Southern Historical Association, 459-476.

Houpt, David W. "Securing a Legacy: The Publication of James Madison's Notes from the Constitutional Convention," *The Virginia Magazine of History and Biography.* Vol. 118, No. 1, Richmond, The Virginia Historical Society, 2010.

Ketcham, Ralph L. "William Cabell Rives, Editor of the *Letters and Other Writings of James Madison,*" *The Virginia Magazine of History and Biography.* Vol. 68 (April 1960) No. 2

Kiracofe, David James. "The Jamestown Jubilees: State Patriotism and Virginia Identity in the Early Nineteenth Century," *The Virginia Magazine of History and Biography*. 2002, Volume 110, No. 1, Richmond, The Virginia Historical Society.

Lawrence, Abbott. "Letters from the Hon. Abbott Lawrence to the Hon. William C. Rives of Virginia," Boston, Eastburn's Press, 1846.

Lay, K. Edward, and Stockton, Martha Tuzson. "Castle Hill: The Walker Family Estate," *The Magazine of Albemarle County History*. Vol. 52, (1994), Charlottesville, Albemarle County Historical Society.

Mackay-Smith, Alexander. "Cleveland Bays and Hunter Breeding in Virginia Before the Civil War," *The Horse*, Washington D.C., published by the American Remount Association, March-April, 1937.

Moore, John Hammond. "Amélie Louise Rives and the Charge of the Light Brigade." *The Virginia Magazine of History and Biography*, Vol. 75, No. 1, Richmond, The Virginia Historical Society, January 1967.

Moore, John Hammond. "Judith Rives of Castle Hill," *Virginia Cavalcade*. Vol. XIII, No. 4, Spring 1964.

Moore, John Hammond. "The Rives Peace Resolution March 1865." *West Virginia History*. Charleston, West Virginia, V. 26 (1964-65), 153-65.

The New Yorker. review of Irmscher, Christopher. *Louis* Agassiz. March 11, 2013, 75.

"The Park Horse, Imported Emperor," *Wallace's Monthly*, Vol. II, June, 1876.

Pease, Sir Alfred E. "The Cleveland Bay and Yorkshire Coach Horse," reprinted from *Yorkshire Agricultural Journal*, 1937.

Rives, Judith Page. "Observations on Washington Society: Mrs. William C. Rives – Miss Maria L. Gordon Letters 1842," *Papers of the Albemarle Historical Society*. Vol. XI, Charlottesville, Albemarle Historical Society, 1951.

Rives, William Cabell and Francis Robert. Articles on the Cleveland Bay horse breed, lime, and sheep, in *The Southern Planter*. Vols. II (1842), XIII (1853), XIV, (1854), XV (1855), XVI, (1856), XVI, (1856), XVII (1857),

Rives, William Cabell. "Address of William C. Rives to the People of Virginia," Charlottesville, James Alexander, 1839.

Rives, William Cabell. "Connection of Agriculture with Free Political Institutions... an address delivered at Saratoga Springs September 23, 1853," Albany, J. Munsell, 1853.

Rives, William Cabell. "Correspondence," Printed pamphlet request from T. J. Wertenbaker and others that Rives represent Albemarle at the Virginia Secession Convention and Rives' reply, January 12, 1861.

Rives, William Cabell. "Discourse Before the Young Men's Christian Association of Richmond On the Ethics of Christianity December 7, 1855," Richmond, John Nowland.

Rives, William Cabell. "Discourse on the Character and Services of John Hampden and the great struggle for popular and constitutional liberty in his time," Richmond, Shepherd and Colin, 1845.

Rives, William Cabell, "Discourse on the Uses and Importance of History, illustrated by a comparison of the American and French Revolutions," Richmond, Shepherd and Colin, 1847.

Rives, William Cabell. "Letter of Hon. William C. Rives giving his reasons fro preferring Mr. Clay to Mr. Van Buren for next President," New York, Greeley and McElrath, 1844.

Rives, William Cabell. "Letter from the Hon. William C. Rives of Virginia, February 15, 1840," Washington, 1840.

Rives, William Cabell. "Letter from the Hon. William C. Rives to t Friend on the Important Questions of the Day," Richmond, Printed at the Whig Book and Job Office, 1860.

Rives, William Cabell. "Letter in Regard to a Portrait of Franklin." *Virginia Magazine of History and Biography*, Vol. 40, (1932), Richmond, The Virginia Historical Society.

Rives, William Cabell. "Letter of Hon. William C. Rives to Mr. Boteler of the House of Representatives on the National Crisis," 1860 printed broadside.

Rives, William Cabell. "Letters of William Cabell Rives to Thomas Walker Gilmer," *Tyler's Quarterly Historical and Genealogical Magazine*. Volumes 5, 6 & 7 (1923-25), Richmond, Whittet and Shepperson.

Rives, William Cabell. "Speech of William C. Rives at a public dinner given him at Louisa CH, Virginia on 7th September, 1839," Charlottesville, James Alexander, 1839.

Sowle, Patrick. "The Trials of a Virginia Unionist: William Cabell Rives and the Secession Crisis 1860-61," *The Virginia Magazine of History and Biography*, Vol. 80 (January 1972) Richmond, The Virginia Historical Society, No. 1.

Rives, William Cabell. "Speech of Hon. William C. Rives on the Proceedings of the Peace Conference and the State of the Union," Richmond, Printed at the Whig Book and Job Office, 1861.

Rives, William Cabell. "Speech on the Resolution for the Annexation of Texas, February 15, 1845." (no printer given)

Rives, William Cabell. "Virginia and Her Interests," *Plough, the Loom and the Anvil*, New York, published by Myron Finch, January 1852.

Shulman, Holly C. "Dolley Madison and the Publication of the Papers of James Madison, 1836-1837," *The Virginia Magazine of History and Biography*. Vol. 118, No. 1, Richmond, The Virginia Historical Society, 2010.

Tallmadge, Nathaniel P. "Senate Speech February 8, 1838." Washington, Printed at the Madisonian Office, 1838

Thomas, Mary Elizabeth. "William Cabell Rives and the British Abolitionists," *The Virginia Magazine of History and Biography*. Vol. 89, No. 1, (1981) Richmond, The Virginia Historical Society.

Urofsky, Melvin I. "The Virginia Historical Society: The First 175 years 1831-2006," *The Virginia Magazine of History and Biography*. Vol. 114, No. 1, Richmond, The Virginia Historical Society, 2006.

Webster, Daniel. "Speech of March 12 in Answer to Mr. Calhoun." Boston, John H. Eastburn, 1838.

Winthrop, Robert C., "Remarks on the Death of Hon. W. C. Rives and Hon. Edward Coles," *Proceedings of the Massachusetts Historical Society*, Series 1, Vol. 10 (1867-1869) 397-402.

BOOKS AND DISSERTATIONS

Alexander, Thomas B., and Beringer, Richard E., *The Anatomy of the Confederate Congress*. Nashville, Vanderbilt University Press, 1972.

Auchincloss, Louis. *A Writer's Capital*. Boston, Houghton Mifflin Company, 1979.

Bagby, George W. *John M. Daniel's Latch-Key*. Lynchburg, J.P. Bell & Co., 1868

Benton, Thomas Hart. *Thirty Years View*. Vol. I, New York, D. Appleton and Company.

Bernier, Olivier. *Lafayette, Hero of Two Worlds*. New York, E. P. Dutton Inc. 1983.

Brown, Alexander. *The Cabells and Their Kin*. 1895, Reprinted by Cabell, Randolph W. Franklin, North Carolina, Genealogy Publishing Service, 1994.

Bruce, Philip Alexander. *History of the University of Virginia 1819-1919*. Vol. I, New York, The MacMillan Company. 1920.

Bruce, Philip Alexander. *The Virginia Plutarch*. Vol. II, Chapel Hill, University of North Carolina Press, 1929.

Bruce, William Cabell. *John Randolph of Roanoke 1773-1833*, Vol. II. New York, G. P. Putnam's Sons, 1922.

Cappon, Lester J. editor, *The Adams-Jefferson Letters*. Vol. II 1812-1826, Chapel Hill, University of North Carolina Press, 1959.

Childs, James Rives. *Reliques of the Rives*. Lynchburg, J. P. Bell Company, 1929.

Chittenden, Lucius E. *Personal Reminiscences Including Lincoln and Others 1840-1890*. New York, Richmond Crosup and Company, 1893.

Chittenden, Lucius E. *A Report of the Debates and Proceedings in the Secret Sessions of the Conference Convention for Proposing Amendments to the Constitution of the United States held at Washington D.C. in February A.D. 1861.* New York, D. Appleton and Company, 1864.

Clay, Henry. *Private Correspondence of Henry Clay.* Edited by Calvin Colton, Boston, Frederick Parker, 1856.

Cole, Donald B. *Martin Van Buren and the American Political System.* Princeton, Princeton University Press, 1984.

Crofts, Daniel W. *Reluctant Confederates, Upper South Unionists in the Secession Crisis.* Chapel Hill, University of North Carolina Press, 1989.

Crapol, Edward P. *John Tyler The Accidental President.* Chapel Hill, University of North Carolina Press, 2006.

Current, Richard N., Williams, T. Harry, Friedel, Frank, Brownlee, W. Elliot. *The Essentials of American History.* 3rd Edition, New York, Alfred A. Knopf, 1980.

Dabney, Virginius. *Mr. Jefferson's University A History.* Charlottesville, University of Virginia Press, 1981.

Dingledine, Raymond C., Jr. "The Political Career of William Cabell Rives," PhD. Dissertation, University of Virginia, 1947. University of Virginia Library Call # Diss. 0513.

Evans, Eli N. *Judah P. Benjamin The Jewish Confederate.* New York, The Free Press, 1988.

Freehling, William W. *The Road to Disunion, Volume I :
Secessionists at Bay 1776-1854.* New York, Oxford, Oxford
University Press, 1990.

Freehling, William W. *The Road to Disunion, Volume II:
Secessionists Triumphant 1854-1861.* New York, Oxford, Oxford
University press, 2007.

Freehling, William W., and Simpson, Craig M., editors.
*Showdown in Virginia: The 1861 Convention and the Fate of the
Union.* Charlottesville, University of Virginia Press, 2010.

Freeman, Douglas Southall. *Lee's Lieutenants A Study in
Command.* Vol. III "Gettysburg to Appomattox." New York,
Charles Scribner's Sons, 1944.

Freeman, Douglas Southall. *R. E. Lee A Biography.* Vol. I, New
York, Charles Scribner's Sons, 1934.

Friedman, Jean E. *The Revolt of the Conservative Democrats An
Essay on American Political Culture and Political Development
1837-1844.* UMI Research Press, 1979.

Gallagher, Gary W. editor, *Fighting for the Confederacy The
Personal Recollections ofr General Edward Porter Alexander.*
Chapel Hill, University of North Carolina Press, 1989.

Gallagher, Gary, and Sheldon, Rachel A., editors, *A Political
Nation: New Directions in Mid-Nineteenth-Century American
Political History.* Charlottesville, University of Virginia Press,
2012.

Genovese, Eugene D. *Roll Jordan Roll, The World the Slaves Made*. New York, Vintage Books (a division of Random House) 1976.

Gunderson, Robert G. *Old Gentlemen's Convention The Washington Peace Conference of 1861*. Madison, University of Wisconsin Press, 1961.

Heidler, David S., Heidler, Jeanne T. and Coles, David J. editors, *Encyclopedia of the American Civil War: A Political, Social, and Military History*. New York, W. W. Norton and Company, 2000.

Heidler, David S. and Jeanne T. *Henry Clay The Essential American*, New York, Random House, 2010.

Holt, Michael F. *The Rise and Fall of the American Whig Party: Jacksonian Politics and the Onset of the Civil War*. New York, Oxford, Oxford University Press, 1999.

Jackson, Andrew. *Correspondence of Andrew Jackson*. Vol. 5, Edited by John Spencer Bassett, Washington, D.C., Carnegie Institution of Washington, 1926-35.

James, Marquis. *The Life of Andrew Jackson*. Complete in one Volume, Indianaoplis, New York, The Bobbs-Merrill Company, 1938.

Jones, Newton Bond. *Charlottesville and Albemarle County 1819-1860*. 1950 University of Virginia Dissertation.

Jordan, Daniel. *Political Leadership in Jefferson's Virginia.* Charlottesville, University of Virginia Press, 1983.

Jordan, Ervin L. *Charlottesville and the University of Virginia in the Civil War.* Lynchburg, H. E. Howard Inc., 1988.

King, Margaret Rives, *Ancestors and Ancestral Homes.* Cincinnati, Robert Clarke and Company, 1890.

Kirwan, Albert, editor. *The Confederacy.* New York, Meridian Books, 1965

Krick, R. E. Lee. *Staff Officers in Gray.* Chapel Hill, University of North Carolina Press, 2003.

Lankford, Nelson D. *Cry Havoc!: The Crooked Road to Civil War.* New York, Viking, 2007.

Latner, Richard B. *The Presidency of Andrew Jackson.* Athens, University of Georgia Press, 1979.

Lincoln, Abraham. *Complete Works of Abraham Lincoln.* Vol. I, Edited by John Nicolay and John Hay, New York, Francis D. Tandy Company, 1922.

Lucey, Donna M. *Archie and Amélie Love and Madness in the Gilded Age.* New York, Harmony Books, 2006.

Madison, James. *Letters and Other Writings of James Madison.* In 4 Volumes, [editors Rives and Fendall], Philadelphia, J. B. Lippincott and Company, 1865.

McCoy, Drew R. *The Last of the Fathers: James Madison and the Republican Legacy.* Cambridge, Cambridge University Press, 1989.

Meacham, Jon. *American Lion, Andrew Jackson in the White House.* New York, Random House, 2008.

McPherson, James M. *Battle Cry of Freedom.* New York, Ballantine Books, 1988.

McPherson, James M. *Ordeal by Fire The Civil War and Reconstruction.* New York, Alfred A. Knopf, 1982.

Mead, Edward C. *Historic Homes of the Southwest Mountains Virginia.* Philadelphia, J. B. Lippincott Company, 1899.

Moore, John Hammond. *Albemarle, Jefferson's County 1727-1976.* Charlottesville, University of Virginia Press, 1976.

Nicholas, Richard L. *Sheridan's James River Campaign of 1865 through Central Virginia.* Charlottesville, Historic Albemarle, 2012.

Niven, John. *Martin Van Buren The Romantic Age of American Politics.* New York, Oxford University Press, 1983.

O'Brian, Gerard, "James A. Seddon Prototype of the Old South," University of Maryland MA Thesis, Seddon Papers, University of Virginia Special Collections, Accession #14847.

Page, Richard Channing Moore. *Genealogy of the Page Family in Virginia*. 2nd Edition 1893, Reprinted Harrisonburg, Va. C. J. Carrier Company, 1972.

Perdue, Charles L., Barden, Thomas E., and Phillips, Robert K. editors, *Weevils in the Wheat: Interviews with Virginia Ex-Slaves*. Charlottesville, University of Virginia Press, 1976.

Pierson, Rev. Hamilton Wilcox. *Jefferson at Monticello. The Private Life of Thomas Jefferson*. Charlottesville, University of Virginia Press, 1967 (8th printing 1988).

Perlik, Annabel Shanklin. "Signed L. M. D. Guillaume." Masters Thesis for George Washington University, 1979. University of Virginia Special Collections Library Accession # ND1329. G845P471979.

Peterson, Norma Lois. *The Presidencies of William Henry Harrison and John Tyler*. University Press of Kansas, 1989.

Rakove, Jack N. *James Madison and the Creation of the American Republic*. Third Edition, New York, Pearson Longman, 2007.

Remini, Robert J. *Andrew Jackson and the Course of American Democracy*. Vol. III, New York, Harper and Row, 1984.

Rives, Barclay. *A History of Grace Church, Cismont*. Cismont, Grace Church, 2010.

Rives, George Lockhart. *Genealogical Notes*. New York, (privately printed) 1914.

Rives, George Lockhart. *The United States and Mexico*, Vol. I, New York, Charles Scribner's Sons, 1913.

Rives, Judith Page. *Autobiography.* (*Grandmamma's Autobiography for Her Grandchildren*). 1861, Rives Papers, Library of Congress, Box 103, also in Rives papers, University of Virginia Special Collections, Accession #2313, Box 1.

Rives, Judith Page. *Home and the World.* New York, D. Appleton and Company, 1857.

Rives, Judith Page. *Tales and Souvenirs of a Residence in Europe.* Philadelphia, Lea and Blanchard, 1842.

Rives, William Cabell. *History of the Life and Times of James Madison.* Vol. I, 1859, Vol. II, 1866, vol. III, 1868, Boston, Little Brown and Company.

Ritter, Charles F., and Wakelyn, John L. *Leaders of the American Civil War: A Biographical and Historiographical Dictionary,* (online ebook), Westport, Connecticut, Greenwood Publishing Group, 1998.

Sale, Edith Tunis. *Manors of Virginia in Colonial Times.* Philadelphia, J. B. Lippincott Company, 1909.

Schlesinger, Arthur M., Jr. *The Age of Jackson.* Boston, Little Brown and Company, 1953.

Simms, Henry H. *The Rise of the Whigs in Virginia 1824-1840.* Richmond, William Byrd Press, Inc., 1929.

Tyler, Lyon G. *The Letters and Times of the Tylers.* Vol. II, New York, Da Capo Press, 1970.

Warner, Ezra J., and Yearns, Wilfred Buck, *Biographical Register of the Confederate Congress,* Baton Rouge, Louisiana State University Press, 1975.

Wiencek, Henry. *An Imperfect God, George Washington, His Slaves, and the Creation of America.* New York, Farrar Straus and Giroux, 2003.

Wiencek, Henry. *Master of the Mountain Thomas Jefferson and His Slaves.* New York, Farrar, Straus and Giroux, 2012.

Willson, Beckles. *America's Ambassadors to France, 1777-1927.* London, John Murray, 1928

Woods, Rev. Edgar. *Albemarle County in Virginia.* Charlottesville, The Michie Company, 1901.

Yearns, W. Buck. *The Confederate Congress.* Athens, University of Georgia Press, 1960.

Younger, Edward. editor, *Inside the Confederate Government, The Diary of Robert Garlick Hill Kean.* New York, Oxford University Press, 1957.

Index

de Toqueville, Alexis, 217–18, 219

Dickens, Charles, 175

Dickinson, George, 328–29

Edgehill, 146

Edgewood, 10

Everett, Edward, 186, 221, 237, 254–56 passim

Ewell, Richard S., 297

Ewing, Thomas, 129, 163, 168

Farmington, 33, 34

Fendall, Philip R., 241

Fillmore, Millard, 211–12, 218, 220, 237

Fluornoy, Thomas, 237

Fort Sumter, 2–3, 261, 262, 271, 274

Free Soil Party, 129, 212

Fugitive Slave Act, 219, 235

Gayrard, Paul, 221

Gilmer, George, 11, 21

Gilmer, John Harmer, 315–16

Gilmer, Thomas Walker, 61, 85–86, 102–3, 176, 192, 315; death of, 177; Lieutenant Randolph Outrage, 92–95

Grant, Ulysses S., 6, 309

Grigsby, Hugh, 11

Guillaume, Louis Mathieu Didier, 209, 227–29

Guthrie, James, 266

Half way house, 66, 165, 182

Hampden, John, 209

Hampden-Sidney, 12, 208, 209

Harrison, William Henry, 3, 114, 115, 156, 157, 161

Holcombe, 57–58

Hunter, Robert M. T., 262, 285, 292, 296, 318

Irving, Washington, 73

Jackson, Andrew, 1–2, 4–5, 47, 54, 77, 131; bank issue, 98–100, 112–14; election of, 61

Jackson, Stonewall, 297

Jefferson, Thomas, 1, 35–36, 51, 61, 84, 341; death of, 57; tutor, 4, 14, 16–22

Jenkins, Micah, 304

Johnson, Andrew, 47, 326, 327, 331

Johnson, Reverdy, 331

Johnson, Richard Mentor, 5, 26, 114–16

Kansas Nebraska Act, 244

Kean, Robert Garlick Hill, 317

Lafayette, 3, 48–51, 69–74, 78–79, 107

Lawrence, Abbott, 209

Lee, Robert E., 3, 78, 241, 305, 309, 320; letter of condolences, 339–40; letter to Rives, 297–98; surrender, 321